Footprint Handbook
Kilimanjaro &
Northern Tanzania
LIZZIE WILLIAMS

This is
Kilimanjaro
& Northern
Tanzania

Vast, uncrowded and home to a staggering range of animals, Tanzania offers visitors what most expect to see on a visit to the continent: the drama of the wildebeest migration unfolding along an infinite savannah, the gleaming snows of Mount Kilimanjaro and the proud Maasai warriors stalking the plains. Huge areas of Tanzania are dedicated to national parks and game reserves, and most visitors go on safari (which means 'journey' in Kiswahili). The principal draw card is the Big Five: lion, leopard, elephant, rhino and buffalo, but there are other fascinating species too, as well as good birdlife and varied landscapes.

The most popular region is the parks that make up the Northern Circuit, which are some of East Africa's most reliable destinations to spot the animals most people want to see. These are the vast plains of the Serengeti where the annual wildebeest migration is staged, the natural beauty of Lake Manyara tinged pink by thousands of flamingos, the dry-season retreat of Tarangire trampled by hundreds of elephants, and the animal-stuffed Ngorongoro Crater that has World Heritage status as the largest unbroken caldera in the world. In contrast to the flat grasslands and soda lakes of the Rift Valley, Northern Tanzania's other main attraction is a mountain that needs no introduction, snow-capped Kilimanjaro. For many people, scaling the continent's tallest peak to watch the sun rise over Uhuru Peak is one of Africa's most satisfying achievements.

Arusha, the safari capital of Tanzania, is the starting point for trips to the Northern Circuit parks that lie to the west. Moshi, at the base of Kilimanjaro and only 80 km to the west of Arusha, is the departure point for all expeditions to the top. Both are served by Kilimanjaro International Airport, strategically located midway between the two. Northern Tanzania is not only easily accessible, but also offers an extraordinarily diverse menu of things to do and see – from photographing lion or cheetah and trekking on lush mountainsides, to shopping for trinkets in the lively markets and meeting the stately Maasai in their traditional homes – all in one quintessentially African and neatly contained region.

Lizzie Williams

Best of
Kilimanjaro & Northern Tanzania

top things to do and see

❶ Arusha

The gateway to the Northern Circuit parks, Arusha may be noisy and crowded with traffic and people but it has an infectious vibrancy and, in addition to being the place to organize a safari and some interesting cultural experiences, it also has some excellent places to stay, eat and shop. Page 42.

❷ Mount Meru

Kilimanjaro's sister peak and Tanzania's second tallest mountain provides a scenic backdrop to Arusha. Its pretty forested lower slopes can be explored on gentle walks or on game drives in Arusha National Park, or the active can attempt the three-day climb to the icy summit. Page 73.

❸ Tarangire National Park

Dominated by the life-giving Tarangire River, this scenic park of huge baobab trees and gently sloping hills is the domain of huge elephant herds and some unusual species of antelope. The swamps, tinged green year-round, offer exceptionally good birdwatching. Page 78.

❹ Lake Manyara National Park

This small park's diverse range of habitats includes giant trees where lions famously drape themselves along the branches, but it's the view of the colourful flamingos on the lake that is most impressive, especially from the Rift Valley escarpment that looms above. Page 87.

5

KENYA

NAIROBI

Lake Victoria

Musoma

Maasai Mara National Reserve

Mara River

C12

Nairobi National Park

Lake Magadi

C58

A109

Bundu

TANZANIA

Lake Natron

Amboseli National Park

Namanga

B144

Serengeti National Park

6 **7**

Ngorongoro Conservation Area

Longido

Mt Longido (2629m)

A104

Oloitokitok

Eugaruka Ruins

Kilimanjaro National Park

8

Olduvai (Oldupai) Gorge

5

Ngorongoro Crater

Mto wa Mbu

Arusha National Park

2

Mt Meru (4572m)

Mt Kilimanjaro (5896m)

Lake Chala

Taveta

Shinyanga

Lake Manyara National Park

4

B144 A104

Lake Manyara

Arusha Airport

1

Arusha

Kilimanjaro International Airport

Moshi

A23

Himo

Same

Lake Eyasi

Wembere River

Mt Leya (2417m)

3

Tarangire National Park

A104

Babati

Pare Mountain

Pangani River

N

Mt Hanang (3417m)

Kolo

Maasai Steppe

10 km

10 miles

Singida

Kondoa

❺ Ngorongoro Crater

Nothing can prepare visitors for the spectacular, jaw-dropping view down into this steep-walled caldera (collapsed volcano), or the world-class game-viewing on its grassy floor where the animals congregate around vehicles with comfortable familiarity. Page 102.

❼ Balloon safaris

The extra expense of a balloon trip over the Serengeti (and Kenya's Maasai Mara) is more than worth it for most safari-goers. Nothing beats the space, silence and wonderful views over the plains and watching the sunrise bathe the landscape in extraordinary colours. Page 120.

❽ Mount Kilimanjaro

Africa's highest peak might be the world's tallest mountain that can be walked up, but don't underestimate the challenging multi-day ascent. However, those who do reach the top agree, it's an unforgettable and deeply rewarding personal achievement. Page 144.

❻ Serengeti National Park

While it might be most famous for the wildebeest migration – singularly the largest land mammal movement on earth – the vast Serengeti is a year-round safari destination for its wonderful diversity of wildlife, dramatic scenery and fabulous selection of lodges and tented camps. Page 109.

Safari
adventures

❝❞ Dawn sunlight seeped through the bush, a glowing tangerine tide that gilded the acacia trees and sparkled through dew-laden grasses. When it reached the lions, huddled together in a clearing, they responded instantly to its warmth. One of the males stood and stretched, while the rest of the pride rolled in the grass, pawing and flirting in a tangle of tawny-gold limbs and black-tipped tails. They barely glanced in the direction of our Land Cruiser. We were parked just a few metres away, yet the big cats seemed completely unfazed by our presence. They briefly contemplated a distant herd of impala, then sauntered off, single-file, into the dense scrub. The softly berating call of a turtle dove infiltrated the silence that followed the lions' departure. Then somewhere close by we heard the sound of branches snapping and splintering. Lions and elephants in a single morning's game drive… and the sun was only just clear of the horizon.

The Great
Migration

66 99 Mid-August in the Maasai Mara. Our Land Cruiser is parked beside a river, no more than 100 m wide and flowing in shallow rapids between low banks of crumbling sand. At any other time of year, we'd barely have given it a second glance – pausing only, perhaps, to look for hippo or the iridescent flash of a kingfisher. Today, however, the Mara River has us transfixed. The reason is overwhelmingly clear: we have a front-row seat for one of the most spectacular wildlife events on earth: the Great Migration.

Migration calendar
Monthly highlights

January The migration settles in the short-grass plains of the southern Serengeti, near Lake Ndutu. The short rains usually fall here in November and December (sometimes as early as October), luring herds from the central Serengeti in search of fresh pasture. Nourished by phosphorous-rich volcanic soils, the grasslands offer nutritious grazing. Wildebeest, zebra and gazelle begin calving at the end of the month.

The Ndutu region is the best base.

February Calving continues, with up to 500,000 wildebeest born on the southern plains during a two- to three-week window. Far from being static, the wildebeest move around the plains.

You should be in easy driving distance of the herds from Ndutu and Kusini. Due to its central position in the Serengeti, Seronera can be used as a base for viewing the migration from about November to June.

March Several weeks of grazing have taken their toll on the southern plains. There are rumblings of thunderstorms to the north and west; soon the herds will be following their noses in search of rain and fresh grass.

The Ndutu region is still the best base.

April The migration moves towards the Western Corridor of the Serengeti National Park as the long or heavy rains set in. It's a slow plod through patchy woodland and long-grass plains, the herds streaming past Moru Kopjes and the Mbalageti River.

Bases around Moru Kopjes are the best bet.

May As the long rains dwindle, columns of wildebeest continue to enter the Western Corridor of the Serengeti. There is a sense of expectation as the migration piles into the narrow wedge of land between the forest-lined river courses of the Mbalageti and Grumeti.

Properties in the Seronera region are still a good bet. As the month progresses, everyone wants to be based near the Grumeti River.

June By June the rains have stopped and the wildebeest rut is well underway. The grasslands reverberate to the bellows and grunts of testosterone-fuelled males as they chase rivals and round up females. The migration begins to coalesce into a 'mega herd', bunched up along the southern bank of the Grumeti River. Crossings can start early in the month, herds splashing through what is usually a series of pools and channels rather than a continuous, flowing river. As the frequency of crossings intensifies during June, Grumeti's large crocodiles enjoy their annual glut of wildebeest and zebra flesh.

The lodges in the Grumeti Game Reserve and those further south towards the river are the prime spots.

July With the Grumeti River in their wake, the herds push northwards, the sweet scent of the Mara grasslands in their nostrils. They spread out on a broad front that extends from the Grumeti Game Reserve and Ikorongo Game Controlled Area to northern reaches of the Serengeti National Park. The migration can enter the Mara as early as mid-June; in other years wildebeest can linger in the northern Serengeti well into August and September. You can stake out likely Mara River crossing points in both the Serengeti and Masaai Mara throughout July and August.

The best bases are between the Mara River and the Kenyan border, the Lamai Wedge and around the Mara River.

August The northward thrust continues. In a typical year, you can expect the migration to reach the Maasai Mara by early August. River crossings often reach their frenzied climax this month as large herds take a leap of faith into the Mara River, sometimes doubling back on themselves a few days later – much to the delight of waiting crocs and lions.

The camp in the western half of the Maasai Mara are within easy reach of the river crossing points, but all camps in the wider Mara can organize trips into the national reserve.

September The focus of the migration is firmly in Kenya where the wildebeest edge slowly eastwards through the Maasai Mara. They'll wander wherever there is fresh grass, so you can also expect to encounter large herds in the conservancies surrounding the reserve.

October The herds begin to move with renewed purpose. Any week now, rains start falling on the short-grass plains of the southern Serengeti and the wildebeest need to be there when fresh green shoots have pushed to the surface. And so begins the long trek south.

The Kuka Hills in the Loliondo Controlled Area and lodges a little further south make ideal bases.

November The herds pick up the pace as the short rains lure them southwards. They form long columns stretching from Lobo to the Serengeti's central Seronera area.

Any lodges from Lobo to Seronera are good options, but as the month progresses the further south the better.

December The herds reach the southern Serengeti, completing the cycle.

Lodges and camps in the Seronera and Ndutu areas once more become the focus of migration viewing.

In focus
mammals

On safari the first animals that you will see are almost certainly antelope, including the ubiquitous wildebeest. They come in all sizes, ranging from eland, which stand nearly 2 m at the shoulder to the Kirk's dik-dik at just 40 cm.

Nearby are the hunters – lions, leopards and cheetahs – often resting in the shade with their cubs before exploding with lightning speed and cunning to snare their prey. Hanging around the fringes are the scavengers – hyenas, jackals and wild dogs – planning a pack attack of their own.

Meanwhile going about their own business are herds of elephant, the most complex and intelligent of animals, and noisy troops of baboons. And of course you will notice giraffes grazing on the acacia trees or galloping gracefully across the savannah. At waterholes along the rivers, hippopotamus cool off in the water while huge crocodiles lie on the banks.

Sadly, it is now almost too late to catch sight of black rhinocerous – poachers have all but killed them. There are only around 35 left in the whole country.

Rock hyrax
Heterohyrax brucei
Engaging and fairly common. Lives in communities.
Habitat Crevices in rocky areas
Diet Grass, leaves, bird eggs

Olive baboon
Papio anubis
Large, heavily built, the males have a well-developed mane.
Habitat Savannah
Diet Grass, leaves, fruit

Thomson's gazelle
Gazella thomsonii
69 cm. Among the most numerous of antelopes.
Habitat Savannah
Diet Grass

Eland
Taurotragus oryx
183 cm. The largest of the antelopes. Seen in small herds.
Habitat Savannah
Diet Grass

Topi
Damaliscus korrigum
127 cm. Dark patches at the top of its legs. Seen in large herds.
Habitat Savannah
Diet Grass

Impala
Aepyceros melampus
107 cm. Has a unique tuft of thick black bristles, just above heels.
Habitat Savannah
Diet Grass

African wild dog
Lycaon pictus
Packs run down prey; dominant female in clan society.
Habitat Savannah, woodland
Diet Mainly antelopes

Lion
Panthera leo
Up to 3.3 m long; weighs up to 260 kg; the only truly sociable cats.
Habitat Savannah, woodland
Diet Porcupines to giraffes

Hippopotamus
Hippopotamus amphibious
Lower canines can reach 45 cm in length; males can weigh 3200 kg.
Habitat Rivers, lakes, swamps
Diet Nocturnal grazer

Leopard
Panthera pardus
Solitary, adaptable predator; hides kills in trees out of reach of lions.
Habitat Exploits all
Diet Hares to antelopes

Cheetah
Acinonyx jubatus
Daytime hunter, can sprint at 112 kph over short distances.
Habitat Open savannah
Diet Small mammals, gazelles

African elephant
Loxodonta africana
Savannah elephant can weigh 5000 kg; forest elephant is smaller.
Habitat Desert, savannah, forest
Diet Grass, leaves, bark, fruit

Giraffe
Giraffa camelopardalis
Males can reach a height of 5.5 m and have horns on their heads.
Habitat Savannah with acacias
Diet Acacia leaves

Zebra
Equus burchelli
Smaller than Grevy's zebra with thicker stripes.
Habitat Arid savannah
Diet Grass

Spotted hyena
Crocuta crocuta
92 cm. Matriarchal. Has the strongest jaws in animal kingdom.
Habitat Savannah
Diet Wildebeest, zebra

Kirk's dik-dik
Madoqua kirkii
Tiny, only 35-45 cm in height; large glands near eyes.
Habitat Arid thornbush
Diet Leaves, shoots, berries

Warthog
Phacochoerus africanus
Curved upper tusks; males have prominent warts behind eyes.
Habitat Savannah, woodland
Diet Rhizomes, roots, seeds

Coke Hartebeest
Alcelaphus buselaphus cokii
122 cm. Post sentinels on ant hills to watch out for predators.
Habitat Savannah
Diet Grass

In focus
birds

Tanzania is one of the richest areas of birdlife in the world. The total number of species exceeds 1100, and it is possible and not too difficult to see 100 species in a day. You will find that a good pair of binoculars is essential. The camps often have a good library of field guides.

If you are not going on a dawn game drive, still try and get up early and sit quietly outside your tent with a cup of tea and just wait. You'll be amazed at how active the dawn chorus is with birds of all types and sizes coming quite close to you.

After lunch, instead of retreating for a snooze, take advice from the camp guides and find a quiet spot in the trees alongside a waterhole or stream. Swallows will amaze with their acrobatics as they do spin turns over the water while smaller birds flit from tree to tree. Look out for butterflies as they add another dimension.

Overhead, the bigger birds – eagles, vultures and the like – seek out thermals to survey the surrounding area for prey or carcasses, ready to clean up after the cats.

Crowned crane
Balearica pavonina
Around 100 cm, in flight legs trail behind and neck extends. Flocks fly in loose V-shaped formations.
Habitat Moist areas

Greater flamingo
Phoenicopterus ruber
142 cm. Larger and paler than the lesser flamingo. Has a pink bill with a black tip.
Habitat Soda lakes

Fish eagle
Halieaeetus vocifer
76 cm. Often perches on tops of trees. It has a wild yelping call which is often uttered in flight.
Habitat Lakes

Speckled mousebird
Colius striatus
36 cm. Seen in small flocks following each other from bush to bush. Tail is long and graduated.
Habitat Moist areas

Helmeted guineafowl
Phacochoerus africanus
55 cm. Lives in flocks. Has dark slaty and white spotted plumage and bony 'helmet' on its head.
Habitat Dry, open woodland

Red-billed oxpecker
Buphagus erythrorhynchus
18 cm. Hunts for ticks on game and cattle, spending time clinging to and hopping over the animals.
Habitat Open plains

Ground hornbill
Bucorvus cafer
107 cm. Looks like a turkey from afar, usually seen in pairs. Female has red and blue skin around eye.
Habitat Open plains

White-backed vulture
Gyps africanus
81 cm. Often seen circling overhead, look out for the white band on the underside of the wing.
Habitat Open plains

Pied kingfisher
Ceryle rudis
25 cm. The only black and white kingfisher, it hovers over water before plunging in.
Habitat Rivers, lakes, swamps

Paradise fly-catcher
Terpsiphone viridis
33 cm. Has a very long tail and bright chestnut plumage. Female has shorter tail.
Habitat Wooded areas

Superb starling
Speo superbus
18 cm. Widespread and seen hopping around on the ground. Often seen near habitation.
Habitat Dry, open woodland

White-crowned shrike
Eurocephalus rueppelli
23 cm. Occurs in small flocks in acacia country, it is rather thickset. Appears brown and white.
Habitat Dry, open woodland

Lilac-breasted roller
Coracias caudatas
41 cm. Perches on bare branches, so easily spotted. Its tail has two elongated streamers.
Habitat Dry, open woodland

Secretary bird
Sagittarius serpentarius
110 cm. Often seen in pairs as it hunts for snakes, which form its main food source.
Habitat Open plains

Ostrich
Struthio camelus
2 m. Sometimes seen singly but also in family groups, this large bird stalks across the grasslands.
Habitat Open plains

Red bishop
Euplectes orix
13 cm. Quite brilliantly coloured with brown wings and scarlet feathers on its rump.
Habitat Dry, open woodland

Red-cheeked cordon-bleu
Uraeginthus benegalus
13 cm. They are seen in pairs or family parties. Quite tame and often seen around lodges.
Habitat Dry, open woodland

Scarlet-chested sunbird
Nectarinia senegalensis
15 cm. Often perches on overhead wires, it is sturdy and thickset with a short tail.
Habitat Urban

66 99 While the diversity of wildlife on an African safari is something to be marvelled at, it's worth slowing down, or staying put, for a morning or afternoon and observing a single group of animals. After several hours in the company of a herd of zebra or a family of cheetah you'll observe all kinds of behaviour and begin to synch with their natural rhythms – something that's all too often missed on safari.

Planning
a safari

Will Gray, author of Footprint's *Wildlife Travel*, offers some tips

Safaris have become hugely popular, but planning one can leave you wallowing in logistics like a proverbial hippo. Are you looking for 'safari chic' at an upmarket lodge, or is roughing it with a tent and some fire sticks more your kind of thing? Then there are the seasons to consider, what gear to take, the costs, modes of transport, independent trip versus package or tailor-made and whether you really need to pack one of those multi-pocketed khaki waistcoats. See also box, page 58.

Armed with just your senses and a pair of binoculars, you'll return home intoxicated with vivid sights, sounds and smells. You'll have heard the bewitching 'whoop' of a hyena, studied the grafitti of tracks around a waterhole, and felt the electric anticipation of a big cat sighting. The names of hundreds of birds will be fresh in your mind, while the pepper-sweet tang of the bush will linger for days.

But having said all that, let's not forget the dust, the pre-dawn wake-up calls and those buttock-numbing, three-hour game drives when all you see is the retreating posterior of a lone warthog, its perky tail held aloft like a defiant flag of victory. Safaris are not for everyone, but then again, those who have 'gone bush' in Africa invariably come back for more.

A typical day

A typical day on safari usually starts with an early wake-up call. You'll need to be up and about when it's cool and the wildlife is most active. Game drives generally last around three to four hours. There will be lots of bumping around on rutted tracks and perhaps some frustrating periods when you see very little. But this will be far outweighed by the excitement of your first encounter or the titbits of bushlore that you glean from a good guide. You may well stake out favoured wildlife haunts, such as waterholes or fruiting trees, or if regulations allow, take a short walk in the company of an armed scout. Back at your lodge or camp, a large breakfast or brunch will be waiting. Then you have a few hours to lie low during the hottest part of the day when much of the wildlife has also retreated to the shade. By late afternoon it's time for another game drive. At dusk, you might stop for a sundowner, before continuing your safari on into the night when a new cast of nocturnal creatures emerges. Dinner may well be served around an open fire – perfect for stargazing.

Package versus tailor-made

Tailor-made safaris are obviously more expensive than package trips, but they do allow you full control of your plans. If you opt for a package safari, be sure to find out what's included. A 'bargain' safari may conceal hidden extras, such as national park fees. On cheap safaris you could also be fighting for a window seat in a crowded vehicle or be frustrated by a driver-guide who is more 'driver' than 'guide'. Good guides will take you away from big groups of other vehicles. They'll also know the best spots for wildlife and will be able to tell you more about what you're seeing.

Where to stay

Accommodation is largely a matter of personal preference and budget. Lower-cost camping safaris, in which you take an active role in pitching tents, cooking, etc, are excellent value and can be great fun – particularly if you're travelling alone. Lodges and camps often have swimming pools and offer night drives and other activities. Generally, the smaller and more remote the lodge or camp is, the higher the rates.

Aren't safaris really expensive?

Not when you consider the logistics of maintaining a camp in an area of remote wilderness. Some camps are seasonal and have to be dismantled and reassembled each year. Then there are the high standards of accommodation, food and guiding, the high staff to guest ratio, inclusive activities and – for top-end camps – the inevitable price of exclusivity. And remember costs vary hugely depending on duration, season, where you stay and how many are in a group. If flying and staying in top-end places expect to pay in excess of US$500 per person per day. This can fall to US$180-250 per person per day staying in national park campsites and sticking to road travel.

I never get any decent photos

Most of the dramatic close-up shots of African wildlife you see are the result of hours spent in the bush and a good pinch of luck. Give your photography a boost by spending longer on safari, ideally in a single location to become familiar with the wildlife, or shoot less demanding subjects such as landscapes, camp life and lodge interiors. See also Improve your travel photography, page 38.

Will I spend half my holiday in a vehicle?

Yes, this can happen. Most parks are some way from departure points so if you go on a three-day safari by road, you will often find that at least one day is taken up with travelling to and from the park, often on bad bumpy and dusty roads – leaving you with less time on safari in the park itself. Flying is the way to avoid this, if you can afford it.

Route planner

putting it all together

Tanzania's Northern Circuit is one of the most celebrated safari areas in Africa, and the sheer concentration of Africa's big game is simply phenomenal. Most itineraries are designed around the world-famous Serengeti and the Ngorongoro Crater, which are the most popular 'pairing' logistically too – to get to the Serengeti from Arusha, the route passes right through the Ngorongoro Conservation Area. Then there are the other parks of Lake Manyara and Tarangire – lesser known but rewarding in their own right – and towering above it all is Kilimanjaro, arguably Africa's toughest challenge. You can opt for an organized road safari from Arusha, or have the luxury of flying between lodges and tented camps, or intrepid self-drivers with a sturdy vehicle can explore at their own pace. How long you go for depends on how many parks you want to visit, how many nights you want to stay in each, and whether you want to climb to the top of a very tall mountain.

Four to seven days

park life and panoramas

The **Ngorongoro Crater** and the **Serengeti National Park** can be done in four days and three nights. This would allow one night at a lodge or campsite either at the top of the crater within the Ngorongoro Conservation Area, or at one of the accommodation options around Karatu in the Ngorongoro Highlands, and would factor in an excursion down on to the crater floor itself. Then a minimum of two nights is recommended to be in the Serengeti – more if possible, especially to see the migration. The road to both also passes along the Rift Valley escarpment, where every safari vehicle stops to admire the views of **Lake Manyara National Park**. But another night here allows time for game driving too. If you add **Tarangire**, a dry-season retreat for many animals, to these three, you will need a minimum of six days and five nights. Also allow for one night's accommodation in **Arusha** before and at the end of your safari – although those flying into the parks could save time by cutting out some road journeys to be able to organize onward flights.

If you also want to add a mountain climb to your safari – not only Kilimanjaro, but Mount Meru too offers a summit challenge and is quieter than the Kili climb – then you need to factor in extra time. **Kilimanjaro** can be climbed on a five-day organized trekking expedition, which involves camping or staying on mountain huts for four nights. However, because of acclimatization issues, it's usually recommended to spend an extra night on the mountain (on a six-day trek), which greatly increases the chances of reaching the top. You will have to stay in **Moshi** or around on the night before your early morning departure up Kilimanjaro, and another after your return to recover and enjoy a cold beer and hot shower. The **Mount Meru** climb typically takes three days, but there are other options that might appeal if you don't want to especially reach a summit. There are several day tours to the foothills of these mountains from both Arusha and Moshi, especially to rural villages, coffee plantations and waterfalls, or you can spend a day exploring **Arusha National Park**. You may also want to spend a day in the towns themselves to enjoy a wander around, a meal in a nice restaurant, relaxing by a hotel swimming pool, or indulging in a bit of shopping.

Two to three weeks
local peoples and wildlife encounters

If budget and time allows, consider a longer safari at the **small tented camps** which are tucked away from the busy areas. These are found in the Serengeti in particular, the mobile or seasonal camps, or those in the concession areas bordering the park, and offer circuits that either follow the migration or where you will have time to spend on walks with Maasai guides or relax at camp to enjoy the wilderness. Flying between these is the most logical option and more than a week on a slower safari is a fine way to enjoy the Northern Circuit at its natural pace. Away from the tourist hotspots, the region is also home to a variety of different cultures including the Maasai and Wahadzabe people. In many areas the red-blanketed Maasai graze their cattle with the wildlife or you can meet the local people on excursions to the Rift Valley **Lakes of Eyasi** and **Natron**, both of which are also the breeding grounds for large flocks of flamingos. If coming from Nairobi, it's also possible to arrange a safari to Kenya's **Maasai Mara National Reserve** too, which adjoins and shares the same ecosystem as the Serengeti. The minimum time for a Mara safari from and returning to Nairobi is three days and two nights. See pages 122 and 160 for details.

When to go

… and when not to

Thanks to its location near the equator, Tanzania has a moderate climate and long sunny days for most of the year, although there are variations depending on topography and elevation. In the parks of the Northern Circuit daytime temperatures average between 25 and 30°C throughout the year. Generally, the hottest months are January and February and the coolest months are May to August. Most of the rain falls roughly between late October and May, and is generally split into the short rains, *mvuli*, usually from the end of October to early December, and the long rains, *masika*, usually from the end of March to May. However this pattern of rainfall is not that predictable – in wetter years, rain falls more continuously October to May than is indicated by average rainfall figures, while in other years there may be a longer spell of dry weather between the two typical rainy seasons, especially around January and February. But even in the wet months, there is an average of four to six hours of sunshine each day before or after the clouds gather for a downpour; although March to May are the wettest months when day-long storms may occur. On peaks above 1500 m the climate becomes cooler as the altitude increases, with permanent snow on the highest peaks of Kilimanjaro and sometimes Meru, where night-time temperatures drop well below zero.

Safaris to the Northern Circuit operate all year round, and each season offers something different. In terms of avoiding the rains, the best time to visit is between late-June and October. These drier months are the best time of year for

Weather Tanzania

January	February	March	April	May	June
34°C	34°C	32°C	31°C	29°C	28°C
21°C	22°C	22°C	22°C	21°C	20°C
148mm	143mm	184mm	157mm	62mm	14mm

July	August	September	October	November	December
28°C	28°C	29°C	30°C	29°C	29°C
20°C	21°C	21°C	22°C	22°C	23°C
8mm	8mm	15mm	34mm	92mm	151mm

game viewing as vegetation cover is at a minimum and a lack of water forces animals to congregate around rivers and waterholes, making it easier to spot them. The wildebeest migration in the Serengeti usually occurs from December to July, but the peak times of seeing high concentrations of

wildebeest, zebra and gazelle and the associated predators on the move is June and July as they are returning to Kenya's Maasai Mara, which they usually reach around August.

The disadvantage of the wet seasons is that the thicker vegetation and the wider availability of water mean that the wildlife is more spread out and more difficult to spot; also, driving conditions are far harder in deep mud as none of the park roads are paved. The wetter months however have their highlights too; the parks are transformed into beautiful, thriving green landscapes, and animals will be in good condition after feeding on the new shoots and there are chances of seeing breeding displays and young animals. Wetter landscapes also attract the migrant birds to Tanzania. It's also low season, meaning less crowded parks and many of the safari lodges drop their rates significantly; sometimes by as much as 50% in April and May. But this is also the time of year when the parks are at their wettest and can make travel difficult, and seasonal tented camps close; not only because of the weather, but to make repairs and refurbishments.

What to do

Going on safari is the top activity in this region – with the Serengeti's wildebeest migration and high concentration of predators and the Ngorongoro's Big Five experience being the main attractions; for further information, see pages 8-24. But a traditional vehicle safari can be complemented by birdwatching or walking or you can survey the game-studded landscape from a hot-air balloon. There's also the opportunity to meet the people on cultural excursions and climbing Kilimanjaro or Meru makes a contrasting experience to exploring the savannahs. Details of local tour operators are listed in the relevant chapters.

Ballooning

The **Serengeti National Park** is the top spot for a gentle float over the animals in a balloon and, for many, this excursion (albeit expensive) is the highlight of a visit to the park. Most of the lodges and camps in the Seronera and Western Corridor can organize this activity. Tourists are picked up around 0500 and driven to the site where the lift-off will take place. Watching the balloon inflate is part of the experience. Once the balloon rises, passengers can watch the sunrise high above the plains when the grasslands turn from blue to gold. This is quite a spectacular experience, especially during the months of the wildebeest migration. Flights last 60-90 minutes and cost US$540 per person, which includes a bush breakfast with champagne. For more information, see www.balloonsafaris.com.

Birdwatching

Apart from all the mammals, Tanzania also boasts a vast selection of birds with 1100 recorded species, of which 22 are endemic and a further 43 are near-endemic. Migrants are present from November to April. Birdwatching is a popular pastime and can easily be combined with wildlife watching in all the Northern Circuit parks. In particular **Arusha National Park** has an amazing diversity of habitats, which attract an incredible list of 400 species in a small area, while **Lake Manyara** is home to a good variety of waterbirds and **Tarangire** is well-known for its raptors. Most tour operators will be able to arrange safaris particularly aimed at birdwatchers, while bird checklists for Tanzania can be found at www.tanzaniabirding.com or www.tanzaniabirds.net.

Climbing and hiking

Kilimanjaro tops the list as Africa's most famous – and highest (5895 m) – mountain to climb, with organized treks that take five to six days. But Northern Tanzania also has other options that vary from the dramatic crater of **Mount Meru** and the active volcano of **Ol Doinyo Lengai**, to tamer options such as Kilimanjaro and Meru **foothills** and the comparatively gentle slopes of the **Ngorongoro Crater Highlands**. Tour operators and trekking companies will put together an itinerary that suits your preferences and abilities. Bear in mind, there are no mountaineering or outdoor outfitters in Tanzania, so you'll need to bring most of your own gear. Many safari lodges also offer guided game walks, often with the Maasai, which while not particularly strenuous give a great introduction to the bush and are ideal for birdwatching and perhaps spotting the smaller mammals.

Cultural tours

Several villages around **Arusha**, **Moshi**, **Mto wa Mbu**, and other regions of Tanzania, have initiatives that are part of the **Tanzania Cultural Tourism Programmes**. These promote community-based tourism in which the local people are directly involved in designing and organizing tours and showing tourists the areas they live in. Profits from each are used to benefit community projects. Most are in rural areas and you can go on walks, village tours, and get involved in traditional activities such as farming, ceremonies or handicraft-making. It's a great way to engage with the local people. The head office is in Arusha (see page 66) or some of the programmes are listed in the relevant chapters; www.tanzaniaculturaltourism.com.

Riding

There are a few opportunities to go horse or camel riding, especially around **Arusha** and **Moshi**. These include fun short camel rides from the **Meserani Snake Park** (page 63) and longer seven-day horse safaris for experienced riders in the foothills of **Kilimanjaro**. On horseback it's possible to get very close to wildlife, as animals do not have an inherent fear of horses.

Where to stay

from secluded tented camps to business hotels

There is a wide range of accommodation on offer in Tanzania, from luxurious and secluded tented camps that charge US$300-1000 per couple per day, to mid-range safari lodges for around US$150-250 for a double room, standard small town hotels used by local business people for around US$50-100 per room, and basic board and lodgings used by local travellers at under US$20 a day.

Generally, accommodation booked through a European agent will be more expensive than if you contact the establishment directly; most of Tanzania's hoteliers have websites and there are many Tanzanian-run hotel and lodge groups. Hotels in the towns and cities usually keep the same rates year-round, but safari lodges have seasonal rates depending on weather, periods of popularity with overseas (especially European) visitors, and events such as the wildebeest migration in the Serengeti. Accommodation seasons are as follows: high is December to February and June to August; mid or shoulder season is March and September to November; low season is April and May.

Non-resident rates and prices

Like in the other East African countries, two-tier pricing applies in most of Tanzania and there are different (higher) rates for visitors ('non-residents') than for those living in Tanzania and neighbouring countries ('residents'). As such for more expensive hotels, airlines, tour operators, national park and game reserve

Price codes

Where to stay	Restaurants
$$$$ over US$300	$$$ over US$30
$$$ US$100-300	$$ US$15-30
$$ US$50-99	$ under US$15
$ under US$50	

Unless otherwise stated, prices refer to the cost of a double room including tax, not including service charge or meals.

Prices refer to the cost of a main course with either a soft drink, a glass of wine or a beer.

entrance and camping fees, tourists are charged approximately double the rate locals are charged. Most non-resident rates are published in US dollars, but these can also be paid in Tanzania shillings and other currencies such as GBP and Euro cash – just ensure the exchange rate is fair. If paying a US dollar-set price by credit or debit card, your own bank at home will make a calculation from US dollars to your own currency at the day's exchange rate (plus there will be the associated fees for making a foreign transaction).

Safari options

All safari companies offer basically the same safari but at different prices, depending on what accommodation is booked. For example, you can choose a four-day safari to the Ngorongoro Crater and Serengeti, and the options would be camping (the companies provide the equipment) or a lodge safari, making it considerably more expensive. For those who want to spend more, there is the option of adding flights between destinations or staying at one of the smaller luxury tented camps. Either way, you are likely to have the same sort of game-viewing experiences, but the level of comfort you enjoy on safari depends on where you stay and how much you spend.

Safari lodges vary and may be either typical hotels with rooms and facilities in one building, or individual *bandas* or *rondavels* (small huts) with a central dining area. Standards vary from the rustic to the modern, from the simply appointed to the last word in luxury. Some of the larger lodges in the parks of the Northern Circuit are enormous impersonal affairs with little atmosphere that were built some decades ago, although comfort and service is good. But at the newer ones, efforts have usually been made to design lodges that blend into their environment, with an emphasis on natural local building materials and use of traditional art and decoration. Most lodges serve meals and have lounges and bars, sometimes swimming pools, and they often have excellent views or overlook waterholes or salt licks that attract game.

A luxury tented camp is really the best of both worlds: the comfort of extremely high facilities and service, combined with sleeping closer to the animals. They are usually built with a central dining and bar area, often in a communal 'mess tent', are in stunning well-designed locations, and each tent will have a thatched roof to keep it cool inside, proper beds, a veranda and a small bathroom at the back with solar-heated hot water. The added benefit is that camps are usually fairly small, with just a few tents, so the safari experience is intimate and professional. Most safari lodges and tented camps are full board, although extras such as wine and liqueurs can be very expensive.

There are **campsites** in most national parks. They are extensively used by camping safari companies. Vehicles, guides, tents and equipment, as well as food and a cook, are all provided, but you'll need to take your own sleeping bag and possibly a sleeping mat. Facilities are very basic – the Serengeti campsites, for example, have not much more than a long drop loo (a basic hole in a concrete slab) and a cold shower – but sleeping here at night is really exciting: the campsites are unfenced and are often visited by hyena and lion. At some campsites there may be hot water for showers, but bear in mind it may not be constant – for instance it could only be available if a fire is lit under the boiler or solar panels have heated it up during a sunny day. Do not leave food scraps or containers where they may attract and harm animals, and be careful about leaving items outside your tent. Many campsites have troupes of baboons nearby that can be a nuisance, and a hyena can chew through something as solid as a saucepan. Campsites usually provide running water and firewood, but you will almost always need to be totally self-sufficient, with all your own equipment. Camping should always have minimal impact on the environment. All rubbish and waste matter should be buried, burnt or taken away.

Hotels

Quality of town and city hotels vary widely; some are newly built, modern, comfortable and have good facilities, while others are bland, boring and have dated decor and poor service. Increasingly, the much nicer options are in fact outside the busy and noisy centres, and it is far more pleasant to stay in a peaceful scenic location such as the foothills of the mountains around Arusha and Moshi for example. Hotels at the top end charge US$200-300 for a double room and for this you should expect good en suite facilities, a/c or fans, although this depends on the local climate, mosquito nets, DSTV (satellite TV), Wi-Fi, or internet access elsewhere in the hotel, and breakfast. Mid-range hotels cost around US$100-200 and offer the same but won't be as luxurious or reliable or have as many extras such as a swimming pool. Rooms in the US$50-100 range are often the best value with comfortable accommodation in self-contained rooms, hot water, fans, possibly DSTV, breakfast and perhaps a decent restaurant. At the budget end there's a fairly wide choice of cheap hotels for US$20-50. A room often comprises a simple bed, basic bathroom that is sometimes shared, mosquito net and fan, but may have an irregular water or electricity supply; it is always a good

Tip...
Credit cards are widely accepted at the larger and more expensive hotels, but may attract a surcharge of around 5%. Hotels at the cheaper end will only accept Tanzania shillings, but in the tourist areas, they may also accept US dollars. On all hotel bills, VAT at 20% is added and is included in the bill.

Tip...

The word *hoteli* in Kiswahili means a cheap stall/café for food and drink, rather than lodging. It is better to use the word guesthouse in Kiswahili, *guesti*, when enquiring about accommodation.

idea to look at a room first to ensure it's clean and everything works. It is also imperative to ensure that your luggage will be locked away securely for protection against petty theft. There may be a restaurant serving local food or basics such as chicken or fish and chips, and breakfast could be included but may not be substantial with perhaps a cup of tea/coffee, bread and fruit. At the very bottom of the scale are bare cell-like rooms in concrete compounds often attached to a bar and referred to locally as 'board and lodgings'; these are as little as US$6-8 but are generally not recommended as they are, more often than not, rented out by the hour.

Camping

Away from the campsites in the national parks and game reserves, camping in Tanzania is fairly limited to the road that runs from Kenya all the way to Malawi in the south. This is part of the great African overland route and independent overlanders and commercial trucks on camping safaris travel in either direction. Campsites have sprung up along this route to accommodate the vehicles and campers and some are very good; indeed better than what is on offer in the national parks. The better ones have bars and restaurants, simple sleeping huts for those that don't want to camp, guards for tents and vehicles, and clean ablution blocks with plenty of hot water. However, you should always have your own tent and basic equipment, as these cannot be hired, and have adequate supplies of drinking water and food. For obvious reasons, it's illegal to camp anywhere except a designated campsite in a game park or reserve. Never bush camp on the side of a busy road or near a town; it's an invitation to be robbed in the middle of the night.

Food
& drink

Cuisine on mainland Tanzania is not one of the country's main attractions. Tanzanians are largely big meat eaters, and a standard meal is *nyama choma*, roasted beef or goat meat, usually served with a spicy relish, although some like it with a mixture of raw peppers, onions and tomato known as *kachumbari*. The main staple or starch in Tanzania is *ugali*, a dish of maize flour, millet flour or sorghum flour cooked with water to a porridge or dough-like consistency, which, under various names, is eaten all over Africa. It is fairly bland on its own, but makes a filling meal accompanied with a tasty sauce or stew. Other starch includes *wali* (rice), *matoke* (boiled and mashed plantains) and *chapati* (an unleavened flatbread originally imported from India).

Eating out

Local hotels and restaurants tend to serve a limited and somewhat unadventurous menu of food such as steaks, meat stews, grilled chicken, chips and boiled vegetables. There is a much greater variety of restaurants in the tourist spots or where expats live; in particular Arusha has a good choice of individual restaurants (not connected to the hotels) which are enjoyed for their creative menus and specialist ingredients such as seafood, which is flown up from the coast. Asian eating places can also be a good bet; there are substantial Chinese and Indian communities in Tanzania and authentic cuisine can be found. Most of the larger safari lodges (and beach resorts if you are going to the coast too) offer breakfast, lunch and dinner buffets for their all-inclusive guests, some of which can be excellent while others can be of a poor standard and there's no real way of telling what you'll get. The most important thing is to avoid is food that has been sitting around for a long time on a buffet table, so ensure it's freshly prepared and served. Vegetarians are catered for, and fruit and vegetables are used frequently, although there is a limited choice of dishes specifically made for vegetarians on menus and you may have to make special requests.

Restaurant prices vary depending on where you are eating; it is quite possible to get a plate of simple hot food in a basic restaurant for US$5, while the expensive places with gourmet cuisine will cost more like US$30-40 per person with drinks.

The service in Tanzanian restaurants can be somewhat slower than you are used to and it can take hours for something to materialize from a kitchen. Rather than complain, just enjoy the laid-back pace and order another beer.

Street stalls, shops and markets

Various items can be bought at roadside stalls and from street vendors who prepare and cook over charcoal, which adds considerably to the flavour. It's pretty safe, despite hygiene being fairly basic, because most of the items are cooked or peeled. Snacks include barbecued beef on skewers (*mishkaki*), roast maize (corn), samosas, hard-boiled eggs, roast cassava (looks like white peeled turnips) and *mandazi* (a kind of sweet or savoury doughnut). Fruits include oranges (peeled and halved), pineapples, bananas, mangoes (slices scored and turned inside-out), paw-paw (papaya) and watermelon. These items are very cheap and are all worth trying and, when travelling, are indispensable.

Most food is bought in open-air markets. In the larger towns and cities these are held daily and, as well as fresh fruit and vegetables, sell eggs, bread and meat. In the smaller villages, markets are usually held on one day of the week. Markets are very colourful places to visit and, as Tanzania is very fertile, just about any fruit or vegetable is available. Other locally produced food items are sold in supermarkets, often run by Asian traders, while imported products are sold in the few upmarket supermarkets in the larger cities, such as **Nakumatt**.

Drink

Sodas (soft drinks such as Coca-Cola, Fanta and the like) are available everywhere and are very cheap, and are bought in cans or cheaper refundable 300 ml bottles. Bottled water is fairly expensive, but is available in all but the smallest villages. Tap water is reputedly safe in many parts of the country, but is only really recommended if you have a fairly hardy traveller's stomach. In cafés, freshly squeezed fruit juices are often available, and they are quite delicious, but remember they may be mixed with tap water. **Coffee**, when freshly ground, is the local Arabica variety that grows on the lower slopes of Mount Meru and Kilimanjaro, which has a distinctive, acidic flavour. Most of the upmarket cafés and hotels have coffee machines for cappuccinos, espressos etc, but also look out for

> ## **Best** cup of coffee
> The terrace bar at Arusha Coffee Lodge, page 48
> Among the coffee bushes at The River House, page 52
> In modern Fifi's cafés in Arusha and Moshi, pages 54 and 137
> At the Chagga coffee-growing village of Materuni, page 127
> The coffee-growers cooperative's Union Café, page 138

traditional Swahili coffee vendors with large portable conical brass coffee pots with charcoal braziers underneath (often seen at bus stations and markets). Chai (**tea**) is drunk in small glasses, and is served milky and sweet with the ingredients boiled together, but is surprisingly refreshing. **Local beers** (lager) are decent and cheap and are sold in 700 ml refundable bottles. Brands include Kilimanjaro and Safari lager, tasty Tusker imported from Kenya or Castle from South Africa. Imported **wines** are on the expensive side, but there's a good choice of European or South African labels.

Imported **spirits** are widely available, and local alternatives that are sold in both bottles and sachets of one tot include some rough vodkas and whiskies and the much more pleasant *Konyagi*, a type of scented gin distilled from sugarcane. Going under various names, you may be offered banana wine in the rural and mountain areas: a home-brew of fermented bananas and sorghum that produces a highly intoxicating and foul-tasting alcohol – administer with care.

Improve your travel photography

Taking pictures is a highlight for many travellers, yet too often the results turn out to be disappointing. Steve Davey, author of Footprint's *Travel Photography*, sets out his top rules for coming home with pictures you can be proud of.

Before you go

Don't waste precious travelling time and do your research before you leave. Find out what festivals or events might be happening or which day the weekly market takes place, and search online image sites such as Flickr to see whether places are best shot at the beginning or end of the day, and what vantage points you should consider.

Get up early

The quality of the light will be better in the few hours after sunrise and again before sunset – especially in the tropics when the sun will be harsh and unforgiving in the middle of the day. Sometimes seeing the sunrise is a part of the whole travel experience: sleep in and you will miss more than just photographs.

Stop and think

Don't just click away without any thought. Pause for a few seconds before raising the camera and ask yourself what you are trying to show with your photograph. Think about what things you need to include in the frame to convey this meaning. Be prepared to move around your subject to get the best angle. Knowing the point of your picture is the first step to making sure that the person looking at the picture will know it too.

Compose your picture

Avoid simply dumping your subject in the centre of the frame every time you take a picture. If you compose with it to one side, then your picture can look more balanced. This will also allow you to show a significant background and make the picture more meaningful. A good rule of thumb is to place your subject or any significant detail a third of the way into the frame; facing into the frame not out of it.

This rule also works for landscapes. Compose with the horizon two-thirds of the way up the frame if the fore-ground is the most interesting part of the picture; one-third of the way up if the sky is more striking.

Don't get hung up with this so-called Rule of Thirds, though. Exaggerate it by pushing your subject out to the edge of the frame if it makes a more interesting picture; or if the sky is dull in a landscape, try cropping with the horizon near the very top of the frame.

Fill the frame

If you are going to focus on a detail or even a person's face in a close-up portrait, then be bold and make sure that you fill the frame. This is often a case of physically getting in close. You can use a telephoto setting on a zoom lens but this can lead to pictures looking quite flat; moving in close is a lot more fun!

Interact with people

If you want to shoot evocative portraits then it is vital to approach people and seek permission in some way, even if it is just by smiling at someone. Spend a little time with them and they are likely to relax and look less stiff and formal. Action portraits where people are doing something, or environmental portraits, where they are set against a significant background, are a good way to achieve relaxed portraits. Interacting is a good way to find out more about people and their lives, creating memories as well as photographs.

Focus carefully

Your camera can focus quicker than you, but it doesn't know which part of the picture you want to be in focus. If your camera is using the centre focus sensor then move the camera so it is over the subject and half press the button, then, holding it down, recompose the picture. This will lock the focus. Take the now correctly focused picture when you are ready.

Another technique for accurate focusing is to move the active sensor over your subject. Some cameras with touch-sensitive screens allow you to do this by simply clicking on the subject.

Leave light in the sky

Most good night photography is actually taken at dusk when there is some light and colour left in the sky; any lit portions of the picture will balance with the sky and any ambient lighting. There is only a very small window when this will happen, so get into position early, be prepared and keep shooting and reviewing the results. You can take pictures after this time, but avoid shots of tall towers in an inky black sky; crop in close on lit areas to fill the frame.

Bring it home safely

Digital images are inherently ephemeral: they can be deleted or corrupted in a heartbeat. The good news though is they can be copied just as easily. Wherever you travel, you should have a backup strategy. Cloud backups are popular, but make sure that you will have access to fast enough Wi-Fi. If you use RAW format, then you will need some sort of physical back-up. If you don't travel with a laptop or tablet, then you can buy a backup drive that will copy directly from memory cards.

Recently updated and available in both digital and print formats, Footprint's Travel Photography by Steve Davey covers everything you need to know about travelling with a camera, including simple post-processing. More information is available at www.footprinttravelguides.com

Arusha &
Arusha
National Park

In the northern highlands of Tanzania, at the foot of Mount Meru, Arusha is a sprawling, noisy, traffic-congested city of about 1.6 million. A frenetic, commercial and not particularly attractive place, it is set at a lush altitude of 1380 m above sea level and enjoys a temperate climate. It is also the safari capital of the country, and is the springboard to what is referred to as the Northern Circuit parks – the world-famous Serengeti and Ngorongoro Crater, as well as Lake Manyara, Arusha and Tarangire. Mount Kilimanjaro is also just within striking distance. Arusha can be very busy with tourists, mostly either in transit to, or returning from, these attractions. The dusty streets are filled with 4WD game-viewing vehicles negotiating potholed roads and Maasai warriors in full regalia mingling with tourists clad in crisp khaki. There are lots of good hotels and restaurants, as well as souvenir shops and markets, and tourism has made Arusha a very prosperous city. The 542-sq-km Arusha National Park, situated on Arusha's doorstep, is remarkable for its range of habitats attracting a variety of wildlife and birdlife. It also contains Mount Meru, which offers a quieter trek than Mount Kilimanjaro but equally as demanding in places.

Arusha
& around

What Arusha lacks in conventional sights, it more than makes up for in all the facilities and modern trappings you might need to organize, or recover from, an excursion into the wilds. Some time spent shopping in the souvenir shops and markets, eating in a nice restaurant and strolling around town is recommended. Short jaunts offer opportunities to explore the local countryside and to meet local people through Cultural Tourism Programmes, which organize trips into local villages to observe a different way of life.

Arusha

a busy city with crowded streets

Centre

The centre of town is the **clock tower**, which was donated in 1945 by a Greek resident, Christos Galanos, to commemorate the Allied victory in the Second World War. The German Boma now houses the **National Natural History Museum** ① *north end of Boma Rd, T027-250 7540, 0900-1730, US$5,* opened in 1987. The building was built by the Germans in 1900 and it has an outer wall, with block towers at each corner. Inside the fortifications are a central administrative building, a captain's mess, a soldiers' mess, a guard house and a large armoury.

The museum contains the celebrated **Laetoli Footprints**, dating back 3,500,000 years. Three hominids walking on two legs have left their tracks in solidified volcanic grey ash. The discovery was made at Laetoli, about 45 km south of the Oldupai (Olduvai) Gorge, by Mary Leakey and her team in 1976, and the site was fully excavated in 1978. Another display of interest is the tracing of the evolution of man based on the findings at Olduvai Gorge (see page 93).

The **Tanzanite Experience** ① *on the 3rd floor of the Blue Plaza Building, India St, T0767 600 990, www.tanzaniteexperience.com, Mon-Fri 0900-1700, Sat 0900-1300, free,* is nearby and explains about the history, mining and processing of tanzanite, found only in Tanzania, on the foothills of Kilimanjaro. There's a shop here where you can buy certified gems.

North of the museum, the huge **Arusha International Conference Centre (AICC)** ① *T027-250 3161, www.aicc.co.tz,* is made up of three main blocks – the Kilimanjaro, Ngorongoro and Serengeti wings. It has been an important centre for international deliberations, with events such as the International Criminal Tribunal for Rwanda (ICTR)

BACKGROUND
Arusha

The current site of Arusha was first settled as a trading post by the Maasai in the 1830s and the Maasai are today still the dominant community in the region. It was conquered by the Germans in 1896, who established a permanent presence in 1900, when they built a *boma* (fort) with a military garrison and a few shops around a grassy roundabout. The British took Arusha after the First World War, and from the 1920s, it grew from its backwater status to a prosperous service town and centre for colonial administration as British and Greek settlers took over the former German farmlands and plantations of northern Tanzania. It has been an important place in the making of modern Tanzania: documents ceding independence to Tanganyika were signed in Arusha in 1961, and in 1967 the Arusha Declaration was signed – the government's policy on socialism and self-reliance. Its prominence increased further when it became the host town for the International Criminal Tribunal for Rwanda (ICTR) in 1994 and the headquarters of the East African Community in 2000. The Arusha International Conference Centre (AICC) has witnessed the signing of some of the most important peace treaties and international agreements in modern African history. Arusha gained city status in 2006 and, today, it is the busiest Tanzanian city after Dar es Salaam.

from 1994 to 2014 and the Arusha Peace and Reconciliation Agreement for Burundi from 1995 to 2000 taking place here. The centre also has a bank, post office, foreign exchange bureau and cafeteria, as well as various tour operators and travel agents.

Old Moshi Road

In the colonial period Europeans settled in the area adjacent to the River Themi, along Old Moshi Road and to the north and south of it. The Asian community lived near their commercial premises, often over them, in the area between Boma Road and Goliondoi Road. Africans lived further to the west on the far side of the Naura River. On the north side of the Old Moshi Road is **Christ Church Anglican Cathedral**, built in the 1930s in traditional English style of grey stone with a tiled roof and a pleasant interior. The cathedral is surrounded by a vicarage and church offices. Further along the road there are several bungalows with red tile roofs and substantial gardens, which once housed government servants.

Makongoro Road

The **Arusha Declaration Monument** is set on a roundabout past the police station on the Makongoro Road. Also commonly referred to as the Uhuru (Freedom) Monument, it has four concrete legs that support a brass torch at the top of a 10-m column. Around the base are seven uplifting scenes in plaster. The Declaration of 1967 outlined a socialist economic and political strategy for Tanzania. The nearby **Arusha Declaration National Museum** ① *T027-250 7800, 0900-1700, US$3.70*, is dedicated to this landmark in Tanzania's history, outlining the evolution of Tanzania's political and economic development. It also has historic photographs of the German period and a display of traditional weapons including clubs, spears and swords. South of the museum is a small park containing the **Askari Monument**, dedicated to African soldiers who died in the Second World War.

Essential Arusha and Arusha National Park

Finding your feet

The gateway airport to Arusha and the Northern Circuit parks, as well as Moshi and Mount Kilimanjaro, is **Kilimanjaro International Airport** (KIA). It lies to the south of the A23 road, 40 km east of Arusha and 55 km west of Moshi, and has a full range of facilities including restaurants, cafés and shops, plus ATMs and bureaux de change. It is well served by domestic flights and some international airlines (see Practicalities, page 157). A taxi from the airport to Arusha will cost around US$50, or you can pre-arrange an airport transfer with your hotel, tour operator or safari company for a similar price for up to four people. If you fly into KIA with **Precision Air** or **Fastjet**, you can make use of their shuttle

buses that meet incoming flights and go to their offices in central Arusha; both of which charge about US$10 for the service. The Nairobi–Arusha–Moshi shuttle buses also call in at the airport (see Practicalities for further information). Closer to town is the smaller **Arusha Airport**, 9 km west off the A104 road to Dodoma. This is mostly used for charter flights and scheduled services to the airstrips in the Northern Circuit parks. Any *dala-dala* heading along the Dodoma road can drop you at the junction, from where it's a 1.5 km walk – with luggage, it's best to get a taxi which costs around US$8 from the city centre. The 625-km road between Arusha and Dar es Salaam (which goes via Moshi) is smooth tar all the way, and the journey by bus takes around nine hours.

Arusha is also only 273 km south of Nairobi, with the Kenya/Tanzania Namanga border being roughly halfway. An alternative arrival point for those visiting the north of Tanzania is Nairobi's Jomo Kenyatta International Airport, and the two cities are linked by twice daily shuttle buses which normally take around six hours to Arusha. There are also several one-hour flights per day between Jomo Kenyatta International Airport and Kilimanjaro International Airport with either **Kenya Airways** or **Precision Air** (see Practicalities for further information).

Tip...

Touts on the streets in Arusha (known as 'fly-catchers') can be very persistent and will try and take you to a tour operator's offices in the hope of getting a commission. This can be intimidating, especially when they latch onto and follow you, but they are usually harmless. To get them off your back, tell them you have already booked a safari, even if you haven't.

Listings Arusha *map p46*

Tourist information

Tanzanian Tourist Board
Information Centre, 47E Boma Rd, T027-250 3842/3, www.tanzaniatourism.com. Mon-Fri 0800-1600, Sat 0830-1300.
A useful source of local information with leaflets and free city maps of Arusha and Moshi to pick up. It also can help make arrangements for the **Tanzania Cultural Tourism Programmes** (see page 66) and

holds a list of registered tour and safari companies as well as a 'blacklist' of rogue or unlicensed ones (see page 59).

Ngorongoro Conservation Authority Information Office
Boma Rd, T027-253 7019, www.ngorongorocrater.go.tz. Mon-Fri 0900-1700, Sat 0900-1300.
A couple of doors along from the tourist information office. There's not much to pick

Getting around

The city centre, which is easily walkable but not advised at night, is in two parts, separated by a small valley through which the Naura River runs. The upper part, to the east, contains the government buildings, post office, most of the top-range hotels, safari companies, airline offices, curio and craft shops, and the huge **Arusha International Conference Centre (AICC)**. Further down the hill and across the valley to the west are the commercial and industrial areas, the Central Market, small shops, many of the budget hotels and the bus stations. In the middle of the centre is the clock tower and roundabout. From here, Sokoine Road neatly bisects the town to the west and continues further out of town to become the main A104 road that goes to both Dodoma and the parks of the Northern Circuit. To the southeast of the clock tower is Old Moshi Road, along which some of the better hotels are located. *Dala-dalas* run frequently up and down the main throroughfares, costing US$0.50. Taxis are everywhere and should cost little more than US$4-6 for a short journey around town – remember fares should always be agreed upon at the start of a journey. There are also motorbike taxis – known as both *boda-bodas* and *piki-pikis* in Arusha – and short ride costs around US$2.

Tour operators can help you trek Mount Meru or explore Arusha National Park.

Safety

Arusha is a moderately safe city, but precautions should always be observed. Occasional muggings and pickpocketing are the greatest risks so ensure you do not flash your wealth and keep valuables hidden, if you have to carry them at all. Be extra vigilant along congested parts of Sokoine and Old Moshi roads and in the market areas and bus stations. Taxis are advised at night and if you are in a vehicle, ensure that it is securely locked.

When to go

Arusha is mostly warm and sunny and accessible at any time of year. Be aware though tht Mount Meru can be tough to climb in the rainy season from the end of March to May, when the going is hard, slippery and sometimes dangerous; the summit, at over 4000 m, can be cold at any time of year.

Time required

One or two days will be needed to sort out safari arrangements and see the town; add on another day for a trip around the Arusha National Park, three days to climb Mount Meru and one day to recover.

up here in the way of leaflets, but it does sell some books and maps of the national parks, and there is an interesting painting on the wall that shows all the parks in the Northern Circuit, which gives a good idea where they all are in relation to each other. There is also a model showing the topography of the Ngorongoro Crater.

Tanzania National Parks Authority (TANAPA)
*Dodoma Rd, T027-250 3471, www.
tanzaniaparks.com. Mon-Fri 0800-1600.*

TANAPA's head office can provide information about the national parks if required, although the park gates themselves are the better bet to pick up maps and brochures.

Where to stay

There is a reasonable choice of accommodation in and around Arusha, given that it's usual to spend at least a night here before and after going on safari. The board and lodgings type places in the

Arusha

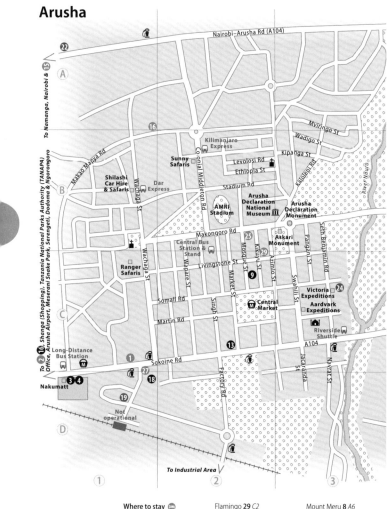

Where to stay 🛏

The African Tulip **13** *D5*
Arusha **19** *C4*
Arusha Backpackers **27** *C1*
Arusha Coffee Lodge **2** *C1*
Arusha Crown **25** *B2*
Arusha Naaz **18** *C4*
Bay Leaf **6** *C6*
East African **4** *D5*
Equator **28** *B5*

Flamingo **29** *C2*
Ilboru Safari Lodge **7** *A6*
Impala **11** *D6*
Karama Lodge **5** *D6*
Le Jacaranda **12** *D6*
L'Oasis Lodge
  & Restaurant **14** *A6*
Masai Camp &
  Barafu Art Lounge **3** *D6*
Meru House Inn **1** *C1*

Mount Meru **8** *A6*
Naura Springs **31** *A4*
New Safari **21** *C4*
Onsea House &
  Country Inn **9** *A6*
Outpost Lodge **23** *D5*
Palace Hotel Arusha **10** *B4*
Pepe One & Pepe's
  Restaurant **32** *B5*
Sakina Campsite **15** *A1*

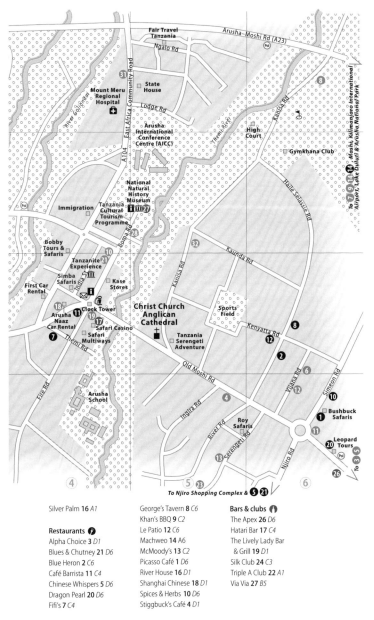

Silver Palm **16** *A1*

Restaurants 🍴
Alpha Choice **3** *D1*
Blues & Chutney **21** *D6*
Blue Heron **2** *C6*
Café Barrista **11** *C4*
Chinese Whispers **5** *D6*
Dragon Pearl **20** *D6*
Fifi's **7** *C4*

George's Tavern **8** *C6*
Khan's BBQ **9** *C2*
Le Patio **12** *C6*
Machweo **14** *A6*
McMoody's **13** *C2*
Picasso Café **1** *D6*
River House **16** *D1*
Shanghai Chinese **18** *D1*
Spices & Herbs **10** *D6*
Stiggbuck's Café **4** *D1*

Bars & clubs 🍸
The Apex **26** *D6*
Hatari Bar **17** *C4*
The Lively Lady Bar
 & Grill **19** *D1*
Silk Club **24** *C3*
Triple A Club **22** *A1*
Via Via **27** *B5*

downtown market area and around Sokoine Road are cheap and handy if you want to be in the city centre and close to the bus stages, but can be noisy and suffer from Arusha's griminess. The better option is to travel to the outlying suburbs, where places are often set in their own attractive gardens, or stay in the peaceful country hotels in the foothills of Mount Meru. If you are going on an organized safari, the tour operators will usually pick up and drop off at your chosen accommodation even if it's out of town.

$$$$ Arusha Coffee Lodge
5 km west of town on the Dodoma (A104) road near Arusha Airport, T027-250 0630, www.elewanacollection.com.
One of the most luxurious options in Arusha, set on a working coffee estate, with 30 stunning spacious chalets with balconies, fireplaces, facilities to make coffee, enormous beds with mosquito nets, hardwood floors and wooden decks, Zanzibar-style furniture and Persian rugs. Very elegant lounge and a restaurant for fine dining (see below) with dressed up tables and leather sofas, plus a swimming pool.

$$$$ Onsea House
Baraa Rd, about 5 km outside Arusha off the Moshi (A23) road, T0784-833 207, www.onseahouse.com.
In a beautiful location overlooking the hills and Mount Meru, this boutique hotel owned by the Belgian Janssen family has 13 super-stylish rooms either in the main house or cottages. All are elegantly furnished with tribal artwork on the walls, elaborate designer chandeliers, walk-in showers, furniture made from coconut trees, private verandas or balconies, and there's a swimming pool in tranquil gardens. Excellent restaurant on the terrace, see below.

$$$ The African Tulip
44/1 Serengeti Rd, T027-254 3004, www.theafricantulip.com.
Hotel owned by **Roy Safaris** with 29 rooms decorated in smart contemporary style with an African safari theme, all with either balconies or large windows with window seats overlooking the grounds, DSTV, Wi-Fi and minibar. There's the chic Zanzibar Lounge bar, which also serves afternoon tea, a Baobab-themed restaurant and a pool in lawned gardens.

$$$ The Arusha Hotel
Near the clock tower, T027-250 7777, www.thearusha hotel.com.
Formerly the site of an old German hotel built in 1894, of which the splendid restaurant is the only surviving feature. The 86 elegantly decorated rooms, with a/c, DSTV and Wi-Fi, have balconies overlooking the swimming pool or the beautiful gardens running down to the Themi River. There's a gym, bar with garden terrace, restaurant serving Italian and Indian dishes, and the spacious lobby is a good place to drop into even if not staying as it has a lounge with high-back chairs and leather sofas, Wi-Fi, a coffee bar, and good book, gift and jewellery shops.

$$$ The Bay Leaf
102 Vijana Rd, T027-254 3055, www.bayleaftz.com.
This popular boutique hotel is set in a charming house in a quiet leafy street just a few mins' walk from the centre. It has just 5 individually decorated suites, some with colonial antiques and luxurious drapes, modern bathrooms with power showers, Wi-Fi, no pool but a mini-garden and terrace. Best known for its superb gourmet restaurant (see below) and the high standard of food carries through to the fantastic breakfasts for overnight guests.

$$$ East African Hotel
Between the clocktower and Impala roundabouts on Old Moshi Rd, T0786-066 060, www.eastafricanhotel-arusha.com.
Aimed predominantly at the conference market, but will appeal to those looking for a large, modern, purpose-built (some would say anonymous) hotel with good facilities, the 144 rooms are spacious with satellite

TV and Wi-Fi and some have mini-kitchens. There's a bar and coffee shop, restaurant, and rates include a generous buffet breakfast, swimming pool and gym.

$$$ Ilboru Safari Lodge
2 km northeast of the centre off the Nairobi-Arusha (A104) road, T0754-270 357, www.ilborusafarilodge.com.
This popular and stylish Dutch-run lodge is set in beautiful flowering gardens and has 38 comfortable rooms either in the main house or in thatched cottages, some triple and family rooms, decorated with well-chosen African art and bright white linen. There's an excellent restaurant (see below) and the large swimming pool is open to non-guests (0900-1800) for a small fee. Interesting activities offered include traditional tingatinga painting and Swahili cookery classes.

$$$ Impala Hotel
At the Impala roundabout on Old Moshi Rdr, T027-254 3082/7, www.impalahotel.com.
A well-run hotel with several useful amenities. The 177 rooms are in a modern block with DSTV and Wi-Fi, and there's a pleasant garden and patio, swimming pool, 4 good restaurants, including an excellent Indian one, 3 bars/coffee shops, 24-hr room service, gift shop and bureau de change. Mountain bikes for hire.

$$$ Karama Lodge & Spa
3 km from town off the Old Moshi Rd, turn off just past Maasai Camp, T0754-475 0188, www.karama-lodge.com.
22 thatched stilted log cabins built on the hillside in a pretty tract of forest. It's close enough to town but is very peaceful and has good views of Meru and Kilimanjaro. Colourful rooms have hanging chairs on the balcony. There's a rustic bar, and the restaurant uses ingredients from the garden. A popular choice for a rest after climbing Kilimanjaro or Meru and, although it doesn't have a full spa as such, it does have a swimming pool and offers massages, body scrubs and yoga.

$$$ Naura Springs Hotel
East Africa Community Rd, T027-205 0001, www.nauraspringshotel.com.
Unmissable 14-storey, blue-glass building on the corner of the Moshi (A23) road and about 500 m north of the AICC. Beautifully crafted wooden carvings decorate the communal areas and there are good views of Meru, but, beyond that, the place has little character. However the 125 rooms are spacious, have DSTV and Wi-Fi, there are lawns and a pool, and a decent choice of bars and restaurants.

$$$ New Safari
Boma Rd, T027-254 5940, www.newsafarihotel.com.
Although first established in 1935, the New Safari is now a smart modern building, with a nice terrace restaurant on the 1st floor with good views of Meru. The 46 rooms with a/c, DSTV, Wi-Fi, and minibar with soft drinks are good-value from US$125 for a double and US$180 for a triple. Staff are friendly and helpful and it's very close to everything around the clocktower.

$$$-$$ Mount Meru
Kanisa Rd, T027-254 5111, www.mountmeruhotel.com.
Arusha's most luxurious large hotel, this glassy block set in spacious grounds has 178 rooms, from twin/doubles to 2-room suites, with a/c, DSTV, Wi-Fi, bright modern décor and floor-to-ceiling windows, many of which overlook Arusha's golf course or the large pool. There are 3 excellent restaurants, plus bars and a café in the lobby, and a spa. Everything you'd expect of a professionally run 4-star hotel and the highlight is the peaceful, park-like environment so close to the city centre.

$$$-$$ Palace Hotel Arusha
Corner of Boma and Makongoro rds, T027-554 5800, www.palacehotelarusha.com.
A shiny tall new block and very centrally located with 97 modern rooms with Wi-Fi, a/c, room service, DSTV and views of Mount Meru from the higher floors,

including the gym which is on the top floor. The 1st floor **Turaco Bar** with its balcony and large windows looks down Boma Rd, a good place for a drink even if not staying, plus there's the reasonable **Twiga Restaurant** and **Orchids Coffee Shop**.

$$ Arusha Crown
Makongoro Rd, T027-250 8523,
www.arushacrownhotel.com.
A modern hotel and very centrally located (though at first glance it seems a pretty rough and ready backstreet), with 38 good standard rooms on 6 floors with DSTV and Wi-Fi and a decent coffee shop/restaurant that is also open to non-guests. A single is US$54, a twin or a double US$72, excellent value in this price range. The rooms facing north overlook Meru and directly into the stadium – if there's a match on you can watch the football from bed.

$$ The Equator
Near the Natural History Museum, Boma Rd,
T0754-040 810, www.equator-hotel.com
Although very central at the end of Boma Rd, this is on a jungly plot next to the Themi River and is surprisingly quiet. It's old-fashioned but well-kept with 24 fairly large rooms, all with balconies and DSTV, bar and restaurant offering decent buffet breakfasts and mostly Indian meals, a garden, and a car park (rare in the city centre).

$$ Silver Palm
Makao Mapya Rd, T0767-286 630,
www.silverpalmhotel.com.
A low-budget modern option north of the downtown area and not too far from the bus stations, with 45 rooms with DSTV, tiled floors, decent cubicle showers and sound-proofed windows, plus there's a large lobby with lounge seating. Standard doubles start from US$60, and a good buffet breakfast is included in the rates, although there have been poor reports about mediocre food and slow service in the restaurant at other meal times.

$$-$ Arusha Naaz Hotel
Near clock tower on Sokoine Rd,
T027-250 2087, www.arushanaaz.net.
Once you get through the bizarre shopping centre entrance and head up the small staircase, the 21 single, double and triple (US$45/60/75) a/c rooms are centred around a little internal courtyard and are clean, with en suite bathrooms, 24-hr hot water, fans and mosquito nets, and there's a restaurant with Indian snacks and buffet lunches (closed in evening), though there are better eating options close by. You can also hire cars from here.

$$-$ Le Jacaranda
Vijana Rd, T027-254 4624,
www.lejacarandahotel.com.
This cheerful lodge has 23 African-themed rooms, small but clean and decorated with Maasai artwork, some are in the main building, which was a colonial farmhouse, while others are dotted around the gardens. Facilities include Wi-Fi, comfortable bar area with sofas on a terrace overlooking the gardens, a rather bizarre 'home-made' but fun crazy golf course, and the restaurant serves everything from Chinese to Swahili with plenty of vegetarian options (see page 53). Doubles from US$55.

$$-$ L'Oasis Lodge & Restaurant
2 km out of town, in the quiet residential area of Sekei, off the Moshi (A23) road,
T027-250 7089, www.loasistanzania.com.
Good all-round setup catering for budget travellers, with 28 rooms, some in thatched rondavels, some in the main building, plus a row of 12 smaller twin budget rooms with shared bathrooms, although some are a little dark and dreary. Good restaurant with continental and vegetarian dishes (the Greek-inspired salads are good) and there's a casual laid-back lounge and bar by the swimming pool which serves burgers and pizzas. The lovely garden has a pond with fish and wading birds.

$$-$ Outpost Lodge
41 Serengeti Rd, off Old Moshi Rd, near Impala Hotel, T027-254 8405, www.outpost-lodge.com.
Good and long-established friendly budget option with 28 simple but neat rooms in spacious garden cottages, plus dorms/family rooms in the main house sleeping up to 4 (US$20 per person), with reliable hot water, mosquito nets and fans and a full English breakfast included. There's a swimming pool and **Café Mambo** is a cheerful café and bar, with chilled music and Wi-Fi around the pool area.

$ Arusha Backpackers
Sokoine Rd, T0715-377 795, www.arushabackpackers.co.tz.
This is a popular low-budget option with good facilities, including a lively bar and restaurant on the top floor with Wi-Fi, the 34 rooms share toilets and showers and are sparsely furnished and some are like windowless cells with nothing but bunk-beds and a chair, but good value at US$20 for a double including breakfast. There are also some dormitories with 2 sets of bunk beds for US$10 per person.

$ Hotel Flamingo
Kikuyu St, near the market, T0754-260 309, flamingoarusha@gmail.com.
A good low-budget option, with 9 spotlessly clean, light and airy rooms with mosquito nets and own bathrooms. Friendly staff and a pleasant bar area that serves soft drinks only, and can serve very early breakfasts (toast, tea and fruit) if need be; if you're catching an early bus, for example.

$ Hotel Pepe One
Just off Kanisa Rd, T0784-365 515, www.hotelpepeone.co.tz.
This popular restaurant also has 5 rooms, all off the main reception area, which are simple but with good, modern, tiled bathrooms, nets, Wi-Fi and DSTV. Tidy and clean but a bit cramped. Lively restaurant serving a varied menu (see below) and it's in a quiet location in pretty grounds. Good value at US$45 for a double; breakfast is an extra US$5.

$ Meru House Inn
Sokoine Rd, T027-250 7803, www.meruhouseinn.com.
One of Arusha's cheapest options, but like the nearby Arusha Backpackers (above), it's on a horribly noisy and busy section of Sokoine Rd. Nonetheless, it's secure and friendly, the en suite rooms on 3 floors above a row of shops are clean with nets and good new bedding, the front ones have balconies, and there's Wi-Fi in reception, a bar and small restaurant for breakfast and pizza later on in the day. Single US$25, double US$40 and triple US$50.

Camping

Masai Camp
3 km along Old Moshi Rd, T027-250 0358, www.masaicamptz.com.
This long-established camp is deservedly popular with budget travellers, backpackers and overlanders and offers shady camping spots on grassy terraces (US$8 per person), 2 en suite cottages with little patios (US$50 double/twin), plus some basic huts with single beds and mosquito nets that share bathrooms with campers (US$10 per dorm bed, US$25 for a twin). The ablutions are spotless, with steaming hot water, and there's a fantastic restaurant and lively bar (see below), with good food, Wi-Fi and a sociable atmosphere around the giant fireplace.

Sakina Campsite
5 km northwest of the centre on the Nairobi-Arusha Rd (A104), T073-979 050, www.sakinacampsite.com.
A little bit out of town, but a secure spot at a house in a walled compound and a good option for budget travellers and those with vehicles. 5 rooms with shared bathrooms in configurations of doubles, triples and dorm rooms from US$10 per person, or you can camp on the lawns for US$5 and there are hot showers. Self-catering kitchen, bar and home-cooked meals are available. Plenty of *dala-dalas* run into town from the main road outside.

Restaurants

Arusha has some of the best dining options in the region, many of which are found in the restaurants of the upmarket hotels.

$$$ The Bay Leaf
See Where to stay, above.
Open 0800-1400, 1800-2200.
Excellent-quality food in this stylish boutique hotel, including the quartet starter – a sample of 4 of the starter dishes – and gourmet mains using lamb, duck and rabbit, plus fresh ravioli and gnocchi, liqueur coffees and good choice of wines. There's also a separate Indian menu offering some delicate Punjabi cuisine. Expensive, but a very inventive menu for Arusha and nice for a treat in the smart dining room.

$$$ Machweo
At Onsea House, see Where to stay, above, T0784-833 207, www.machweo.com. Open for brunch, lunch and dinner, bookings essential.
The Belgian head chef and sommelier here, Axel Janssens, prepares a daily changing menu of gourmet, beautiful-presented brasserie dishes that are Belgian/French with an African influence, accompanied by fine wines. He is passionate about using locally sourced and the freshest ingredients (seafood is only on the menu if it has been flown up from Dar es Salaam that morning for example). Expensive, but a sophisticated treat. Tables are on a terrace or around the swimming pool, from where there are good views of the Monduli Mountains and Mount Meru.

$$$-$$ Arusha Coffee Lodge
See Where to stay, above. Open 0800-2200.
In a fabulous setting at this luxurious lodge, the main **Bacchus Restaurant** is in the main building, Plantation House, which overlooks the swimming pool and offers lunchtime buffets with at least 4 main courses to choose from, and a dinner menu of gourmet dishes and fine wines. **3 Degrees South** is a bistro-style venue with outside decks and offers lighter meals including good pizzas, and its bar also offers excellent coffees from the estate.

$$$-$$ Chinese Whispers
Njiro Rd, T0688-969 669. Open 01000-2200.
The best and most upmarket of Arusha's several Chinese restaurants, this is on the second floor at the Njiro Shopping Complex (see Shopping below). Smart decor with white linen-clad tables, good winelist, swift proficient service and an extensively long menu of everything from duck pancakes and dim sum to sizzling prawns and whole steamed tilapia fish. Dishes are beautifully presented and ideal to share.

$$$-$ The River House
5 km west of the centre on the Dodoma road (A104), near Arusha Airport, T0689-759 067, www.shanga.org. Open 0930-1630, buffet lunch is served 1130-1430.
This is the restaurant at Shanga (see Shopping below), and has lovely lawns surrounded by coffee bushes that make up the Burka Coffee Estate, Arusha's oldest coffee plantation. Tables are set up in open-air pagodas and the lunchtime buffet (about US$20; reservations recommended) includes at least 4 main dishes of barbequed fish, chicken, and beef, plus salads, vegetables and desserts. You can also pop in for tea/coffee and cakes before or after an interesting tour of the Shanga workshops and spot of shopping.

$$ Barafu Art Lounge
At Masai Camp, see Where to stay, above. Open 1000-late.
This hugely popular restaurant and bar at the Masaai Camp offers a great atmosphere and good food including Tex Mex, burgers, pasta, salads, sandwiches and nachos but is best known for its brick-oven baked pizzas. There are plenty of lounge areas, usually a roaring fire going, pool tables and a separate cocktail bar opens in the evening. An excellent place to hook-up with other travellers and swap safari tales, and there's Wi-Fi.

$$ Dragon Pearl
Old Moshi Rd, near the Impala Hotel,
T027-254 4107. Mon-Fri 1100-1500,
1800-2230, Sat-Sun 1230-2245.
Tasty and fairly authentic Chinese food and
swift service with outside tables in lovely
gardens. Specialities include fried wonton
and sizzling dishes, or try the crispy chilli
prawns or hot and sour chicken. It's a good
choice for vegetarians and serves wines
from South Africa.

$$ George's Tavern
50 Hallie Selassie Rd, T0782-943 690.
Open 1000-2200.
Very tasty Greek food from mixed mezes
and Greek salad to beef and lamb kleftiko
and traditional moussaka, plus a few Italian
dishes such as pizzas and lasagne, and
some rich and gooey chocolate desserts.
The blue-and-white checked tablecloths
and cheerful Greek music create a lovely
atmosphere and George and his team offer
friendly, professional service.

$$ Ilboru Safari Lodge
See Where to stay, above. Open 0600-2300.
Popular spot serving a mix of international
and Swahili cuisine, along with some Dutch
dishes; try the Swahili stews, which include
a delicious veggie option, or the excellent
sweet and savoury pancakes. There's a relaxed
atmosphere in the Masaai-inspired restaurant
or eat outside next to the swimming pool.

$$ Le Jacaranda
See Where to stay, above. Open 0900-2200.
Restaurant and bar on an attractive upstairs
wooden deck, lounge area downstairs,
surrounded by pretty gardens. Continental,
Indian, Chinese and Swahili meals, grills and
steaks, and a wide selection of vegetarian
options and desserts. The downside is
service can be very slow.

$$ Pepe's
At Hotel Pepe One, see Where to stay, above.
Open 1200-1500, 1800-2230.
A lively Italian and Indian restaurant, well
known for its pizzas and lasagne but the

tandoori and tikka dishes are worth a try
too and are served with buttery naan bread.
Tables are set in pretty gardens or in the
restaurant with Maasai artwork.

$$ Shanghai Chinese Restaurant
Sokoine Rd near the bridge, beside
Meru Post Office, T0756-659 247.
Open 1200-1500, 1800-2230.
This long-established Chinese has an
extensive and fairly authentic menu; the
hot and sour soup is highly recommended,
service is quick and portions large. There
are pleasant outdoor tables under thatch
on a terrace with potted palms.

$$ Spices & Herbs
Simeon Rd, a few metres north of the Impala
Hotel, T0754-818 533. Open 1100-2300.
Long-established, informal Ethiopian
restaurant with good vegetarian options
made from lentils, peas and beans, very
good lamb and continental food (steaks,
chops and ribs) and of course injera (spongy
flat bread). Set in a beautifully landscaped
garden full of birds, with good, friendly
service, full bar and sometimes live music at
the weekend. Also has a dozen or so rooms
for accommodation at the back (**$**). They
are simple with not much more than a bed,
wardrobe and floor mat, and you cannot
pre-book, but are cheap and clean with
reliable hot showers.

$$-$ Alpha Choice
In the TFA Shopping Centre (see page 57),
Sokoine Rd, T0688-813 954. Mon-Sat 1000-
2300, Sun 0800-1600.
Next to Nakumatt, this is a shop for seafood
and fish, which is flown up daily from the
coast, and also has a neat little café and
takeaway for excellent fish and chips,
shawarmas and burgers – the double cheese
burger with guacamole is especially filling
and delicious. Most surprisingly for Arusha,
also serves nicely presented well-priced sushi
and there's a teppanyaki hot plate to grill
king prawns and calamari.

$$-$ Fifi's
Themi Rd, T0789-666 518, www.fifis tanzania.com. Open 0800-2200.
As close to a modern coffee shop as you can get, always busy Fifi's is only 300 m from the clock tower. Offers a full range of barista-style coffees and has a bakery for bread, cakes and pastries, plus a variety of breakfasts from full English to American pancakes, and more substantial meals for lunch and dinner like burgers, pasta, steaks and fish. Also does takeaway lunch boxes for people going on safari. Wi-Fi and it's also an outlet for **iheartz** – a gift and clothing brand specializing in local fabrics.

$$-$ Le Patio
Kenyatta Rd, just off Haile Selassie Rd, T0783-701 704. Open 0830-2300.
Set in a delightful garden setting with tables scattered under giant fig trees and around an outdoor fireplace, this is part formal restaurant, part café-bar and nightspot. The menu starts with hearty cooked breakfasts and moves on to exceptionally good cakes and pastries and light lunches during the day, to more sophisticated grills and fish dishes for dinner. There are plenty of lounge areas, good music and a DJ cranks up things up on Fri and Sat nights when the bar is open to 0100.

$$-$ Picasso Café
By Kijenge Supermarket, Simeon Rd, T0756-448 585, www.picassocafe.info. Open 0900-2300.
A modern a/c café and a great place for an upmarket breakfast or brunch, with a full English for US$7. It's also a popular lunch spot, serving sandwiches, crêpes, burgers and delicious cakes and more substantial meals in the evening. Wine and beer served too and has Wi-Fi.

$ Khan's BBQ
Mosque St. Mon-Fri 1830-late, Sat-Sun 1630-late.
On the edge of the Central Market and popular with locals and visitors alike, Khan's has been around for decades and is a cross between a *nyama choma* joint and an Indian takeaway (it's actually a vehicle spare parts shop during the day). For about US$6 per plateful, you can fill up with tasty skewered grilled meat, roast chicken, tandoori kebabs, naan bread and salad, and can wash it down with either a cold beer or fresh fruit juice.

$ McMoody's
On the corner of Sokoine and Market St, T027-254 4013. Tue-Sun 1000-2200.
McDonald's-inspired fast food for those hankering after fries and milkshakes in a refreshing swoosh of a/c. The menu offers burgers – beef, chicken and vegetarian and naturally there's a McWhopper – plus slices of pizza, Indian snacks and decent cappuccinos and iced coffees.

Cafés

Blue Heron
Haile Selassie Rd, T0785-555 127, www.blue-heron-tanzania.com. Mon-Thu 0900-1600, Fri-Sat 0900-2200.
A colourful house set in beautiful gardens, the outside bar is built around a frangipani tree and tables are set on the lawns or under a giant sail-cloth on the terrace. All-day breakfasts, cakes, coffees, filled paninis, wood-fired pizzas, and a good choice of pastas, steaks and sauces on Fri and Sat evenings. Children are well catered for with a kids' menu and jungle gym, plus there's an outlet of **Schwari Collectables** here (ladies and children's clothing, handbags and shoes made from local beading and hand-died textiles).

Blues & Chutney
Leganga Rd, off Njiro Rd, T0732-971 668, www.bluesandchutney.com. Mon-Sat 0900-1700.
Set in a 1950s' colonial house in a spacious garden, this charming café is part of a B&B – the 6 rooms (**$$**) are neat and comfortable and either have en suite or shared bathrooms. The house is decorated in an interesting mix of art deco antiques and modern paintings, many of

which are for sale in the gift shop. Food includes soups, homemade baguettes for sandwiches, generous salads, and brownies, biscuits and cakes. There's Wi-Fi and a day spa in a couple of rooms around the back (www.bodysensetz.com).

Café Barrista
Sokoine Rd, T0754-288 771, www.cafe barrista.com. Mon-Thu 0700-1830, Fri-Sun 0730-2200.
This comfy a/c café is really in the heart of things, just near the clock tower roundabout, and is always buzzing with tourists drinking lattes and checking their emails (it has Wi-Fi and computer terminals, plus a printing and scanning service). The long menu offers coffees, juices, ice cream, pastries and muffins and main meals such as pizza and crispy fried chicken. The super friendly staff are a good source of tourist information.

Stiggbucks Café
In the TFA Shopping Centre, see Shopping below, Sokoine Rd, T0754-375 535. Mon-Sat 0900-1700.
Behind **Nakumatt**, this small friendly café has outside seating under trees and offers all-day breakfasts including good filled omelettes, crunchy salads, sandwiches, coffees, assorted teas, thick milkshakes, fresh juices, and there's free Wi-Fi.

Bars and clubs

There are a number of popular places in town and almost all the hotels and many of the restaurants have bars. If you are looking for a party with other travellers the best places to go are the Meserani Snake Park (page 63) and Masai Camp (page 51).

The Apex
Old Moshi Rd, just past the Impala Hotel, T0765-047 901. Thu-Sat 1800-0600.
A popular club with dance floors, several bars, and what is probably the biggest outdoor stage in Arusha for concerts of local bands and regular events like hotly-contested karaoke competitions.

Hatari Bar
The Arusha Hotel, near the clock tower, T027-250 7777, www.thearushahotel.com. Open 1200-0100. Happy hour daily 1700-1900.
A relaxed bar in **The Arusha Hotel** and named after the 1960 'safari' movie Hatari, on account of it being the favourite watering hole of John Wayne and other cast members during its filming. Offers a full range of drinks including cocktails, plus coffees, an all-day menu of light meals and shows sports on TV. In the hotel lobby is **Freshly Ground**; a coffee bar and patisserie (0700-1030).

The Lively Lady Bar & Grill
Range Rd, turn off Sokoine Rd into the dirt road behind Arusha Backpackers, T0713-650 777. Mon-Sat 1700-2400.
This friendly and tiny bar, with its even tinier kitchen, is lively indeed and is a fun and vibrant place to meet local people and has a wide selection of drinks from beers to shooters. Serious drinking gets going at about 2300, but get there early to grab a table and enjoy some Indian snacks or *nyama choma* (including unusual pork steaks).

Silk Club
Seth Benjamin Rd, T0713-123 359. Wed-Sat 2200-0400.
Formerly the Crystal Club (and it's still called the Crystal Club Building), what is considered as Arusha's oldest nightclub has 2 large dance floors with separate DJs playing anything from soul ballads to upbeat hip-hop, pool tables and several bars including a quieter covered outside one that shows sports on TV.

Triple A Club
5 km northwest of the centre on the Nairobi-Arusha Rd (A104), T0655-998 87. Open 2000-0600.
This is easily the largest and most popular nightclub in Arusha with sophisticated lighting and sound, a big range of music including R&B and hip hop, enormous dance floor, pool tables, 2 bars, regular event nights, and also runs its own FM radio station.

Via Via

Boma Rd, T076-562651. Mon-Sat 0930-2300, Sun 1300-2300.

A popular bar in the gardens of the Natural History Museum, arranged in a series of thatched *bomas* with garden seating. A DJ plays a mashed up mix of both local and international music, and Thu night is the liveliest when there's a live band and it closes much later. The sandwiches and snacks are passable but the hot meals are poor, so eat elsewhere first.

Entertainment

Casino

Safari Casino, *at The Arusha Hotel (see Where to stay, above).* Open from 1200 for the slot-machines and from 1700 for the gaming tables and stays open until 0400 or 0500.

Cinema

Century Cinemax, *in the Njiro Shopping Complex, 3 km out of town on Njiro Rd (see page 57), T0755-102 221, www.century cinemaxtz.com.* A 2-screen cinema showing movies from 1300, either Hollywood or Bollywood. Tickets are around US$6 and Mon is half price. Popcorn and cold drinks are available and there's a food court and restaurants in the centre itself.

Shopping

There are plenty of curio shops and stalls in the streets around the clock tower; especially along Goliondoi Rd, India St and Fire Rd. These have a good choice of Maasai beads and blankets, as well as animal carvings, masks, batiks and jewellery. All prices are negotiable.

Arts, crafts and curios

Cultural Heritage Centre, *3 km west of the centre on the Dodoma road (A104), T027-250 7496, www.culturalheritage.co.tz. Mon-Sat 0900-1700, Sun 1000-1500.* This one-stop art and curio 'department store' is in a massive structure built to resemble a giant Maasai

Tip...

For tanzanite gemstones and jewellery, go to **Tanzanite Experience** on India Street (www.tanzaniteexperience.com) or **Swala Gem Traders** in **The Arusha Hotel** (www.swalagemtraders.com).

spear and shield ensemble and it's a popular stop for all safaris on the way to the Northern Circuit parks, although, of course, it is very expensive. The items however are of very high quality: carvings, musical instruments, cloth, beads and leatherwork from all over the continent, plus there's a tanzanite and precious stone counter, and shops selling Tanzanian tribal antiques and spices from Zanzibar. They can arrange shipping back to your home country and there are desks for both DHL and Fedex on site. The restaurant here offers a long menu from teas and coffees to Swahili dishes and Indian curries.

Shanga, *5 km west of the centre on the Dodoma road (A104), turn off on the right after the Cultural Heritage Centre, T0689-759 067, www.shanga.org. Open 0900-1630.* On the Burka Coffee Estate, this began in 2006 as an initiative to train local disabled artists in beadwork – Shanga is the Kiswahili word for bead – made from wine and other drinks bottles collected from safari lodges around Arusha. Today it has grown into a clutch of workshops and shops selling some beautiful items made from recycled glass, paper, fabrics, aluminium and plastic. Products include jewellery, glassware, crockery and clothes. The majority of today's artists – which you can meet and watch work – are physically disabled or deaf, and the project has gone a long way to provide paid employment and teach skills such as glass-blowing or tailoring. Additionally 10% of profits go towards assistance for disabled children in schools – providing wheelchairs in classrooms for example. Also here is **The River House** restaurant (see Restaurants above), so a visit can include coffee or lunch combined with a visit to the workshops and shops.

Bookshops

A Novel Idea, *TFA Shopping Centre, see below, T0272-547 333, www.anovelideatz.com. Mon-Sat 0900-1730, Sun 0900-1400.* Stocks a wide range of up-to-date novels, coffee table books on Africa, guide books, maps, intelligent Africana titles, as well as wrapping paper and greeting cards. Prices are steep as everything is imported, but nevertheless one of the best ranges of books in Tanzania and there's another branch in Dar es Salaam.

Kase Book Stores, *Boma Rd, T027-250 2640. Mon-Fri 0900-1730, Sat 0900-1400.* A very large shop with a good selection of books in English and Kiswahili. It's a bit chaotic but if you search among the textbooks you'll find novels, wildlife and cookery books, stationery and postcards.

Markets and shopping centres

Central Market, *behind the bus station along Market St and Somali Rd.* A colourful and lively place to visit (though, as in any market, be wary of pickpocketing), and the range of fresh produce is very varied as you can buy just about every imaginable fruit and vegetable in Tanzania. Also sells locally made basketware, wooden kitchenware and spices, and look out for chips mayai (chips in omelette), a tasty market snack. Be prepared to haggle hard and visit a variety of stalls before deciding on the price. Market boys will help carry goods for a fee. In the rainy season watch where you are stepping – it becomes a bit of a quagmire.

Njiro Shopping Complex, *Njiro Rd, 4.7 km south of the clock tower roundabout.* Not quite a fully fledged shopping mall, but this modern centre with a car park has a few useful shops, a pharmacy, ATMs, a number of restaurants in a food court with central open-air tables and the **Century Cinemax** (see Entertainment, above). Also here is **The Village Supermarket**, *open 0900-2100.* Has a good range of imported items and an excellent butchery.

TFA Shopping Centre, *Western end of Sokoine Rd, beyond Meru Post Office and*
opposite the long-distance bus station. This is home to Nakumatt, Arusha's largest supermarket (a branch of the hugely successful Kenyan chain) selling just about anything you might be looking for (Mon-Sat 0830-2200, Sun 1000-0900). The centre also has banks with ATMs, an internet café, an ice cream parlour, restaurants and several other shops, including a wine and cheese shop and a branch of **Woolworths**, a South African chain for quality clothes, and the bookshop **A Novel Idea** (see above). TFA stands for the Tanganyika Farmers' Association, which owns the centre.

What to do

Golf

Arusha Gymkhana Club, *Kanisa Rd, bordering the Mount Meru Hotel, T0782-777 077, www. arushagymkhanaclub.com.* 9-hole golf course established in 1953. Temporary membership is available and clubs and caddies can be hired. There are also facilities for tennis and squash and a 25-m swimming pool, plus a clubhouse with bar and restaurant.

Horse riding

Kaskazi Horse Safaris, *based on a farm adjacent to the Nduruma Polo and Country Club near Usa River, T0766-43 27 92, www. kaskazihorsesafaris.com.* Offer day rides, and 3- to 14-day horse safaris around Kilimanjaro and Lake Natron as well as Amboseli National Park in Kenya. These are for experienced riders, as several hours a day are spent in the saddle. A real opportunity to explore terrain where vehicles cannot go. Full-board rates, inclusive of meals and fly camping, start from US$350 per day.

> **Tip...**
>
> For camel riding around Arusha guided by the local Maasai, see **Mkuru Camel Safari Cultural Tourism Programme**, page 68, and the **Meserani Snake Park**, page 63.

ON THE ROAD
How to organize a safari

- Figure out how much money you are willing to spend, how many days you would like to go for, which parks you want to visit and when you want to go.
- If you have the time before arriving in Arusha, check out the websites and contact the safari operators with questions and ideas. Decide which ones you prefer from the quality of the feedback you get.
- Pick three or four tour operators in your price range.
- Shop around. Talk to the companies. Notice if they are asking you questions in order to gain an understanding of what you are looking for, or if they are just trying to book you on to their next safari (regardless of what would be the best for you). Also, are they open about answering your questions and interested in helping you get the information you need. Avoid the ones that are pressuring you.
- Listen to them too. They have current news about which parks are best at the moment. If they recommend you a different itinerary than you originally planned, it is probably the best itinerary for game viewing. They know the best areas to visit depending on the time of year and where the animals are in their yearly migrations.
- Make sure you understand what is included in the price, and what is not. Normally, breakfast on the first day and dinner/accommodation on the last day is not included.
- Ask what kind of meals you can expect. If you are on a special diet, confirm that they can accommodate your needs.
- Ask how many people will be on the safari. Make sure there is enough room in the vehicle for people and equipment.
- Talk to the guide. Make sure that he is able to communicate with you, and that he is knowledgeable.
- If possible, inspect the vehicle you will be using beforehand. If you are going on a camping safari or trek, ask to see the equipment (tents, sleeping bags, etc).
- Get a contract with all details regarding itinerary, conditions and price before handing over any money.

If you want to swim, some of the hotels allow non-guests to use their pools for a small fee or if you visit for lunch; try the **Mount Meru Hotel**, **Il Boru Safari Lodge** or **Impala Hotel**.

Tour operators

There are over 100 tour operators and safari companies based in Arusha who organize safaris to the different national parks in the Northern Circuit, such as the Serengeti, Ngorogoro, Manyara, etc (see Northern Circuit Game Parks). Most also offer local day trips to nearby destinations such as Lake Duluti and Arusha National Park, Mount Kilimanjaro and Meru treks, holidays in Zanzibar, hotel and lodge reservations, vehicle hire, charter flights, arrangements for **Tanzania Cultural Tourism Programmes** (see page 66) and safaris to the other parks in southern and western Tanzania and across the border in Kenya. The list below is far from comprehensive. It is just a matter of finding one you like and discussing what you would like to do. Many have adopted cultural or environmental policies – supporting local communities, schools or empowerment projects – which is also worth thinking about when choosing an operator. Give yourself at least a day or two to shop around and organize everything – see box, above, for further information on how to organize a safari – and remember safaris usually return back to Arusha later in the day, so allow for at least one night in Arusha on the final day.

It needs to be highlighted that in the low season and quieter times, rival or similarly-priced tour operators sometimes 'double up'. This means that safari clients – as singles or in groups of 2-4 – may well be sharing the same vehicle, guide and accommodation arrangements, simply because its more cost effective for the tour operators to combine their clients on one trip. This is usually not a problem, but check that you are paying no more than other people on your safari and be wary of itineraries that are changed at the last minute without agreement. Along the same vein, at the **Tanzanian Tourist Board Information Centre** on Boma Rd (see below) is a notice board for tour operators advertizing seats on safaris to fill up vehicles – you may well be able to get a last minute bargain.

In the past, Arusha was well known for its bogus tour operators, and many tourists fell victim to well-organized scams by paying in advance for a safari that never actually materialied. Although this is a rare occurrence these days (Arusha's tourist industry is fairly well self-regulating), there are a couple of ways to check the credentials of your chosen tour operator. At the **Tanzanian Tourist Board Information Centre** on Boma Rd (see page 44), there is both a list of accredited tour operators and safari companies, and a blacklist of rogue and unlicensed ones and the names of people who have been reported for cheating tourists. You can also check the website of the **Tanzania Association of Tour Operators** (**TATO**): www.tatotz.org. This not only provides collective representation in the tourism industry in Tanzania, but also promotes high quality and standards among its members – any Arusha tour operator worth its salt, will be a member of TATO.

Aardvark Expeditions, *Swahili St, T0784-424 905, www.aardvark-expeditions.com.*
Adventureland Safaris, *Sokoine Rd, T0754-866 339, www.adventurelandsafari.com.*
African Heart Expeditions, *off the Nairobi-Arusha (A104) road near Ilboru Safari Lodge, T0732-975 428, www.africanheart.com.*
African Trails, *Njiro Rd, T0784-428 355, www.africantrails.com.*

Angoni Safaris, *AICC, T0784-282 117, www.angoni.co.tz.*
Bobby Tours & Safaris, *Goliondoi Rd, T027-250 3490, www.bobbytours.com.*
Bushbuck Safaris, *Simeon Rd, T027-254 3336, www.bushbuckltd.com.*
Classic Tours & Safaris, *Impala Hotel, see Where to stay, above, T027-254 3082, www.theclassictours.com.*

Duma Explorer, *Njiro Rd, T0787-079 127,*
www.dumaexplorer.com.
Eastern Sun Tours & Safaris, *PO Box 14236,*
T0784-279 996, www.easternsuntours-
safaris.com.
Easy Travel & Tours, *New Safari Hotel,*
see Where to stay, above, T0754-400 14161,
www.easytravel.co.tz.
Fair Travel Tanzania, *Almizo St, off Ngalo Rd,*
T0786-025 886, www.fairtravel.com.
Fortes Safaris, *Nairobi-Arusha (A104) road,*
T027-250 6094, www.fortes-safaris.com.
Good Earth Tours & Safaris, *Moshono Baraa*
Rd, T0732-902 655, www.goodearthtours.com.
Hoopoe Safaris, *India St, T027-250 7011,*
www.hoopoe.com. Safaris and climbs and also
run luxury mobile tented camps, **Kirurumu**
Under Canvas (www.kirurumu.net).
JM Tours, *Plot 15, Olorien, off Njiro Rd,*
T027-254 3310, www.jmtours.co.tz.
Laitolya Tours & Safaris, *Meru Plaza, Esso Rd,*
T0754-264 845, www.laitolya.com.
Leopard Tours, *Old Moshi Rd, T027-254 8441,*
www.leopard-tours.com.
Lions Safari International, *Nairobi-Arusha*
(A104) road, T027-250 6423, www.lions-safari-
intl.com.
Nature Discovery, *PO Box 10574, T0732-971*
859, www.naturediscovery.com.
Predators Safari Club, *Namanga Rd,*
Sakina, T0784-562 254, www.predators-
safaris.com.
Ranger Safaris, *Wachagga St, T027-250 3023,*
www.rangersafaris.com.
Roy Safaris, *2 Serengeti Rd, T027-250 2115,*
www.roysafaris.com.
Safari Multiways, *TFA Building, off Fire Rd*
next to Arusha Hotel, T0767-317 805,
www.safarimultiwaystz.com.
Shidolya Safaris, *AICC, T027-254 8506,*
www.shidolya-safaris.com.
Simba Safaris, *between Goliondoi Rd and*
India St, T027-254 9115, www.simbasafaris.com.
Sunny Safaris, *Col Middleton Rd, T027-250*
8184, www.sunnysafaris.com.
Takims Holidays Tours and Safaris, *Uhuru*
Rd, T027-250 8026, www.takimsholidays.com.

Tanzania Serengeti Adventure, *corner*
Kanisa and Old Moshi Rds, T027-250 4069,
www.tanzaniaserengetiadventure.com.
Tanzania Travel Company, *AICC, T027-250*
3349, www.tanzaniatravelcompany.com.
Tropical Trails, *Maasai Camp, Old Moshi Rd,*
T027-250 0358, www.tropicaltrails.com.
Victoria Expeditions, *Seth Benjamin Rd,*
T027-250 0444, www.victoriatz.com.
Wayo Africa, *Sekei Village Rd, T0784-203 000,*
www.wayoafrica.com.
Wildersun Safaris and Tours, *Joel Maeda Rd,*
near the Njiro Shopping Complex T027-
254 8847, www.wildersun.com.
Wild Spirit Safaris, *Moshono Village,*
near Baraa Primary School, T0784-654 624,
www.wssafari.com.

Transport

Air
Kilimanjaro International Airport (**KIA**),
T027-255 4252, www.kilimanjaroairport.
co.tz, is 40 km east of Arusha and 55 km
west of Moshi to the south of the A23. It is
served by a number of international airlines
(see page 44) and domestic and regional
carriers; **Air Excel**, **Air Tanzania**, **Fast Jet**,
Precision Air, **Regional Air** and **Tanganyika**
Flying Co. (TFC). Closer to town is the smaller
Arusha Airport, 9 km west off the A104 road
to Dodoma. This is mostly used for charter
flights and scheduled services to the airstrips
in the Northern Circuit parks. It is served by
Air Excel, **Air Tanzania**, **Auric Air**, **Coastal**
Aviation, **Flightlink**, **Precision Air**, **Regional**
Air, **Tanganyika Flying Co. (TFC)** and **ZanAir**.
For details of destinations and contacts, see
Practicalities, page 157, and getting to and
from the airports, see Essential Arusha and
Arusha National Park, page 44.

Bus, *dala-dala* and shared taxi
Local There are 2 bus stations in Arusha.
The **Central Bus Station and Taxi Stand** is
on Makongoro Rd just to the north of the
market and buses from here mostly go to
places not too far away. Buy your ticket from

the driver. There are regular buses and *dala-dala* to **Moshi**, 1½ hrs, US$1.50. You can also get a shared taxi (usually a Peugeot estate car), which will be a little more expensive, about US$3, given that they only seat 7 passengers. Alternatively, and much more comfortably, is to jump on one of the Nairobi–Moshi shuttle buses in Arusha for US$15; see page 44.

Long distance Long-distance buses go from the main long-distance bus station along Makao Mapya Rd opposite the **TFA/Nakumatt Shopping Centre** at the western end of Sokoine Rd. Buses will only leave when completely full. Note: buses are not permitted to travel at night, so except for those to nearby destinations, departures are early in the morning. As such, this bus station gets very busy from as early as 0500 (when it's still dark), when buses are preparing themselves to leave their overnight parking spots, and the roads around are teeming with people being spewed from taxis and

dala-dalas. Petty theft has been known to occur at the Arusha bus stations so guard your possessions fiercely.

Buses to **Dar es Salaam** (10 hrs: US$17) depart at least every 15 mins between 0600 and 1000, and also pick up in Moshi an hour so later (note though you cannot get on a long-distance bus between Arusha and Moshi – the alternatives are above). Buses on this route offer a complementary bottle of soda or water, and they stop for 30 mins-1 hr for lunch at a petrol station (usually in Mombo or Same) where there's a canteen-like restaurant, takeaway, shop etc.

If you are getting off the bus take everything with you – although main luggage is locked securely beneath the bus, it's not unheard of for things to go missing from overhead shelves inside. There are numerous bus companies, but for the Arusha-Dar route, **Dar Express**, Wachaga St, T0784-555 208 and **Kilimanjaro Express** (also known as **KLM Express**), Colonel Middleton St, T0755-233 077 are recommended for their relatively new a/c buses. More usefully is that both have offices near the bus station so you can book your ticket the day before.

There are also buses to **Dodoma** (11 hrs); **Lushoto** (6 hrs); **Tanga** via Moshi (7 hrs); **Mwanza** via Singida (12 hrs); and **Musoma** (12 hrs), but the Musoma buses pass through the Serengeti National Park and the Ngorongoro Conservation Area and non-residents/foreigners must pay the park entry fees – this makes it a very expensive bus journey and the better option is to go to Mwanza first and then make your way north to Musoma and around.

To Kenya *Dala-dalas* and Peugeot taxis depart from the main long-distance bus station to the Namanga border. You then cross the border on foot and then catch another vehicle to Nairobi, where they arrive and depart from the corner of River Rd and Ronald Ngala St. This will cost roughly about US$12, but the minibuses only leave when full and not to a timetable and there will be a problem of the vehicles accommodating luggage (it might have to go on your knees). The better option are the through shuttle services, see page 44.

Car hire

You can either self-drive or hire a driver at additional cost. Remember you'll need a 4WD to go to the parks and types of vehicles available include Suzuki Vitara, Toyota RAV4, Toyota Land Cruiser, Land Rover and Nissan Patrol. Also ask if the companies can provide tents and other equipment if you want to camp. See page 166 for more details about hiring a car in Tanzania. Most of the tour operators listed above can organize car hire. Also try: **Arusha Naaz Rent a Car**, at the **Arusha Naaz Hotel**, Sokoine Rd, T027-250 2087, www.arushanaaz.net. **Drive Tanzania**, PO Box 11117, Arusha, T0789-667 182, www.drivetanzania.com. **First Car Rental**, Goliondoi Rd, T027-250 9108/9, www.firstcarrental.co.tz. **Fortes Safaris & Car Hire**, on the Nairobi-Arusha Rd (A104), T027-250 6094, www.fortes-safaris.com. **Roadtrip Tanzania**, 5 Sekei Village Rd, T0682-075 622, www.roadtriptanzania.com. **Shilashi Car Hire & Safaris**, Makao Mapya Rd, T0755-373 111, www.shilashicarhire.com.

Around Arusha

lakes, snakes and other native species

Meserani Snake Park

25 km west of Arusha on the Dodoma road (A104), on the way to the Ngorongoro Crater and Serengeti, T0754-440 800, www.meseranisnakepark.com, 0730-1800, entry to both the Snake Park and Maasai Cultural Museum US$10, 30-min camel ride US$7. See also Camping, page 66. Any dala-dala running along the A104 to the village of Monduli (which lies north of the A104) will drop and pick up at the gate.

A popular stop with safari operators on the way to the parks, Meserani is run by Barry and Lynn Bale from South Africa, and is a project that works very well with the local community at the local Maasai village. The Snake Park houses mostly local species, with the non-venomous snakes housed in open pits, and the spitting cobras, green and black mambas and boomslangs kept behind glass. It's also home to other reptiles including monitor lizards, chameleons, tortoises and crocodiles. The Bales provide antidote treatment for snake-bites and other basic health services for the Maasai and other local communities free of charge, as well as providing antivenom for much of Tanzania. Also here, the excellent Maasai Cultural Museum has mock-ups of Maasai huts and models wearing various clothing and jewellery, and a Maasai guide will explain the day-to-day life of the Maasai. Additionally there are pleasant gardens, a campsite, a restaurant and bar, local craftspeople sell their goods, and camel rides and walks can be arranged to meet the people in the nearby Maasai village.

Lake Duluti

About 15 km from Arusha along the Moshi road (A23), this small crater lake, fringed by forest, provides a sanctuary for approximately 130 species of birds, including pied and pygmy kingfishers, osprey and several species of buzzards, eagles, sandpipers, doves, herons, darters, cormorants,

Tip...
If in the area, it is well worth walking the scenic circuit through Lake Duluti's fringing forest.

storks, kingfishers and barbets. Reptiles, including snakes and lizards, are plentiful too. There are wonderful views of Mount Meru and, occasionally, the cloud breaks to reveal Mount Kilimanjaro. From both the hotels here – **Lake Duluti Serena Hotel** and **Lake Duluti Lodge** (see Where to stay, below) – walks are available that go through the surrounding coffee plantations and circumnavigate the lake, and they are accompanied by guides who are knowledgeable about the flora and birds. If you're not staying overnight, you can visit for lunch and organize activities. Alternatively make arrangements for exploring the Lake Duluti area with the **Tengeru Cultural Tourism Programme** ⓘ *Akheri Rd, 350 m north of the Moshi Rd (A23), T0754 960 176, www.tengeruculturaltourism.org,* in the village of Tengeru, which straddles the A23 just north of the lake. Walks, canoeing on the lake, coffee tours and village visits can be organized from US$25 for about four hours.

Listings Around Arusha *map p70*

Where to stay

$$$$ Lake Duluti Lodge
14 km east of Arusha off the Moshi Rd (A23), turn right at the sign and follow the road through a coffee plantation, T0759-356 505, www.dulutilodge.com.
One of the most luxurious places to stay on this side of Arusha, with 18 stunning chalets set among indigenous trees on a coffee farm, each has DSTV, Wi-Fi, walk-through showers and contemporary African decor. There's a dining room, wooden deck and bar (sundowners can be taken at an outdoor lounge area on the lakeshore), swimming pool and lovely gardens. Can organize guided nature walks, canoeing and day trips to Arusha National Park. The whole lodge is wheelchair accessible.

$$$ Arumeru River Lodge
20 km east of Arusha, off the Moshi (A23) road, near Usa River, T0732-979 908, www.arumerulodge.com.
In a rural setting in the Usa River region, with 21 chalets set in pleasant gardens full of birds, 6 are more upmarket, with large terraces and Wi-Fi, and there's a 2-bed family cottage with kitchen. Bar and restaurant with good wholesome farm-style food, large solar-heated swimming pool, activities include forest and village walks with Maasai guides.

$$$ Kigongoni Lodge
10 km east of Arusha, 1 km before Tengeru, 1 km off the Moshi (A23) road, T027-255 3087, www.kigongoni.net.
On a 70-acre coffee farm with good views of Kilimanjaro and Meru, the lodge has

18 cottages, built with local materials, with fireplaces, verandas and 4-poster beds. The restaurant serves a set 3-course meal each night and there's a bar with Wi-Fi and a swimming pool on top of a hill with fantastic views. Revenues from the lodge support a local foundation for mentally disabled children and their families. Guided walks available.

$$$ Lake Duluti Serena Hotel
14 km east of Arusha along the Moshi Rd, turn right at the sign, T027-255 3049, www.serenahotels.com.

Quality lodge in an old colonial homestead nestled in a coffee plantation and overlooking Lake Duluti (see page 64). 42 thatched stone cottages with hand-carved African animals on the doors, lovely flowering gardens, elegant dining room, relaxed open terrace bar, library and impeccable service. Activities on offer include guided walks, canoeing and mountain biking.

$$$ Moivaro Lodge
7 km east of Arusha off the Moshi (A23) road,T027-255 3242, www.moivaro.com.

A relaxing country retreat with good Meru views and 40 lovely double- or triple-bed cottages with verandas and fireplaces, set in gardens on a coffee plantation. There's Wi-Fi, a swimming pool, good restaurant with 4-course set meals, a bar, children's playground, massages, and a jogging/walking trail through the plantation. Informative village visits can be arranged with local guides.

$$$ Mount Meru Game Lodge
20 km east of Arusha off the Moshi (A23) road, near Usa River, T0689-706760, www.mtmerugamelodge.com.

Well run establishment with 15 comfortable thatched bandas in a garden setting with 4-poster beds and verandas, charming atmosphere and very good restaurant, lounge and bar with fireplace in the main house. Established in 1959, the animal sanctuary for orphaned or injured animals is today home to zebra, ostrich, and numerous birds and monkeys. Staff of the lodge will take guests on walks around the town of Usa River and the surrounding coffee-producing villages.

$$$ Ngare Sero Mountain Lodge
20 km east of Arusha off the Moshi (A23) road, near Usa River, T027-255 3638, www.ngare-sero-lodge.com.

Formerly the farm of August Leuer, a colonial administrator from the German period, the main house here dates to 1905 and he named it Ngare Sero which means 'sweet waters'. Today it's a fine and peaceful country retreat with 12 cottage rooms in magnificent mature gardens with bougainvillea and jacarandas and an estimated 200 bird species. Good food, a pool, spa, stables for horse-riding, you can play croquet on the lawns or try trout-fishing in the lake.

$$$ Rivertrees Country Inn
20 km east of Arusha, 3 km off the Moshi (A23) road, near Usa River, T0732-971 667, www.rivertrees.com.

Set in natural gardens along the picturesque Usa River, this is a very elegant country lodge with personal service, 4 individually decorated rooms in the farmhouse and 2 garden cottages with additional decks and fireplaces, swimming pool, and horse riding, village visits and walking trips can be arranged. The charming restaurant with its riverside deck and tasty farm cuisine is open to non-guests (daily 1200-2130) but reservations are required.

$$$-$$ Ngurdoto Mountain Lodge
27 km east of Arusha, 3 km off the Moshi (A23) road, T027-254 2217, www.thengurdoto mountainlodge.com.

A large resort-style place with a good range of facilities on a 140-acre coffee estate and good views of Kilimanjaro and Meru. 139 rooms in the main building or double-storey thatched rondavaals, 3 restaurants, 2 bars, a coffee shop, 9-hole golf course, gym, tennis courts, swimming pool, and children's play area. On the downside, it's dated and fixtures and fittings are worn, so is overdue for a refurbishment.

Camping

Meserani Snake Park
25 km west of Arusha on the Dodoma road (A104), on the way to the Ngorongoro Crater and Serengeti, T0754-440 800, www.meseranisnakepark.com.

A hugely popular spot with backpackers, independent overlanders and overland trucks; just about any safari company on the way to the parks will stop here. Lively atmosphere and friendly, the bar serves very cold beers. The campsite has hot showers and vehicles are guarded by Maasai warriors. Meals from simple hamburgers to spit roast impala are on offer (see also page 63).

Tanzania Cultural Tourism Programmes

community-based, insightful tourism

Several villages around Arusha, Kilimanjaro, Iringa, Pangani, Mbeya and other regions of Tanzania have initiatives that are part of the Tanzania Cultural Tourism Programmes. Right from its inception, the policy has been to promote community-based tourism in which the local people are directly involved in designing and organizing tours and showing tourists aspects of their lives in the areas they live in. Today Tanzania has almost 50 cultural tourism programmes and profits from each are used to improve primary schools, kindergartens, clinics and the like, and provide jobs at a community grassroots level. Originally set up in 1996 with the assistance of the NGO, the Netherlands Development Organization (SNV), these programmes are now largely self-sustainable but also receive support from the Tanzania Tourist Board and the Ministry of Tourism.

The head office is in Arusha at the **National Natural History Museum** ① *on Boma Rd (see page 42), T027-205 0025, www.tanzaniaculturaltourism.com, Mon-Fri 0800-1600, Sat 0830-1330*. The office has leaflets outlining each programme, and it is best to go in and make reservations and arrangements here before going out to the individual locations. You can also book at the Tanzanian Tourist Board office, see page 44, or the other option is to discuss with your tour operator what you would like to do and they may be able to incorporate one or more of these programmes into a longer safari. The websites listed below are also good sources of information. Most of the tours are well off the beaten track in rural areas and give a very different and enjoyable tourist experience. Visitors gain an insight into traditional customs, beliefs, values and ways of life, and above all it's an opportunity to engage with the local people in their own environments. They in turn benefit economically from the experience. Costs vary depending on the programme and group size, but expect to pay in the region of US$12-18 for a half day tour; US$20-30 for a full day tour; and US$30-40 for a full day and overnight tour. On most, traditional meals or a limited choice of Western food are provided. Overnight accommodation is in local homesteads or camping. Some examples of tours around Arusha and in the foothills of Mount Meru are listed below.

ee-Yeiyo Cultural Tourism Programme
25 km from Arusha, off the Moshi (A23) road and then off the road to Momela Gate of Arusha National Park. www.ee-yeiyoboma.com.

The villages in this area at the foot of Mount Meru are inhabited by the mainly agricultural Wameru people who are believed to have migrated here around 300 years ago from the Usambara Mountains in the Tanga region further south. A half day tour with this programme includes a tour of the ee-Yeiyo village and farms where you can try your hand at various domestic tasks from feeding chickens and goats to extracting honey from beehives. Longer walks go through the forests on the edge of Arusha National Park to waterfalls and the source of the River Usa, while the guides identify medicinal plants and herbs along the way.

Ng'iresi Cultural Tourism Programme

7 km from Arusha north of the Moshi (A23) road, transportation by pickup truck can be arranged at the Arusha office. www.arusha-ngiresi.com.

Ng'iresi is a village inhabited by the Wa-arusha people, after which Arusha is named. A Maasai clan that settled on the southwestern side of Mount Meru from the 1830s, over time they have gradually shifted from pastoralism to agriculture – while some still depend on their cattle, others have cultivated large plots on the steep slopes of the mountain. This programme offers half-day guided tours of the village and farms, where you can see the various styles of traditional Maasai and Wa-arusha dwellings and local development projects, such as irrigation, soil terracing and fish nurseries. Longer tours can involve camping at a farm and a climb of **Kivesi**, a small volcano with forests where monkeys and antelope live.

Ilkiding'a Cultural Tourism Programme

7 km north of Arusha along the road signposted to Ilboru Safari Lodge from the Moshi (A23) road. www.ilkidinga.com.

Another Maasai village in the foothills of Meru, on a half day tour here you will be welcomed in a traditional *boma*, be able to visit craftsmen and a traditional healer, and walk through farms to one of several viewpoints overlooking Arusha or into **Njeche Canyon**. It is also possible to visit the primary school, which is funded by money generated by the programme. A three-day hike is also available, camping or staying in local homesteads, stopping at various villages and culminating in a visit to a Maasai market.

Longido Cultural Tourism Programme

The town of Longido lies 86 km north of Arusha on the main A104 road to Namanga and Kenya. Take a dala-dala *from Arusha towards Namanga; the journey to Longido should take about 1½ hrs. www.tanzaniaculturaltourism.com.*

Mount Longido (2629 m) rises up steeply from the plains just under 100 km north of Arusha on the border with Kenya and forms an important point of orientation over a wide area. The **Longido Cultural Tourism Programme** offers several walking tours of the environs, including a half-day 'bird walk' from the town of Longido across the Maasai plains to the *bomas* of Ol Tepesi, the Maasai word for acacia tree. The one-day walking tour extends from Ol Tepesi to Kimokonwa along a narrow cattle trail that winds up the slopes of Mount Longido to an altitude of around 1600 m. On clear days there are views of Kilimanjaro and Meru and, from the north side, extensive views of the plains into Kenya. There is also a more strenuous two-day climb to the top of the steep Longido peak, which at 2629 m is good practice for the ascents of Kilimanjaro or Meru.

Mulala Cultural Tourism Programme

About 30 km from Arusha; the turn-off is just before Usa River; follow signs for the Dik-Dik Hotel; after the hotel, the road climbs for about 10 km. www.tanzaniaculturaltourism.com.

The Mulala village is a typical rural setting on the southern slopes of Meru at an altitude of 1600 m and this programme is organized by the Agape women's group – it is in fact the only Tanzania Cultural Tourism Programme to be developed and implemented solely by women. There are walks through the coffee and banana farms to Marisha River, or to the top of Lemeka hill for views of Meru and Kilimanjaro, and on to the home of the village's traditional healer. The women will also demonstrate cheese- and bread-making.

Mkuru Camel Safari Cultural Tourism Programme

The camp is 5 km from Ngarenanyuki Village, which is 5 km north of the Momela Gate of Arusha National Park. www.mkurucamelsafari.com.

Mkuru is a Maasai village on the north side of Meru, where the communal herd of 25 or so camels are led into the plains to forage and back to the village to be milked. Visitors can go on camel safaris, which combine camel-riding and walking alongside, on a number of itineraries from one day to up to one week. Routes go towards the foothills of Kilimanjaro, to Mount Longido, or even further to Lake Natron. Alternatively, there are walks through the acacia woodland looking for birds, or up the pyramid-shaped peak of Ol Doinyo Landaree. Mkuru Camel Camp itself has safari walk-in tents for overnight visitors with basic toilets and showers, and meals are prepared over a campfire.

Babati and Mount Hanang

Kahembe's Trekking and Cultural Safaris i T0784-397 477, www.kahembeculturalsafaris.com, or make arrangements through the Tanzania Cultural Tourism Programme (above). There are regular bus services from Arusha to Babati (172 km) from 0730, 3 hrs; once there, ask for Kahembe's Guest House, a 5-min walk from the main bus stand.

Babati is 172 km southwest of Arusha on the A104 road to Dodoma. It's a small market town straddling the main road, and the mainstay of the economy is maize farming. The plains around the town are home to cattle herders and, among these people, the Barbaig's traditional culture is still unchanged and unspoiled. The women wear traditional goatskin dresses and the men walk around with spears. A number of imaginative local tours can be arranged for around US$45 per person per day, and English-speaking guides who know the area will help you around, while a Barbaig-born guide will tell you about Barbaig culture. There is the chance to participate in local brick- and pottery-making and beer brewing, and to visit development projects like cattle and dairy farming, or piped water projects. The small **Lake Babati** is about a 10-minute walk from the town, and you can organize canoe rides to see the few pods of hippos and the birdlife. Arrangements include full-board accommodation in local guesthouses and in selected family homes.

Lying to the southwest of Babati, **Mount Hanang** (3417 m) is the ninth-highest peak in East Africa and the fourth highest in Tanzania and is a challenge for more adventurous trekkers. **Kahembe's Trekking and Cultural Safaris** can arrange a trek up Mount Hanang along the Katesh route for around US$130 per person. The Katesh route can be completed in one day, with the ascent and descent taking a minimum 12 hours in total, but this is not recommended for inexperienced hikers, and an overnight on the mountain is usually arranged, sleeping in tents or caves. Independent exploration of the area is possible but not common.

Arusha
National Park

The park encompasses three zones: the highland montane forest of Mount Meru to the west, where black-and-white colobus and blue monkeys can be spotted; Ngurdoto Crater, a small volcanic crater inhabited by a variety of mammals in the southeast of the park; and, to the northeast, Momela Lakes, a series of seven alkaline crater lakes, home to a large number of water birds. There are numerous hides and picnic sites throughout the park, giving travellers an opportunity to leave their vehicles, and this is one of the few of the country's parks where walking is permitted.

Ngurdoto Crater

From Ngurdoto Gate a road leads east towards the Ngurdoto Crater. This area is known as the 'park within the park' – rightly so. The road climbs up through the forest until it reaches the rim. At the top you can turn left or right to go around the crater clockwise or anti-clockwise. However the track does not go all the way round the rim of the crater so you will have to turn round and retrace your tracks back to the main road. The crater is about 3 km in diameter, and although there are no roads down, there are a number of viewing points around the rim from which you can view the animals on the crater floor. These include Leitong Point (the highest at 1850 m), Glades Point, Rock Point, Leopard Hill, Rhino Crest and Mikindani Point. From this latter point you will be able to see Mount Kilimanjaro in the distance.

Arusha National Park & around

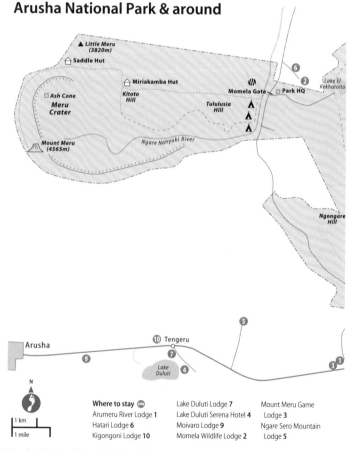

Where to stay
Arumeru River Lodge 1
Hatari Lodge 6
Kigongoni Lodge 10

Lake Duluti Lodge 7
Lake Duluti Serena Hotel 4
Moivaro Lodge 9
Momela Wildlife Lodge 2

Mount Meru Game
Lodge 3
Ngare Sero Mountain
Lodge 5

Momela Lakes route

From Ngurdoto Gate, if you take the left track you will reach the Momela Lakes. This track goes past the Ngongongare Springs, Lokie Swamp, the Senato Pools and the two lakes, Jembamba and Longil. At the peak of the dry season they may dry up but otherwise they are a good place to watch the animals and, in particular, the birdlife. At various spots there are observation hides. At **Lake Longil** there is a camping and picnic site in a lovely setting.

Tip...

Canoeing on Small Momela Lake, where there are several hippos and interesting birdlife, is also an option for the active, and allows you the chance to see wildlife from a slower, quieter perspective. Many Arusha and Moshi tour operators that run day safaris to the park include canoeing.

From here, the track continues through the forest, which gradually thins out, and, through the more open vegetation, you will be able to see Mount Meru. There is a small track leading off the main track to **Bomo la Mengi** – a lovely place from which to view the lakes. Unless the cloud is down, you will also be able to see Kilimanjaro from here. The main track continues past two more lakes – **Lake El Kekhotoito** and **Lake Kusare** – before reaching the Momela Lakes.

The **Momela Lakes** are shallow alkaline lakes fed by underground streams. Because they have different mineral contents and different algae, their colours are also different. They contain few fish but the algae attract lots of birdlife. What you see will vary with the time of year. Flamingos tend to move in huge flocks around the lakes of East Africa and are a fairly common sight at Momela Lakes. Between October and April the lakes are also home to the migrating waterfowl, which spend the European winter in these warmer climes.

Mount Meru

The other major attraction of Arusha National Park is Mount Meru (4565 m), the second-highest mountain in Tanzania and fifth-highest in all Africa. Climbing Mount Meru or enjoying the smaller trails that criss-cross its lower slopes is a popular activity for visitors to the park. Although it only takes three days to reach the crater's summit, it's something of a short, sharp shock – a quieter, but some say more

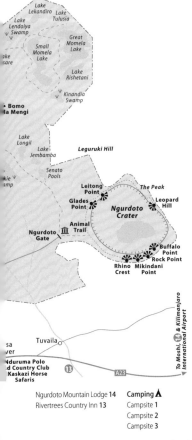

Ngurdoto Mountain Lodge **14**
Rivertrees Country Inn **13**

Camping **A**
Campsite **1**
Campsite **2**
Campsite **3**

BACKGROUND
Arusha National Park

Tanzania's second highest peak and Africa's fifth tallest mountain, Mount Meru (4565 m) is believed to have been formed at around the time of the great earth movements that created the Rift Valley, about 20 million years ago. The crater was formed about 250,000 years ago when a massive explosion blew away the eastern side of the volcano. A subsidiary vent produced the volcano of Ngurdoto, which built up over thousands of years. In a way similar to Ngorongoro, when the cone collapsed the caldera was left as it is today. Ngurdoto is now extinct, while Meru is only dormant, having last erupted about 100 years ago. The lava flow from this eruption can be seen on the northwest side of the mountain. It was at around this time in 1872 that the first European, Count Teleki, a Hungarian, saw the mountain. The Arusha National Park was established in 1960. The Howard Hawks film *Hatari* (meaning 'danger' in Kiswahili) was made here in 1962. Starring John Wayne, Elsa Martinelli, Red Buttons and Hardy Kruger, the movie told the story of a group of adventurers in East Africa engaged in the lucrative but dangerous business of catching wild animals for zoos.

challenging, alternative to the famous peak of nearby Mount Kilimanjaro. Along the lower slopes, paths through ancient fig tree forests, beside crystal-clear cascading rivers and waterfalls make a relaxing day's hike for visitors who don't want to attempt the longer and more arduous climb. The mountain lies to the west of the Ngare Nanyuki road in the western half of the park. There is a track that leads up the mountain to about 2439 m from **Momela Gate**, passing through an open space called **Kitoto** from where there are good views of the mountain, but vehicles are not allowed to pass this way and it is only open to trekkers on the one and only route up to the summit; the Momela Route.

Listings Arusha National Park *map p70*

As well as staying at the below, consider staying at the accommodation off the A23 between Arusha and Moshi (see page 64).

Where to stay

$$$ Hatari Lodge
About 50 km from Arusha, just outside the northern boundary of Arusha National Park, 4 km to the northeast of Momela Gate, T0752-553 456, www.hatarilodge.de.
Named after the famous 1961 movie *Hatari* starring John Wayne, which was filmed in the area, this 'themed' lodge has fun retro 1960s decor – think bucket chairs, lime green walls and padded headboards. The 9 spacious chalets are set in a grove of yellowwood acacia trees and have fireplaces and verandas with views of Mount Meru. Very good food served in the dining room in an old colonial farm building, swimming pool, canoeing, game drives and walks with the Maasai can be arranged. Rates are full board.

$$$ Momela Wildlife Lodge
Close to Hatari Lodge above, 3 km to the northeast of Momela Gate, T027-250 6423, www.lions-safari-intl.com/momella.html.
John Wayne stayed here and the hotel was the production base for *Hatari*; the lodge will screen the film on request. Beautiful gardens, with a swimming pool, but the 55 simple rondavaals are quite run down now and could do with a refurbishment;

Climbing Mount Meru

The ascent of Mount Meru is usually climbed up and down within three days. Because of its altitude and hiking distances, the Meru trek is an ideal warm up for the longer and higher Kilimanjaro challange, but it also appeals to hikers who prefer a less frequented trek.

From the Momela Gate of Arusha National Park, the first day of hiking goes along a track leading up to the Miriakamba Hut (2500 m), which takes about five to seven hours. You should expect to see giraffe, zebra, buffalo and various antelope and as such an armed ranger accompanies trekkers on this section. On the second day the trail continues as a steady climb through montane forest, where there is an abundance of birds and black-and-white colobus monkeys to Saddle Hut (3500 m). It is a three-to five-hour walk between the two huts but it is a steep climb along the ridge of the saddle. Once there you can spend the afternoon climbing Little Meru (3820 m), which takes about 1½ hours and helps acclimatization. From Saddle Hut the climb up to the rim of Mount Meru and around to the summit usually starts at 0200 in order to see the sunrise from the top. It's a steep climb to Rhino Point (3800 m), before continuing along an undulating ridge of ash and rock to reach Cobra Point (4350 m), and then on to the summit (4565 m). The final ascent from Saddle Hut is difficult, cold and can be dangerous, but the views of the cliffs and crater rim are stunning: you can see the ash cone rising from the crater floor and Kilimanjaro floating on the morning clouds. The descent to Momela Gate is on the same day so expect to hike for around 12 to 14 hours in total. If that's too much, there is the option to take four days to complete the trek and spend another night at Miriakamba Hut on the way back down.

Although these are not quite as expensive as for Kili, nevertheless expect to pay in the region of US$650 for a three-day package, US$750 for a four-day trek, including park fees, guide, porters, food and accommodation in mountain huts. See also pages 30 and 71.

it's overpriced at about US$120 for a double. Nevertheless, the views of Meru and Kilimanjaro are excellent, there are many plains animals and a huge variety of birds nearby, and it's well placed for visits to the Momela Lakes.

Camping

Arusha National Park Campsites
There are 3 public campsites in the park at the base of Tululusia Hill, which are rather unimaginatively named 1, 2 and 3, and have water, long-drop toilets and firewood; US$30, children (5-16) US$5.

Northern Circuit
Game Parks

Everything you imagine Africa to be is here in the Northern Circuit Game Parks, from the soaring masses of wildebeest galloping across the plains of the Serengeti, to the iconic image of a lone acacia tree at sunset, to exclusive *Out of Africa*-style lodges deep in the bush. It is a wild, naturally splendid region of Tanzania, but also the most visited region of the country and as such is extremely experienced in catering for tourists and is able to provide for all budgets from the über-luxurious to camping backpackers.

Despite its popularity, it's still easy to escape the crowds. Tarangire National Park, famous for its elephants and quirky baobab trees, is overlooked by many travellers wanting to head for the big names in game parks, and yet it has a gentle beauty and varied landscapes with tremendous birdlife as well as game. Then there's Lake Manyara National Park, where the lake becomes a blanket of pink, as flamingos come here to feed on their migratory route. Also in this region are the little-visited Lake Natron and Ol Doinyo Lengai Volcano – a challenging climb for robust walkers – both offering a glimpse into the rural lives of the local Maasai.

Ngorongoro Crater never disappoints and, because of its steep sides, it has almost captive wildlife. Even if you see nothing, the stunning landscapes within this 265-sq-km caldera 600 m below its rim are reward enough. And last, but far from least, there's the vast Serengeti. From December to July it's the scene of the world's most famous mass migration, when hundreds of thousands of wildebeest pound the path trodden for centuries to the Maasai Mara – definitely a sight not to be missed.

Essential Northern Circuit Game Parks

Finding your feet

About 80 km west of Arusha on the A104 road towards Dodoma, there is a T-junction at Makuyuni. The entrance to the Tarangire National Park is 20 km to the south of this junction towards Dodoma, while the B144 road that heads due west goes towards Lake Manyara, the Ngorongoro Crater and the Serengeti. This road is tar all the way to the gate of the Ngorongoro Crater Conservation Area, after which it becomes a gravel (sometimes rutted) road beyond, and all the way through the Serengeti. The drive from Arusha to the gate of the Ngorongoro Conservation Area takes about four hours and is a splendid journey. On clear days, you'll have a view of Mount Kilimanjaro as you leave Arusha, arching over the right shoulder of Mount Meru. And then you will go across the bottom of the Rift Valley and, at the small settlement of Mto wa Mbu, the road climbs very steeply up the Rift Valley escarpment and there are wonderful views back down onto Lake Manyara. From here,

Best views

Lake Manyara from the Rift Valley Escarpment, page 89
The changing colours of Lake Natron, page 92
Ngorongoro Crater from the crater rim, page 102
The Serengeti from a hot-air balloon, page 120

Best walks

Escarpment walks from lodges around Mto wa Mbu, page 89
Hiking to the top of Ol Doinyo Lengai, page 92
Exploring Lake Natron and the Ngare Sero River, page 92

the country is hilly and fertile, and you will climb up to the Mbulu Plateau, which is farmed with wheat, maize and coffee. The extinct volcano of Ol Deani has gentle slopes and is a prominent feature of the landscape. Once through the crater gate, you are in wild terrain, and the forested top of the Ngorongoro Crater is lush and brilliantly green.

Getting around

All the safari operators offer, at the very least, a three-day and two-night safari of the crater and Serengeti, most offer extended tours to include Tarangire or Manyara, and some include the less visited Ol Doinyo Lengai and Lake Natron. There is the option of self-drive but, as non-Tanzanian vehicles attract much higher entrance fees into the parks, this is not normally cost effective. There is some public transport to towns near park borders, then you'll need to book day trips into parks. For more information on national park fees, see box, page 82; how to organize a safari, see box, page 58; and safari tour operators in Arusha, see page 58.

When to go

It is warm and sunny for most of the year, although evenings can be cool, especially June to October. It does get hot and sticky before the rains. November and December experience light rains and end of March to May see heavier downpours. There are advantages and disadvantages to visiting during the dry and rainy season but do bear in mind that the roads in the parks can be challenging and often impassable during the rainy season (March-May), with access to the crater floor sometimes restricted.

Time required

You will need at least three days for the Serengeti and a day for Ngorongoro Crater. If you want to go off the beaten track, spend an extra couple of days in Manyara or Tarangire – both are worth exploring.

Tsetse flies in the game parks

The tsetse fly is a little larger than the house fly and is found over much of East Africa, including Tanzania. It is a carrier of the disease known as 'sleeping sickness' or African trypanosomiasis, known as nagana

Best safari lodges

Ngorongoro Crater Lodge, page 103
Lemala Kuria Hills Lodge, page 116
Serengeti Serena Safari Lodge, page 118
Serengeti Sopa Lodge, page 118
Singita Sasakwa Lodge, page 119

Best tented camps

Sanctuary Swala, page 83
Namiri Plains, page 116
Serengeti Migration Camp, page 117
Sayari Camp, page 116
Serengeti Pioneer Camp, page 117

among the people of Tanzania. This disease can be deadly to cattle and is therefore of great economic concern to large rural areas of Africa. The presence of the tsetse fly has meant that large areas of Tanzania are uninhabitable by cattle and, consequently, human beings, as farmers need to live where their livestock grazes. Instead, these regions are left to the wild animals, as interestingly, the tsetse fly does not affect them. Since the colonial era, the areas have been gradually designated as national parks and game reserves. Tanzania is probably the worst affected by tsetse fly of all the countries in East Africa, which goes some way to explain why 23% of the country is in designated parks and reserves. Tsetse flies can also infect humans with sleeping sickness – the disease affects the central nervous system and does indeed make you sleepy during the day – but cases in humans are very rare. Tsetse flies, however, do administer a wicked bite, so try and steer clear of them. They are attracted to large objects and certain smells and dark colours – like cows. If you are riding a horse, a tsetse fly is more likely to bite the horse than you.

Tarangire
National Park

Tarangire National Park, established in 1970, covers an area of 2600 sq km and is Tanzania's fifth largest park. Named after the river that flows through it all year round, Tarangire is the scene of an annual 'mini-migration' of sorts, when during the dry season huge masses of animals stream into the park for its perennial water supply. Unjustifiably considered the poor relation to its neighbouring parks – there are far fewer people here than in Ngorongoro, which is very much part of the attraction. Tarangire may have a less spectacular landscape and does make you work harder for your game, but it also retains a real sense of wilderness reminiscent of more remote parks such as Ruaha and Katavi in southwest Tanzania. It's famous for its enormous herds of elephant that congregate along the river; it is not unusual to see groups of 100 or more, including some impressive old bulls. One of the most noticeable things on entering the park is the baobab trees, instantly recognizable by their massive trunks. Within the park boundaries are a number of hills, as well as rivers and swamps, and so there is a variety of vegetation zones and habitats.

Finding your feet

About 80 km west of Arusha on the A104 road towards Dodoma, there is a T-junction at Makuyuni with the B144, which goes towards Lake Manyara, the Ngorongoro Conservation Area and the Serengeti. The entrance to the Tarangire National Park is 20 km to south of this junction towards Dodoma, of which the last 7 km between the A104 and the gate is not tarred. It is a comfortable two-hour drive from Arusha, so there is no need for air transport. However, charter flights can be arranged from Arusha Airport and to/from the Serengeti airstrips. The Tarangire airstrip is next to the Park Headquarters near the entrance gate.

Getting around

With a game-viewing area that is roughly 10 times the size of nearby Lake Manyara National Park, there are several routes and game-viewing circuits. However, like the visitors, most are concentrated in the northern section. It's wilder and quieter further south or up into the hills on either side of the Tarangire River. The roads are reasonable in the dry season (although high clearance vehicles are essential in the hillier sections); while in the wet 4WD is required.

Wildlife

Tarangire National Park forms part of a bigger wildlife ecosystem covering over 20,000 sq km, which includes Lake Manyara National Park to the north, as well as five other surrounding wildlife controlled areas. Tarangire forms a 'dry season retreat' for much of the wildlife in this area and the key to the ecosystem is the Tarangire River. The main animal movements – often referred to as the Tarangire Migration – begin from the river at the beginning of the short rains around October and November, after which the wildlife is widely spread out over the whole 20,000 sq km area during the long

rains and beyond (remember wildlife is more widely dispersed when there is ground water available). When the wet season ends, the animals begin their migration back south and spend the dry season (July-October) concentrated around the Tarangire River until the rains begin again.

Elephant are Tarangire's main attraction, with up to 3000 in the park during the peak months; you cannot fail to encounter large herds and a number of lone bulls as soon as you go beyond the gate. Other game includes wildebeest, zebra, giraffe, buffalo, lion, cheetah, leopard, striped and spotted hyena, warthog and a wide range of antelope including Thompson's gazelle, eland and hartebeest. Three rare species resident here are the greater kudu, long-necked gerenuk and the fringed-eared oryx. The number of species of birds is around 550, which include herons, storks and ducks, vultures, buzzards, sparrowhawks, eagles, kites and falcons. Endemic to the dry savannah of north-central Tanzania (in which Tarangire geographically falls) are the yellow-collared lovebird, rufous-tailed weaver and ashy starling.

When to go

The first migrating animals start to arrive in the park during early June and will remain in the park until November – just before the start of the short rainy season – when the migration moves north again. The game-viewing from July to October is exceptional, but if you cannot coincide a safari with the migration period it's still worth visiting as many animals (especially elephant) stay in the park all year round, the scenery is lush and there are fewer visitors.

Park information

Tanzania National Parks (TANAPA), www.tanzaniaparks.com, open 0630-1830, US$45, children (5-16) US$15, foreign-registered vehicle US$40, Tanzanian-registered vehicle TSh20,000.

The park is large enough for it not to feel crowded even when there are quite a few visitors. There are a number of routes or circuits that you can follow that take you to the major attractions.

Lemiyon area

Lemiyon is the first part of Tarangire that you reach after entering the gate and is tucked in the northernmost end of the park in a triangular shaped zone with the eastern and western boundaries forming the sides and

Tip...
Lookout for the areas along the riverbanks where the water has receded; these are excellent places to observe elephants digging in the sand to reach the water table just below the surface.

the Tarangire River establishing most of the base. The landscape is comprised of grassland and varied woodlands, and this is where you will see the fascinating baobab trees, with their large silvery trunks, mass of gnarled branches and gourd-like fruits. Also found here are flat topped or 'umbrella' acacia trees; a favourite food for giraffes. Other animals that you may expect to see are wildebeest, zebra, hartebeest, gazelle and lots of elephant.

Burungi Circuit

Covering about 80 km, this circuit starts at the Engelhard Bridge and goes clockwise along the Tarangire River bank. Continue through the acacia trees until about 3 km before the Kuro Ranger Post where you will see a turning off to the right. Down this track you will pass through a section of Combretum-Dalergia woodland as you head towards the western boundary of the park. The route continues around and the vegetation turns back to acacia bush as the road turns right and reaches a full circle at the Englehard Bridge. The route features lovely views of Lake Burungi glittering in the distance to the west, which, like Lake Manyara beyond it, is a shallow soda lake.

Matete Woodlands

Located along the eastern side of the Tarangire River, Matete is a region of tall elephant grass, open acacia woodlands and the occasional baobab tree, and the track along the riverbank is an excellent vantage point to watch animals coming to drink in the dry season. The water is alkaline, but the animals seem to have developed a tolerance for the amount of salinity it contains. There is a mountain that stands outside the park called Lolkisale that can also be seen from this area.

Kitibong Hill Circuit

This track covers the west section of the park and is centred on Kitibong Hill. It includes acacia parkland in the east and Combretum-Dalbergia woodland in the west, the Gursi floodplains and Mamire swamps to the south, and the foothills of Sangaiwe Hills, along the western boundary of the park. This area is home to a variety of plains animals, and various pools of water created in natural depressions made by wallowing buffalo and elephant can be found here even in the dry season. Also look out for the turkey-like ground hornbill sauntering through the woodlands.

Tip...
With 550 bird species, Tarangire has the highest count of any Tanzanian park and about one third of all bird species in the country. It offers especially good raptor-viewing – the hills are home to over 50 raptor species.

Tarangire National Park

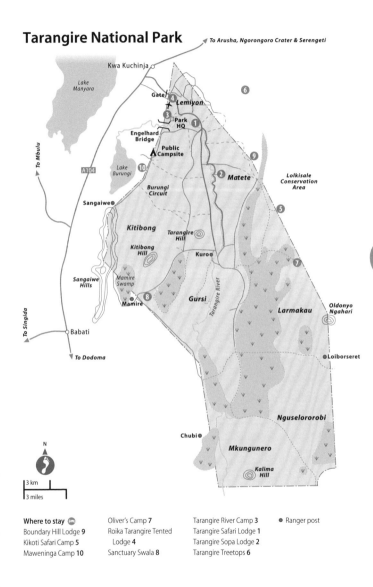

To Arusha, Ngorongoro Crater & Serengeti

Kwa Kuchinja

Lake Manyara

Gate **4** Lemiyon **6**

Park HQ **3** **1**

Engelhard Bridge

Public Campsite

10

Lake Burungi

Burungi Circuit

Matete **2**

9

Lolkisale Conservation Area

5

Sangaiwe

Kitibong

Tarangire Hill

Kuro

7

Kitibong Hill

Sangaiwe Hills

Mamire Swamp

8

Mamire

Gursi

Tarangire River

Larmakau

Oldonyo Ngahari

Babati

Loiborseret

To Singida

To Mbulu

A104

To Dodoma

Chubi

Nguselororobi

Mkungunero

Kalima Hill

N

3 km
3 miles

Where to stay 🛏
Boundary Hill Lodge **9**
Kikoti Safari Camp **5**
Maweninga Camp **10**

Oliver's Camp **7**
Roika Tarangire Tented Lodge **4**
Sanctuary Swala **8**

Tarangire River Camp **3**
Tarangire Safari Lodge **1**
Tarangire Sopa Lodge **2**
Tarangire Treetops **6**

● Ranger post

Park fees

The fees below are for foreign or non-residents; there is a lower fee structure for East African residents, which also applies for expatriate workers (documentation must be shown). If you are on an organized safari your tour operator will pay park entry fees and these costs will be part of the overall price of your safari. You only need pay if you are visiting the parks independently. Entry is per 24 hours. Children's fees are from age 5-16; under 5s go free. Payments are made at the park gates at 'point of sale' machines by Visa or MasterCard credit or debit cards – note: at the time of writing US$ cash was still being accepted, but there are plans to phase out cash payments altogether. For more information contact TANAPA, Arusha, T027-250 3471, www.tanzaniaparks.com.

Serengeti and Ngorongoro Conservation Area
Adult US$60; Children (5-16) US$20

Lake Manyara and Tarangire
Adult US$45; Children (5-16) US$15

Katavi, Kitulo, Mikumi, Mkomazi, Ruaha, Rubondo, Saadani and Udzungwa
Adult US$30; Children (5-16) US$10

Gombe
Adult US$100; Children (5-16) US$20

Mahale
Adult US$80; Children (5-16) US$20

Vehicle entry fees
Up to 2000 kg US$40 (foreign);
TSh20,000 (Tanzanian)
2000–3000 kg US$150 (foreign);
TSh35,000 (Tanzanian)
Only Tanzanian registered vehicles are allowed down into the Ngorongoro Crater itself, for which the additional Crater Service Fee is US$300 per vehicle.

Camping
Public campsites
Adult US$30; Children (5-16) US$5
Special campsites
Adult US$50; Children (5-16) US$10

Gursi and Lamarkau Circuit

The grasslands found in the south of the park are home to many plain-grazing species. You are also likely to see ostrich here. During the wet season a large swamp forms in what is known as Larmakau – a corruption of the Maasai word *o'llakau'*, meaning hippo, which can be seen here.

Without a 4WD you will not be able to see much of the southernmost section of the park and, during the wet season, it is often impassable to all vehicles. There are two areas in the south – Nguselororobi to the east and Mkungunero in the southwest corner. The former is mainly swamp and acts as a giant sponge, which then slowly releases water during the drier seasons so attracts wildlife year-round.

Where to stay

There are accommodation options within the park boundaries, and also just outside in conservation areas established to protect the wet season migration routes. If you are staying outside the park, overnight TANAPA fees do not apply, but you will still have to pay game-driving fees to visit the park during the day. Part of your overnight lodge rate may include a conservation fee.

$$$$ Kikoti Safari Camp
In a conservation area adjoining the east of the park, reservations African Conservancy Company, Arusha, T027-250 8790, www. africanconservancycompany.com.
A small luxury tented lodge built among a landscape of ancient boulders, baobab, mopane and fig trees, with 18 spacious tents with grass roofs and wooden decks. Large eating *boma* with outside campfire and comfortable deck chairs. Bush breakfast and lunches are served in secluded areas, sundowners on Kikoti Rock. Bush walks as well as game drives on offer and visits to the local Maasai village.

$$$$ Oliver's Camp
In the eastern part of the park, reservations Asilia Africa, Arusha T0736-500 515, www.asiliaafrica.com.
Intimate small luxury camp of 10 tents under thatch, with outdoor showers, well spaced out with views of a waterhole. Also a library and drinks tent, open-air dining with the manager and guides who offer walking safaris and game drives during the day. 1 tent is in a secluded location in the bush for honeymooners, carefully designed to blend into the landscape.

$$$$ Sanctuary Swala
On the edge of the Gursi swamp, reservations Sanctuary Retreats, Arusha, T027-250 9817, www.sanctuaryretreats.com.

Comprises 12 extremely comfortable tented suites raised on a wooden deck above the ground under acacia trees, all are within sight of a well-frequented waterhole. Each has its own butler and there's silver service dining in the restaurant that has been constructed around a baobab tree; a stunning infinity pool overlooks the grassy plains and it's a first-class site for birdwatching.

$$$$ Tarangire River Camp
In the Minjingu Maasai community concession area that borders the northwest of the park, 3.5 km from the gate, reservations Mbali Mbali Lodges and Camps, Arusha, T0732-978 879, www.mbalimbali.com.
In a beautiful setting overlooking the river and shaded by a giant baobab tree, are 21 well-equipped tents with 4-poster beds and wooden decks. The main building is an elegant elevated thatch-and-timber structure comprising a main lounge, wildlife reference library, dining room, outdoor fireplace and swimming pool.

$$$$ Tarangire Treetops
Outside the park in the Lolkisale Conservation Area, reservations Elewana Collection, Arusha, T027-250 0630, www.elewanacollection.com.
This pleasantly quirky lodge has 20 enormous rooms in the form of stilt houses, constructed 3-5 m up in huge baobab and marula trees on a wooded hillside overlooking the Tarangire Sand River. It really is a lovely lodge, but its weakness lies in its location, being a considerable distance on rough roads from the main game-viewing areas in Tarangire. Nevertheless, excellent food and service, a swimming pool, walking safaris and night drives on offer.

$$$$-$$$ Tarangire Sopa Lodge
In the northeast of the park, reservations Arusha, T027-250 0630-9, www.sopalodges.com.

If you like intimate lodges, then this might disappoint. A large luxury lodge with 75 suites, opulent lounges, bars and restaurant. Excellent food and barbecues, large landscaped swimming pool on the edge of a rocky gorge and a shop. There are more personal choices of accommodation in the park, but this is a good option for families and offers good out-of-season reductions.

$$$ Boundary Hill Lodge
Outside the park in the Lolkisale Conservation Area, T0787-293 727, www.tarangireconservation.com.
This lodge – part-owned by the local Maasai community and benefiting community projects – has 8 rooms built on the hillside, all affording total privacy with unobstructed views over the savannah and swamps. The rooms are fairly simple but some have outdoor baths and toilets with a view. The restaurant and bar are set on attractive stone terraces. Walking safaris, night drives and fly camping available.

$$$ Maweninga Camp
Outside the northwest boundary of the park, 14 km from the gate, camp T0752-994 7633, reservations Arusha, T0784-228 883, www. maweninga-camp.com.
Built on top of a massive kopje with amazing views over Lake Burungi, the 16 tents are simply decorated and have safari bucket showers but are comfortable and raised on high wooden decks; some are cantilevered from the rocks. Dining room in circular semi-open thatched banda, bar with a natural rock terrace, and a unique outdoor fire pit built into one of the kopje's boulders and reached by a little wooden bridge. Not lavish, more of a high-end budget option with a good bush atmosphere.

$$$ Roika Tarangire Tented Lodge
Just outside the park boundary on the banks of the river about 5 km from the park gate, reservations Arusha, T027-250 9994, www.tarangireroikatentedlodge.com.

Tented camp set in 20 ha, with 20 rooms themed to individual animals, with stunning wood carvings on everything from lamp stands to bedposts. Rather obscure concrete 'animal' baths extend the theme – check out the elephant bath if you can. It's not as scenically striking as its neighbour the **Tarangire River Camp**, and they seem to have gone overboard on the concrete stones in the bar, but it does have a quirky charm and is sensibly priced.

$$$ Tarangire Safari Lodge
10 km into the park from the gate, lodge T027-253 1447, reservations Arusha, T027-254 4752, www.tarangiresafarilodge.com.
This is the oldest lodge in the park and has 35 tents and 5 family-size rondavaals set on an escarpment with stunning views across the Tarangire River and the acacia-studded plains, and perfectly positioned for beautiful sunrises. Not luxurious but comfortable, with a good restaurant and bar, large swimming pool, children's pool with slide, and offers excellent value considering its location within the park.

Camping

TANAPA
Dodoma (A104) road, Arusha, T027-250 3471, www.tanzaniaparks.com.
The park's **Public Campsite** is on the western boundary, 5 km into the park from the gate, and is set amongst a grove of impressive baobab trees. Water and firewood, plus toilet and shower facilities which are simple but above average. US$30, children (5-16) US$5. Pay for camping at the gate. There are also 12 **Special Campsites**, which have to be reserved in advance through TANAPA on an exclusive basis for private use and are often used by the tour operators on camping safaris. At these water and firewood is provided, but unlike standard public campsites they have no facilities whatsoever: you need to be entirely self-sufficient to use them. US$50, children (5-16) US$10.

Mto wa Mbu
to Lake Natron

From the turn-off at the Makuyuni T-junction on the Arusha–Dodoma (A104) road, the road northwest heads through the small town of Mto wa Mbu, home to many distinctive red-clad Maasai. This used to be a popular stop for safari-goers who wanted to rest and have a break from the bumpy road, but now that it is smooth tar all the way to the gate of the Ngorongoro Conservation Area, many safari vehicles carry on straight through. It is, however, a lively place to visit and the closest town to the gate of small and scenic Lake Manyara National Park. Another road goes from here north to the spectacular landscape of Lake Natron.

Mto wa Mbu

banana tasting, curio shopping and views of Lake Manyara

The area around Mto wa Mbu (meaning 'River of Mosquitoes') was dry and sparsely populated only by the Maasai until irrigation programmes began in the 1950s. This transformed the area into an important fruit and vegetable-growing region and attracted people from other regions, and today Mto wa Mbu is a colourful, culturally diverse, busy market town.

Sights

While there aren't many sights in the conventional sense, there is enough to keep you entertained in the town and the environs for a short while. You are likely to be welcomed by people trying to sell the arts and crafts on display in the Maasai central market, a cooperative of about 20 curio sellers, behind which is a fresh food market (look out for the distinctive red bananas for sale). There's also a supermarket, bureau de change (although most of the curio sellers accept US dollars cash), fuels stations, and plenty of bars and cheap eateries along the main street. Thursday afternoon is the biggest market day in town when hundreds of Maasai gather; seeing so many red-robed Maasai men all together is quite a striking sight.

   Mto wa Mbu Cultural Tourism Programme ⓘ *enquire at the Red Banana Café on the main street where the tours start, T027-253 9303; further information available from the Tanzania Cultural Tourism Programme office, or the Tanzanian Tourist Board Information*

Centre, both on Boma Rd in Arusha, see page 59, www.tanzaniaculturaltourism.com, www.mtoculturalprogramme.tripod.com, offers an opportunity to support the local inhabitants and learn about their lifestyle and there are a number of walks on offer or you can hire bikes. You can go through the farms in this surprisingly verdant oasis at the foot of the Rift Valley, and are shown the different varieties of banana grown (there are 32 allegedly) and how the old irrigation system works. You can also walk or cycle to Miwaleni Lake, where papyrus plants grow in abundance, and to one of the waterfalls that cascade down the Rift Valley escarpment for a refreshing dip in the pool below.

Listings Mto wa Mbu

Where to stay

The budget options and campsites in and around Mto wa Mbu are often used by tour operators for the cheaper camping safaris, but if you get to Mto wa Mbu under your own steam, you can stay at these and organize a day trip into Lake Manyara National Park. The more expensive and nicer options are on top of the escarpment beyond town on the way to the crater, which also benefit from lake views (see under Lake Manyara National Park below).

$$$ Migunga Tented Camp
Off the main road, 1.5 km east of Mto wa Mbu, just a couple of kilometres before the gate, reservations Arusha, T027-250 6135, www.moivaro.com.
This lovely, secluded tented camp is set in 14 ha of acacia forest where bushbuck and other antelope are sometimes seen, and has 21 spotless, self-contained tents, dining room and bar under thatch, which are atmospherically lit at night with hurricane lamps. Less luxurious than the normal tented camps, and as it's not on the escarpment there are no lake views, but much more affordable, and rates include meals. Mountain biking, bird walks and village tours can be arranged.

$$-$ Fanaka Campsite & Lodge
Right of the main road in Mto wa Mbu going towards the park, T0753-908 419, www.fanakasafaricamps.co.tz.
A bit newer than most with en suite twin/double/triple rooms in double-storey terracotta-coloured chalets; those on the 2nd floors have balconies, decent grassy gardens surrounded by hedges for camping and spacious tiled bathrooms with hot showers and a kitchen unit with gas cookers. Restaurant, bar with a pleasant terrace and small swimming pool. The friendly staff can organize bike hire.

$$-$ Jambo Lodge & Campsite
In Mto wa Mbu, just a few doors away from Twiga Campsite, T027-2503 5553, www.njake.com.
A well-maintained budget option in pleasant gardens, with 16 en suite rooms in 2-storey houses with fridge, reliable hot water and terrace or balcony. Swimming pool, restaurant and baobab tree bar. Spacious camping ground on a manicured lawn with good ablutions. The downside is it's noisy and dusty given its location on the main road.

$$-$ Kiboko Bush Camp
2 km before town on the Arusha (B144) road, 2 km from the main road, reservations Equatorial Safaris, Arusha, T027-250 2617, www.equatorialsafaris.net.
16 self-contained permanent tents in a lovely tract of acacia forest, set well apart under thatched roofs, although sparsely furnished with small beds and with unattractive concrete showers and toilets, but reasonably good value and there are cheaper beds in ridge tents sharing the campsite bathrooms. The campsite has plenty of space for vehicles, a kitchen area under thatch with cutlery and crockery.

Restaurant and bar in a large thatched building but set meals are uninspiring.

$$-$ Mto wa Mbu Lodge & Campsite
Right of the main road going towards the park, T027-250 6708, www.sunbrighthotels.com.
This pretty campsite is set in lovely gardens dotted with palms and can accommodate 60 tents in all, plus there are 14 small rooms in brick chalets, 9 of which are en suite while the cheaper ones share the bathrooms with campers. Tents and bedding are available to rent, and there are good hot showers, swimming pool and a spacious bar and restaurant under thatch with DSTV. Food is better here than at the other places, and vegetarian dishes and packed lunches can be organized.

$$-$ Twiga Campsite & Lodge
Left of the main road in Mto wa Mbu going towards the park, T027-253 9101, www.twigalodgecampsite.com.

The 24 rooms here vary widely from 'original' and tiny thatched rooms with just a lamp and fan and sharing bathrooms with campers, to 'deluxe' rooms in brick cottages with a/c and en suite bathroom. Plus there some decent grassy tent pitches at the back with plenty of shade and you can hire tents. A good cheap option with bar and restaurant, swimming pool and curio shop but the complex is a bit cramped and can be noisy.

Transport

Mto wa Mbu is 114 km from **Arusha**, and regular *dala-dalas* and buses make the trip from Arusha's main bus station and take about 2½ hrs (although the safari vehicles can do it in under 2 hrs). The town 3 km away from the gate of Lake Manyara National Park.

Tip...
If driving, fill up with fuel in Mto wa Mbu before heading further west.

Lake Manyara National Park
breath-taking escarpment scenery, birdwatching and lakeshore game-viewing

On the way to Ngorongoro Crater and the Serengeti, Lake Manyara National Park is set in the Rift Valley beneath the cliffs of the Manyara Escarpment and was established in 1960. It covers an area of 330 sq km, of which 230 sq km is the lake at its highest. The remaining third is a slice of marshes, grassland and acacia woodland tucked between the lake and the escarpment, whose reddish brown wall looms 600 m on the western horizon. The scenic beauty of Lake Manyara makes it well worth a stop in its own right. Although its compact game-viewing circuit means it doesn't warrant more than a day to see the flamingos and if very (very) lucky, its famous tree-climbing lions.

Routes
With an entrance gate that doubles as an exit, the compact game-viewing circuit in Lake Manyara is effectively a return trip and, except when the water table in the ground forests is especially high, is good enough for most vehicles.

Shortly after the gate, the track crosses the Marere River Bridge, and about 500 m after, the road forks. To the left the track leads to a plain known as **Mahali pa Nyati** (Place of the Buffalo), which has a herd of mainly old bulls cast out from their former herds. There are also zebra and impala in this area. This is also the track to the **Hippo Pool**, formed by the Simba River on its way to the lake and home to hippos, flamingos and many other water birds.

Back on the main track the forest thins out to bush and the road crosses the Mchanga River (Sand River) and Msasa River. Shortly after this latter bridge, there is a turning off to

Essential Lake Manyara National Park

Finding your feet

The only entrance gate is just to the west of Mto wa Mbu, 126 km or 1¾-hour drive from Arusha on the B144 road to the Ngorongoro Crater Conservation Area and the Serengeti. There's an airstrip above the park on top of the escarpment near the Lake Manyara Serena Safari Lodge, which is a 10-minute drive to the gate. The scheduled and charter flight circuits with **Air Excel**, **Auric Air**, **Coastal Aviation**, **Flightlink**, **Regional Air** and **Tanganyika Flying Co** will drop down at Lake Manyara on the way to/from the Serengeti. See page 157 for details.

Getting around

With not much more than 50 km of navigable tracks in the park, Lake Manyara is often visited for half a day on the way to Ngorongoro and the Serengeti. However, if time is not an issue, it's a good park for short game drives with lots of stops to enjoy the lakeshore scenery, birds and picnic spots. Given that it's so close to Mto wa Mbu, an option here, if you are not on an organized safari or in your own vehicle, is to hire a taxi or *dala-dala* from town for the day (remember park entry fees and vehicle costs for Tanzanian residents are much less than for non-residents).

Wildlife

The park's ground water forests, bush plains, baobab-strewn cliffs and algae-streaked hot springs offer incredible ecological variety in such a small area. Lake Manyara's famous tree-climbing lions make the ancient mahogany and elegant acacias their home during the rainy season, and while they are a well-known, they are rather a rare sight so count yourself lucky if you see them lounging above your head. In addition to the lions, the park is home to elephant, leopard, giraffe, buffalo, wildebeest, zebra and antelope including waterbuck, dik-dik, Thomson's gazelle, bushbuck, klipspringer and impala. There is a hippo pool where visitors can get out of their cars and observe from a safe distance, and troops of olive baboons and vervet monkeys inhabit the forest near the entrance gate. There's a huge variety of birdlife – more than 400 species both resident and migratory – and in fact Lake Manyara is so reliable for birdwatching, even first-time visitors might reasonably expect to see 100 species in a day. At certain times of the year, Lake Manyara feeds thousands of flamingos, which form a shimmering pink zone around the lakeshore. Other birds include ostrich, pelicans, African spoonbills, and various species of egrets, herons, ibis, storks and, ducks.

When to go

As with all parks, Lake Manyara's official peak season is from July to October when it is at its driest and less vegetation makes for easier game-viewing. But given that it is such a small park and has reliable water sources, most animals can be seen year-round. The wetter months of December to February and May to July are the best times for birdwatching and for seeing the waterfalls on the cliff faces.

Park information

Tanzania National Parks (TANAPA), www.tanzaniaparks.com, www.lakemanyara.net, 0630-1830, US$45, children (5-16) US$15, foreign-registered vehicle US$40, Tanzanian-registered vehicle TSh20,000.

> **Fact...**
> The first animals you will see on entering the park will undoubtedly be baboons, and the broken forests and escarpment are their perfect habitat. Baboon troops here often number more than 100 individuals, and Lake Manyara is known for having one of the greatest concentrations in Africa.

the left that leads down to the lakeshore, where there is a peaceful picnic spot. Soon after this bridge, the surroundings change to acacia woodland. This is where the famous tree-climbing lions are found, so drive through very slowly and look for a tail dangling down through the branches.

Continue down the main road crossing the Chemchem River and on to the Ndala River. During the dry season you may see elephants digging in the dry riverbed for water. At the peak of the wet season the river may flood and the road is sometimes impassable as a result. Beyond the Ndala River the track runs closer to the Rift Valley Escarpment wall that rises steeply to the right of the road. On this slope are many different trees to those on the plain and, as a result, they provide a different habitat for various animals. The most noticeable are the very impressive baobab trees with their huge trunks.

The first of the two sets of hot springs in the park are located where the track runs along the wall of the escarpment. These are the smaller of the two and so are called simply **Maji Moto Ndogo** (Small Hot Water). The temperature is about 40°C, heated to this temperature as it circulates to great depths in fractures that run through the rocks created during the formation of the Rift Valley. The second set of hot springs is further down the track over the Endabash River. These, known as **Maji Moto**, are both larger and hotter, reaching a temperature of 60°C. You are supposed to be able to cook an egg here in about 30 minutes. The main track ends at Maji Moto and you have to turn round and go back the same way.

Lake Manyara National Park

Map labels:
To Serengeti
Marere River
Msasa River
Chemchem River
Ndala River
Bagayo River
Rift Escarpment
Endabash River
Maji Moto Ndogo
Lake Manyara
Public Campsites 1 & 2
To Mto wa Mbu & Arusha
Gate Bandas
Simba River
Fig Forest
Picnic Spot
Hippo Pools
Picnic Spot
4 WD Only
Ranger posts ●
N
3 km
3 miles

Where to stay
Escarpment Luxury Lodge **1**
Kirurumu Manyara Lodge **2**
Lake Manyara Serena Lodge **3**
Lake Manyara Tree Lodge **4**
Lake Manyara Wildlife Lodge **5**

Listings Lake Manyara National Park

Where to stay

There is only the one luxury lodge within the park – the **Lake Manyara Tree Lodge** – although there are TANAPA campsites. Alternative accommodation is on top of the escarpment beyond Mto wa Mbu, accessed off the B144 on the way to the crater (which is also where the airstrips is), no more than a 10- to 20-min drive to the park gate.

$$$$ Escarpment Luxury Lodge
On the escarpment, reservations Arusha T0767-804 856, www.escarpmentlodge.co.tz.
The 16 chalets here all have large bay windows and terraces with wide views of the lake, tastefully decorated with high ceilings, wooden floors, leather couches in the lounge area, and nice touches include the claw footbaths and outdoor showers. Massages available and the swimming pool is surrounded by a relaxing wooden

BACKGROUND
Lake Manyara

Lake Manyara is a shallow ash-soda lake and is believed to have been formed two to three million years ago when, after the formation of the Rift Valley, streams poured over the valley wall accumulating in the depression below. It has shrunk significantly and was probably at its largest about 250,000 years ago. The name Manyara comes from the Maasai word emanyara, which has in fact nothing to do with a lake, but is a euphorbia species of plant that grows in the region, which the Maasai use to grow a thorny hedge around their homesteads. The lake has alkaline waters and dry spells expose large areas of mud flats. The algae and crustaceans living in such water are eaten by flamingos, which can be seen in great numbers. Seepage from the volcanic rock of the rift wall create freshwater inlets into the lake, and these attract other birds, while hippos, which can only be seen in the northern part of the park, survive because of the freshwater where the Mto wa Mbu River flows into the lake. The park's giant fig and mahogany trees in the ground water forest draw their water from underground springs replenished by rainfall in the Ngorongoro Highlands.

sunbathing deck. Game drives into the park, local walks with the Maasai and an excellent level of service.

$$$$ Kirurumu Manyara Lodge
On the escarpment, reservations Arusha T027-250 2417, www.kirurumu.net.
In a stunning location overlooking the lake, 27 well-appointed tents on solid platforms under thatched roofs, plus 2 honeymoon suites and 2 family cottages, all with splendid views, excellent service and meals. Relaxing bar with sundeck and fire pit, activities include walks with the Maasai, and mountain biking and fly-camping in the Ngorongoro Highlands forests can be arranged.

$$$$ Lake Manyara Tree Lodge
The only lodge within the park, located in the remote southwestern region, reservations Johannesburg, South Africa, T+27-(0)11-809 4300, www.andbeyond.com.
Set in the heart of a mahogany forest and nicely designed to exert minimal impact on the environment, the 10 luxurious treehouse suites here are crafted from local timber and makuti palms, and have outside shower, deck, fans, mosquito nets and butler service. There's a dining *boma* where guests can watch what

is going on in the kitchen, breakfast and picnics can be organized on the lakeshore, and there's a swimming pool. Expensive but for this you virtually get the park to yourself and an impeccable safari experience.

$$$$-$$$ Lake Manyara Serena Safari Lodge
On the escarpment, reservations Arusha T027-254 5530, www.serenahotels.com.
The main attraction here is the lovely infinity pool and observation deck with views over to the lake, while the 67 rooms in circular 2-storey rondavels are comfortable and well-equipped and some triples and interconnecting family rooms are available. Offers mountain biking, forest hikes, nature and village walks, night game drives, canoe safaris when the lake isn't too shallow and children's programmes. Manyara is, perhaps, the weaker of the other Serena lodges in the Northern Circuit in terms of having a luxurious feel, but remains a good and reliable option and is popular with mid-range lodge safaris.

$$$ Lake Manyara Wildlife Lodge
On the escarpment reservations, Arusha, T027-254 4595, www.hotelsandlodges-tanzania.com.

This large but quality safari lodge sits on the very lip of the escarpment and has jaw-dropping views of the lake; especially from the beautiful swimming pool, gardens and the restaurant and terrace bar. The 100 spacious rooms are in a double-storey thatched block and have balconies or patios. As well as game drives, canoeing in the park can be arranged when the water level is sufficiently high.

Camping

TANAPA
Dodoma (A104) road, Arusha, T027-250 3471, www.tanzaniaparks.com.

The park's 2 **Public Campsites** are at the entrance of the park and have water, toilets and showers, US$30, children (5-16) US$5. Pay for camping at the gate. There are also 4 **Special Campsites** further inside the park, which have to be reserved in advance through TANAPA on an exclusive basis for private use and are often used by the tour operators on camping safaris. At these water and firewood is provided, but unlike standard public campsites they have no facilities whatsoever: you need to be entirely self-sufficient to use them. US$50, children (5-16) US$10.

North of Mto wa Mbu

stark, beautiful and inhospitable

The road up from Mto wa Mbu to Lake Natron is very rough and is really only feasible in a 4WD. It is a hot, dusty and desolate journey, but it is also strikingly beautiful in its starkness. Dust cyclones often arise on the horizon, only the occasional Maasai *boma* dots the landscape, and depending on the season, ostriches, zebra and giraffe may be seen wandering slowly across the almost treeless plains.

Engaruka

On the way to Lake Natron and 63 km north of Mto wa Mbu, Engaruka lies at the foot of the Rift Valley escarpment and is one of Tanzania's least known historical sites. In the 15th and 16th centuries the farming community here developed an ingenious irrigation system made of stone-block canals with terraced retaining walls enclosing parcels of land. The site included seven large villages. Water from the rift escarpment was channelled into the canals that led to the terraces. For some unknown reason, the farmers left Engaruka around 1700. Several prominent archaeologists, including Louis Leakey, have investigated these ruins but, to date, there are many questions left unanswered about the people who built these irrigation channels, and why they abandoned the area. The ruins are deteriorating because, with the eradication of the tsetse fly, Maasai cattle now come to graze in this area during the dry season, causing ① extensive damage.

Engaruka Cultural Tourism Programme ① *further details available from the Tanzania Cultural Tourism Programme office, or the Tanzanian Tourist Board Information Centre, both on Boma Rd in Arusha, see page 59, www.tanzaniaculturaltourism.com*, offers day tours from Mto wa Mbu to the ruins or to local farms to see current farming and irrigation methods. A Maasai warrior can also guide you up the escarpment – from where there are views over the ruins and surrounding plains – pointing out trees and plants the Maasai use as food and medicine along the way. In one day you can climb the peak of **Kerimasi** to the north of the village and there is a two-day hike up Kerimasi and then **Ol Doinyo Lengai** volcano (see below). The sodium-rich ashes from the volcano turn the water caustic, sometimes causing burns to the skin of the local Maasai's livestock. Moneys generated are used to exclude cattle from the ruins and to start conservation work, and also to improve the village primary school. There is no formal accommodation but it is possible to camp.

Ol Doinyo Lengai

The closest vehicle access is from Engaresero on Lake Natron in the north (see below). You can organize guided climbs with the Maasai directly with the village council in Engaresero, T0784-710 925, www.oldoinyo-lengai.org, or with the Engaresero Cultural Tourism Programme or with any of the camps at Lake Natron, see below for contact details, or with one of the tour operators in Arusha, see page 58.

> **Tip...**
> On the shifting scree on the lower slopes of Ol Doinyo Lengai the gradient is approximately 30 degrees; as the route ascends on to hard rock covered in tiny stones, the inclination increases to a treacherous 45 degrees.

Ol Doinyo Lengai, the 'Mountain of God' in the Maasai language, is Tanzania's only active volcano and lies to the west of the road to Lake Natron. This 2962-m high active volcano is continuously erupting, sometimes explosively but more commonly just subsurface bubbling of lava. It is the only volcano in the world that erupts natrocarbonatite lava, a highly fluid lava that contains almost no silicon, and is also much cooler and less viscous than basaltic lavas.

The white deposits near the summit are weathered natrocarbonatite ash and lava, and are interpreted by the Maasai as symbolizing the white beard of God. The last violent eruption was in 1926; it lasted for several months and deposited ash more than 100 km away, but lava has occasionally flowed out of the crater since then. Indeed, recent minor eruptions in 2007 and 2008 caused earth tremors in Tanzania and Kenya, the strongest of which measured 6.0 on the Richter scale. Most recently in 2013, a new crack was detected on the summit caused by lava flow and gaseous releases.

Although it is possible to climb the mountain, the trek up to the crater is an exceptionally demanding – no two climbs are the same and only physically fit people should attempt it. The summit is frequently wreathed in clouds, and, in parts, the ground is so soft that one sinks into it when walking. In rainy weather the light brown powdery surface turns white again because of chemical reactions that occur when the lava absorbs water. Climbs are frequently done at night, as there is no shelter on the mountain and it gets extremely hot. You are strongly advised to wear sturdy leather hiking boots to protect against burns should you inadvertently step into liquid lava. Boots made of other fibres have been known to melt. Another safety precaution is to wear glasses to avoid lava splatter burns to the eyes. The ascent usually begins at midnight to reach the peak around dawn, and descending can take just as long; ensure that you have enough water and energy snacks for at least 12 hours. The normal drill is to arrive at Engaresero village in the afternoon in time for a shower, meal and sleep before the guide collects you just before midnight for the 12-km transfer to the base of the mountain. Expect to pay in the region of US$230 for two people, which includes road access fee, climbing permit and the hire of a local Maasai guide; the cost goes down for larger groups.

Lake Natron

This pink alkaline shallow lake is at the bottom of the Gregory Rift (part of the Eastern Rift Valley), touching the Kenyan border about 250 km from Arusha. It lies in a spectacular landscape, surrounded by escarpments and volcanic mountains, with a small volcano at the north end of the lake in Kenya, and the much larger volcano, Ol Doinyo Lengai, to the southeast of the lake (see above).

The lake is fed by the Ngare Sero River and mineral-rich hot springs, but has no outlet, so has an exceptionally high concentration of salts and gets its pink and deep red colours from the billions of cyanobacteria that form the flamingo's staple diet. There are hundreds of thousands of lesser flamingos here, as this lake is their only regular breeding ground in East Africa; successful because the lake's caustic shoreline acts as a barrier against predators trying to reach the nests. Often more of the birds are found here than at either Lake Magadi in Kenya or Lake Manyara. Greater flamingos also breed on the mud flats, and it attracts many other waterbird species, including palearctic migrants. Many of the tour operators in Arusha can include a visit to Lake Natron in their safaris to the Northern Circuit.

Engaresero and nearby walks The only settlement is the sprawling Maasai village of **Engaresero** (which is also spelt Ngare Sero after the river), which lies on the southwest shore of the lake. About a two-hour hike from here and upstream on the Ngare Sero River are a pair of **waterfalls**. This walk winds up through a shady steep-sided gorge and there's a bit of scrambling and splashing though the river involved, but under the second waterfall is an excellent pool for swimming surrounded by doum palms – the walk is well worth it considering temperatures around Lake Natron often exceed 40 degrees.

Engaresero Cultural Tours Engaresero Cultural Tourism Programme ⓘ *guides can be organized at the village council office in Engaresero, T0784-710 925, further details available from the Tanzania Cultural Tourism Programme office, or the Tanzanian Tourist Board Information Centre, both on Boma Rd in Arusha, see page 59, www.engaresero.org, www.tanzaniaculturaltourism.com*, offers day tours around the Lake Natron region, as well as climbs of Ol Doinyo Lengai (above). Some of the options are three-hour trips by 4WD, bike or on foot to see the Engare Sero Footprints (below), some of the lake's hot springs and a spot of birdwatching on the shore, or more challenging four-hour walks up the Rift Valley escarpments for views back down on to the lake (great for seeing the vibrant colours). Visits to Maasai *bomas* around the village can also be arranged, when you may also see how the Maasai herd their cattle into the kraals to milk them.

Engare Sero Footprints The oldest hominid footprints ever found are the Laetoli Footprints, found at Laetoli, which is 45 km south of the Oldupai (Olduvai) Gorge. They were discovered by archaeologist Mary Leakey and her team in 1976. These are the footprints, preserved in volcanic ash, of a man, woman and child walking upright. A cast of these can be seen at the Oldupai (Olduvai) Gorge museum (page 106). But another set of younger footprints have more recently been found within an ancient channel of the Engare Sero River just 1 km from Lake Natron's shoreline. They were first discovered in 1998 by a local Maasai, and were excavated in 2006, and are estimated to represent 18 individuals; mainly women and children who are believed to have walked together on the shores of the lake 120,000 years ago. You can visit them from the village of Engaresero.

Listings North of Mto wa Mbu

Where to stay

$$$ Engare Sero Lake Natron Camp
Near the lakeshore of Lake Natron, 7 km from Engaresero village, info@lake-natron-camp. com, www.lake-natron-camp.com.

This place is set on a flat grassy plain near the lakeshore and has an adventurous Bedouin camp feel to it. The 10 simple tents are under low-level thatched roofs, and the dining and bar mess tent have rugs and cushions scattered on the floor and is located next to a delightful freshwater stream where you can cool off. Follows eco-principles, with, for example, compost toilets and filtered natural spring water to drink. A good range of activities, including sundowners on top of a nearby hill, walks with the Maasai and the climb of Ol Doinyo Lengai, can be arranged. US$20 from each bed night goes to the local Maasai to fund primary school education in the area.

$$$-$ Lake Natron Tented Camp
Close to Engaresero, operated by Moivaro, reservations Arusha T027-250 6315, www.moivaro.com.
A shady spot under a patch of acacia trees, with 9 self-contained spacious permanent tents, plus 4 slight cheaper rustic bandas with flush loos and outdoor showers, and a campsite with a large mess tent to cook in and shelter from the sun; there are tents and bedding for hire. Thatched dining room and bar and lovely rock swimming pool that harnesses the local spring water. Again offers plenty to do including local hikes, visits to Maasai *bomas* and the climb of Ol Doinyo Lengai. Pays a concession fee to the local Maasai community to use their land.

$$-$ Lengai Safari Lodge
Close to Engaresero, T0768-210 091, www.lengaisafarilodge.com.
This fairly new place sits on a little ridge above the village and there are excellent lake and Ol Doinyo Lengai views. Simple accommodation is in 6 stone thatched rondavels or 4 permanent tents or you can camp; it's been built a little haphazardly, the water in the showers doesn't drain away well for example, but comfortable enough and friendly. Tasty set meals and cold beers and the all activities are on offer with the Maasai staff as guides.

$$-$ World View Campsite
Close to Engaresero, T0786-566 133, www.worldviewcampsite.com.
Again on a little hill with views across to the lake, there are plenty of camping pitches here under shady acacias, clean, modern ablution block with cool showers and flush loos, a fire pit to cook on (and you can hire a cook) and a central thatched building with a bar; by the time you read this they may have also have some dorm beds. The Maasai staff will walk you to the Engare Sero Footprints and the river's waterfalls.

Transport

The road to Lake Natron (roughly 120 km north of Mto wa Mbu) is part sand, part small stones, and while wet weather is rarely an obstacle, a high clearance 4WD vehicle is essential. You'll need to fill up tanks in Mto wa Mbu, and carry extra fuel if expecting to do a lot of mileage. You can also drive west from Engaresero if you're in a study 4WD; it's roughly a 5-hr drive to the Serengeti's **Kleins Gate** in the far northeast of the park, but note last entry through this gate is at 1600.

Bus
The only public transport is 1 daily bus from Engaresero to **Arusha** via Mto wa Mbu, which leaves at 0600 and takes 6 hrs; it then returns from Arusha almost as soon as it arrives. There are also occasional buses between Arusha and **Loliondo**, which also stop in Engaresero, but these aren't to be relied upon.

Taxi
4WD taxis (usually battered Land Rovers) make the journey up from Mto wa Mbu to Lake Natron and take around 3 hrs.

Ngorongoro
Conservation Area & Lake Eyasi

With its vast expanses of grassy plains, savannah woodlands and highland forests, the 8292-sq-km Ngorongoro Conservation Area encompasses the Ngorongoro Crater, Oldupai (Olduvai) Gorge, and the Empakaai and Olmoti Craters, while Lake Nduto and Lake Masek mark part of the southern boundary with the Serengeti National Park to the west. The area was established in 1959 as a multi-use area, where wildlife could coexist with the Maasai pastoralists who graze their livestock. In 1978 it was declared a UNESCO World Heritage Site in recognition of its outstanding natural beauty and its importance for archaeological research. The Ngorongoro Crater is often called 'Africa's Eden', and a visit to the crater is a main draw for tourists coming to Tanzania and a definite world-class attraction. With its steep protective walls, abundance of fresh water and good micro-climate, it contains everything necessary for the 25,000 or so large mammals that inhabit the crater floor to exist and thrive. Just outside the remote southern border of the Ngorongoro Conservation Area is Lake Eyasi. Situated at the foot of Mount Oldeani and the base of the western wall of the Rift Valley's Eyasi Escarpment, it is a wild, remote and atmospheric place.

The small but burgeoning town of Karatu lies on the Arusha–Serengeti road (B144) and is 142 km from Arusha, 28 km after Mto wa Mbu, 14 km before the Lodoare Gate of the Ngorongoro Conservation Area, and 115 km before the Naabi Hill Gate to the Serengeti. In the past, the area around Karatu was of great importance to the German colonial administration. The region's cool climate, verdant hills and pleasing views made it popular with settlers and farmers, and coffee was a main crop grown for export. Today, a few large farms that remain in private hands still cultivate the cash crop on the hills and small valleys outside of town.

Essential Ngorongoro Conservation Area

Finding your feet

On the Arusha–Serengeti road (B144), the Lodoare Gate to the Ngorongoro Conservation Area is 156 km west of Arusha, 14 km from Karatu and 101 km before the Naabi Hill Gate of the Serengeti. The 2½-hour drive from Arusha to Lodoare Gate is all on tarmac – in fact the tar stops abruptly at the gate – after which it is gravel all the way through to the Serengeti and beyond. Unless you stay on the main B144 road both in the Ngorongoro Conservation Area and the Serengeti National Park, you are required to have a 4WD vehicle. From the gate the road climbs through dense forest towards the crater rim – look out for leopard and elephant – and the altitude increases and the temperature starts to fall. Your first view down into the crater comes at Heroes' Point (2286 m). Beyond here, the road continues to wind its way around the rim first passing the Lerai crater access road (ascent only), past the access roads to the lodges and on to what is termed as Crater Village. This is the location of the Ngorongoro Conservation Area Authority park headquarters, and there are fuel pumps (not to be relied on), tyre mending facilities, a police post and small *duka* shops (kiosks for very basic supplies). Beyond here is the Seneto crater access road

(descent only). The only other route down into the crater is the Lemala crater access road (descent and ascent) which serves the lodges on the eastern side. Just after Seneto is the Windy Gap viewpoint, and then the road veers west away from the crater and on towards the Olduvai Gorge and Serengeti.

The airstrip is on the crater rim near Crater Village and it is serviced on the scheduled and charter flight circuits to and from the Serengeti from Arusha and Kilimanjaro airports with **Air Excel, Auric Air, Coastal Aviation, Flightlink, Regional Air** and **Tanganyika Flying Co (TFC).** See page 157 for details.

Getting around

Access onto the crater floor is limited to half a day (maximum of six hours) per visitor, and safaris enter either early in the morning or early in the afternoon. While any vehicles can drive through the Ngorongoro Conservation Area (and to the Serengeti beyond), only Tanzanian registered tour operators and vehicles are permitted down into the crater itself and you must be with a guide. As such all visitors go down on a half-day excursion as part of an organized safari from Arusha (see page 58), or join one in Karatu, or organize the trip from one of the lodges on

With completion of the tarred road from Arusha to the gate of Ngorongoro, Karatu has more recently come into its own and now spreads for several kilometres along the highway. It is locally dubbed 'safari junction' and for good reason. All safari vehicles en route to Ngorongoro and the Serengeti pass through here and there are plenty of lodges and campsites in the area. Some offer very good and, in some cases, much cheaper alternatives to staying within the confines of the Ngorongoro Conservation Area. However, the disadvantage is not having the views that the lodges on the rim of the crater afford. As well as the accommodation options listed below, those on an organized camping safari may find themselves staying at one of the many other campsites around Karatu, as the cheaper companies use these instead of the more expensive **Simba Campsite** at the top of the crater (which, incidentally, gets overcrowded, has poor facilities and can be extremely cold). These cheaper campsites cater exclusively to groups who have their own cooks, though there are often also bars to buy beers and soft drinks.

the crater rim. If you are camping at Simba Campsite in your own vehicle, the option is to leave your car there and negotiate to join one of the trips from the lodges.

Wildlife

The crater floor is home to varied and highly concentrated wildlife, and visitors are almost guaranteed to get a good look at some or all of the Big Five. Thanks to the army of pop-up minibuses that go down each day, the animals are not afraid of vehicles and it's not unusual for a pride of lions to amble over and flop down in the shade of a vehicle. About half of the estimated 25,000 large mammals are zebra and wildebeest, but unlike those in the Serengeti, these populations do not need to migrate, thanks to the permanent supply of water and grass through both the wet and dry seasons. There is a dense population of predators; lion, cheetah, hyena and jackal are commonly seen, while leopard, serval and bat-eared fox may be spotted with some good luck. The crater's elephants are mostly old bulls with giant tusks; the females with their young prefer the forested highlands on the crater rim and only rarely venture down into the grasslands. The black rhino here are fairly easily seen as they have a predictable routine of spending the night in Lerai Forest and the day in open grassland. A large number of hippos, flamingos and other water birds can usually be seen at Lake Magadi. Although wayward individuals are occasionally spotted, the crater floor generally has no giraffe, topi or impala as they find it difficult to negotiate the steep crater rim.

Some animals can be found on the rim, too, although not at all as many as down at the bottom. Buffalo and waterbuck are often seen, while elephant, hyena and bush pig are seen on occasion. The montane forests that surround the lodges offer good birdwatching, especially sunbirds, turacos and birds of prey.

When to go

While most of the animals can move in and out using trails from the crater rim, they rarely do and stay on the crater floor, making it well worth visiting all year round.

Park information

Ngorongoro Conservation Area Authority, www.ngorongorocrater.go.tz, 0600-1800, the Seneto descent road closes at 1600, US$60; children (5-16) US$20, note: only Tanzanian-registered vehicles are allowed down into the crater itself, for which there is an additional Crater Service Fee of US$300 per vehicle.

There are three banks in town and all have ATMs. For those on self-drive safaris, this is the last place to buy provisions before entering the Ngorongoro Conservation Area (although there's a far better choice of shopping in Arusha, especially at Nakumatt supermarket on your way out of town). Drivers will also need to fill up in Karatu and fuel stations spread from one end of the main street (B144) to the other. There are plenty of buses, *dala-dalas* and shared Peugeot taxis throughout the day between Arusha and Karatu and the journey takes around two and half hours. One option for budget travellers wanting to visit the Ngorongoro Crater is to catch public transport as far as Karatu, stay overnight and then take a half-day

Tip...
Karatu's market is well worth a visit selling everything from vegetables and spices to Tinga-Tinga paintings and carved wooden curios. However, if you don't have time to stop, vendors trundle little mobile kiosks (on wheels) up and down the main road to sell souvenirs to passing tourists.

Ngorongoro Conservation Area

Where to stay
Acacia Farm Lodge **3**
Bougainvillea Safari Lodge **13**
Country Lodge Karatu **7**
Gibb's Farm **2**
Highview **18**
Kisima Ngeda Tented Camp **5**
Kudu Lodge & Campsite **16**
Lemala Ngorongoro
  Tented Camp **17**
Manor at Ngorongoro **19**
Ndutu Safari Lodge **4**
Ngorongoro Crater Lodge **1**
Ngorongoro Farm House **9**
Ngorongoro Forest Tented
  Lodge **14**
Ngorongoro Serena
  Safari Lodge **6**

safari to the crater the next morning, returning to Arusha the following afternoon. This is considerably cheaper than booking a safari from Arusha.

If you have a bit of time to spare in Karatu, then you can join one of the activities organized by the **Ganako Karatu Cultural Tourism Programme** ⓘ *enquire at the office on the main street at the eastern end of town where the tours start, T0787-451 162; or further information is available from the Tanzania Cultural Tourism Programme office, or the Tanzanian Tourist Board Information Centre, both on Boma Rd in Arusha, see page 59, www.tanzaniaculturaltourism.com*. Options include half day walking tours through farmland and forest on the lower slopes of the Ngorongoro Highlands, and one such hike climbs Mlima Nyoka ('Snake Hill'), where from the top on a clear day you can see Lake Manyara on the eastern side and Lake Eyasi to the west. There's also an informative walk around Karatu itself to the market, maybe a school and church, and to watch how local beer is made and perhaps have a meal in a local home. They can also organize visits by vehicle to Lake Eyasi to meet the Wahadzabe people (see page 107).

Empakaai Crater
○ Embagai

Mount Lolmalasin (3648m)

Lositete ○
○ Kitete
Mbulumbulu ○
○ Rotia
Mto wa Mbu

To Arusha

Manyara ional Park

Lake Manyara

Ngorongoro Sopa Lodge **7**
Ngorongoro Wildlife
  Lodge **8**
Octagon Safari Lodge **15**
Olduvai Camp **10**
Plantation Lodge **11**

Rhino Lodge **12**

Campsites ⌂
Simba Campsite **1**

Where to stay

All the lodges in and around Karatu can organize day trips to the crater, among other safaris and activities such as mountain biking or forest walks. Accommodation is not especially cheap in this area, thanks to Karatu's captive market of people going to Ngorongoro and beyond, but in quiet times you could try negotiating the hefty non-residents rates.

$$$$ Acacia Farm Lodge
Signposted to the right if going out of town towards the crater, 300 m off the main road, T0767-465 557, www.karatuacacialodge.com.
Also in a commanding elevated position overlooking Ngorongoro's forests, this upmarket country lodge on a coffee farm is more of a boutique-style hotel with contemporary decor in the 28 chalets, creatively designed public areas and special treats such as flower strewn pathways and personal butlers in all the rooms. Excellent gourmet food and fine wines and you can eat in the elegant dining room or tables are set up in the gardens or on your veranda. Facilities include coffee shop, swimming pool, spa and gym.

$$$$ Gibb's Farm
4 km from Karatu, T027-253 4397,
www.gibbsfarm.net.
At the edge of a forest facing the Mbulu Hills to the southeast, this charming 80-year-old farmhouse set in lush gardens is still a working farm and coffee plantation, originally built by German settlers in 1929. Super-stylish accommodation is in 22 luxurious farm cottages with private verandas, handcrafted furniture, artwork and open fireplaces. The restaurant produces excellent meals using organic vegetables grown on the farm. And there's a spa with a difference – a traditional Maasai healer provides treatments made from local plants and materials, either in your cottage or in his thatched house, the Engishon Supat.

$$$$ Manor at Ngorongoro
3 km towards the crater, 2 km from the main road, reservations through the Elewana Collection, Arusha T0754-250 630, www. elewanacollection.com.
Reminiscent of a country house with white-washed architecture, the Manor is on a coffee estate that abuts the boundary of the Ngorongoro Conservation Area and has 20 luxurious suites in cottages, plus the double-storey Stable Cottage for families, all with Victorian-style clawfooted bath, private sun terrace and fireplace. Stables for horse rides in the forest, plus mountain biking, picnics on the estate, swimming pool and massages. Pricey from US$500 per person per night, but excellent standards. Often booked as part of a package with the Arusha Coffee Lodge (see page 48).

$$$$ Ngorongoro Forest Tented Lodge
3 km from Karatu on the road to Gibb's Farm, T027-250 8089, www. ngorongoroforestlodge.com.
Also overlooking the Ngorongoro Highlands forest, this stylish lodge has 7 spacious and attractive tented rooms elegantly furnished and with both indoor and outdoor showers and linked by elevated boardwalks. The lounge bar with its vast windows overlooks

a mass of trees, the mango, guava and other fruit trees in particular attract a varied birdlife, and there's a telescope for stargazing.

$$$$ Plantation Lodge
4 km towards the crater, 2 km from the main road, badly signposted so look hard, T0784-397 444, www.plantation-lodge.com.
Accommodation in exquisitely stylish rooms on a coffee estate. A huge amount of work has gone into the safari-style decor. The 16 individual and spacious rooms are in renovated farm buildings throughout the grounds. There are several places to sit and drink coffee or enjoy a sundowner, and you can choose to eat at grand dining tables on your veranda, in huge stone halls, in the garden, or in the main house with the other guests. The honeymoon suite has a vast bed, fireplace, jacuzzi and sunken bath, some units are whole houses which are ideal for families, and there's a swimming pool.

$$$$-$$$ Ngorongoro Farm House
On a 200-ha coffee farm 5 km from the gate to the crater, reservations Tanganyika Wilderness Camps & Lodges, Arusha T0736-502 471, www.tanganyikawildernesscamps.com.
One of the less expensive options outside Karatu, but larger with 52 rooms spread between 3 separate groups of cottages, all attractively decorated in the style of an old colonial farm. In the main thatched building is the restaurant, with a wooden terrace overlooking the farmland and flowerbeds, and excellent food using fresh home-grown vegetables. There's a large swimming pool, and they can arrange farm tours or nature walks with the Maasai.

$$$ Bougainvillea Safari Lodge
Signposted to the left if going out of town towards the crater, 300 m off the main road, T027-253 4083, www.bougainvillealodge.net.
With friendly staff and close to town (though set back from the main road) this has a guesthouse feel and is a good choice for families and mid-range tourists. Fairly newly built with 32 comfortable rooms in brick

chalets with verandas, 2 have adjoining rooms, arranged around a large swimming pool and well-kept lawns and garden. Good meals in the dining room as the chef used to work at **Gibb's Farm**, breakfast and lunch are generous buffets while dinner is a set menu, bar with wicker couches, curio shop and can organize massages.

$$$ Country Lodge Karatu
Signposted to the left if going out of town towards the crater, 300 m off the main road, T027-253 4622, www.countrylodgekaratu.com
Owned by the same friendly management of the **Bougainvillea Safari Lodge** next door, and with similar rates, this is a good mid-range option, with 22 neat and tidy double/twin rooms in stone cottages, with space for extra beds, patios with wicker furniture and good showers with plenty of hot water. The dining room, bar and cosy lounge with fireplace are set in the attractive high-ceilinged central thatched building, and there's a small swimming pool surrounded by lawns.

$$$-$$ Highview Hotel
2 km outside Karatu signposted on the right off the main road towards the Ngorongoro gate, T0752-292 266, www.highviewhotel.com.
Owned by **Zara Tours** in Moshi (a quality and long-standing tour operator for Kilimanjaro climbs), this is popular with safari groups and has friendly hands-on management. The 41 rooms – each named after a different bird – are in a separate block on top of a hill with forest views and are basic but tiled throughout and spotless. Restaurant and take-away lunch boxes available, bar, fire pit in the garden where there is often Maasai dancing or acrobat performances, swimming pool, gift shop and Maasai *bomas* where ladies make crafts.

$$$-$ Kudu Lodge and Campsite
Signposted to the left if going out of town towards the crater, 600 m off the main road, T027-253 4055, www.kudulodge.com.
Established and popular lodge with welcoming staff. Accommodation is in comfortable and well-maintained en suite rondavaals and cottages dotted around the mature tropical gardens, which sleep a total of about 50 people in doubles, triples or 2-bed family units with kitchens; rates start from US$140 for a double. The large shady campsite, often used by safari groups, has separate cooking shelters and good ablution blocks with hot water; camping US$15 per person. Enormous bar with DSTV, pool table, fireplace and lots of couches, and acrobatic shows are put on in the evening, gift shop and good, affordable restaurant. The large swimming pool features a delightful full-size statue of an elephant providing a fountain from its trunk. Safaris and other activities, such as mountain biking, can be organized.

$$$-$ Octagon Safari Lodge
1 km outside Karatu signposted on the left off the main road towards the Ngorongoro gate, T027-253 4525, www.octagonlodge.com.
Set in beautiful indigenous gardens, this cheerful place has 12 wood and bamboo chalets and 2 stone cottages that sleep 4, all with a Maasai theme and terraces. Restaurant, lively bar, can organize walking or mountain-bike tours in the surrounding countryside. Rates from US$65 per person B&B, dinner US$20, and picnic lunch boxes can be arranged. You can also camp here for US$15 per person and there are tents to hire.

ON THE ROAD

Serengeti Darf Nicht Sterben (Serengeti Shall Not Die)

Where the B144 road reaches the rim of the Ngorongoro Crater after entering Lodoare Gate, you will see the memorials to Professor Bernhard Grzimek and his son Michael. They were the German makers of the 1959 documentary film (and book) *Serengeti Darf Nicht Sterben (Serengeti Shall Not Die)*, which was awarded an Oscar for Best Documentary Feature in the same year. Renowned conservationists, they conducted aerial censuses of the animals in the Serengeti and Ngorongoro, which was one of the first-ever surveys documenting the dwindling numbers of numerous species. They were heavily involved in the fight against poachers, and their work, and the film, is widely credited with alerting the world to the plight of Africa's wildlife. Tragically, Michael was killed in an aeroplane accident over the Ngorongoro Crater in 1959. His father returned to Germany, where he set up the Frankfurt Zoological Society. He died in 1987 and requested in his will that he should be buried beside his son in Tanzania. Their memorials serve as a reminder of all the work they did to protect this part of Africa. The crater in Bernhard's words: "It is impossible to give a fair description of the size and beauty of the park, for there is nothing with which one can compare it. It is one of the wonders of the world."

Ngorongoro Crater

the largest unbroken caldera in the world

This crater was once a huge active volcano, probably as large as Kilimanjaro. As recently as 2.5 million years ago the young Ngorongoro Volcano became filled with molten rock that subsequently solidified into a crust or roof. As the lava chamber emptied, the solid dome collapsed and formed the largest perfect caldera in the world. Minor volcanic activity continued, and the small cones that resulted can be seen in the crater floor.

The Ngorongoro Crater has an area of 265 sq km and measures between 16 km and 19 km across. The rim reaches 2286 m above sea level and the crater floor is 610 m below it. From the crater, on a clear day you should be able to see six mountains over 3000 m.

The crater floor is mainly grassy plain, interspersed with a few tracts of sturdy woodland and swamps, and the giant fever trees in the **Lerai Forest** are a good place to see leopard, elephant, waterbuck and flitting sunbirds. Scrub heath and remnants of montane forests cloak the steep slopes. There are both freshwater and brackish lakes, and the main feature is **Lake Magadi**, a large but shallow alkaline lake in the southwestern corner that attracts flocks of pink-winged flamingos and plenty of contented hippos who remain partially submerged during the day and graze on grass at night. There are two picnic and toilet spots – in the Lerai Forest in the south between the ascent and descent roads, and at the Ngoitokitok Springs in the southeast corner. Famously the black kites at Ngoitokitok Springs are so tame, they are known to dive-bomb and steal safari-goers food. The views from the crater rim are sensational, and you can pick out the wildlife as dots on the crater floor.

The name 'Ngorongoro' comes from a Maasai word *Ilkorongoro*, which was the name given to the group of Maasai warriors who defeated the previous occupants of the area, the Datong, around 1800. The sounds of the bells – *'koh-rohng-roh'*– that the Maasai wore during the battle were said to have terrified their enemies into submission. The Maasai refer to the Ngorongoro Southern Highlands as *'O'lhoirobi'*, which means the cold highlands; the Germans also referred to the climate, calling these the 'winter highlands'.

Listings Ngorongoro Crater

Where to stay

These accommodation options are on the crater rim and therefore Ngorongoro Conservation Area entry fees apply.

$$$$ Lemala Ngorongoro Tented Camp
Reservations Arusha, T0736-210 966, www.lemalacamp.com.
A pricey option but a tented camp experience on the crater rim and an alternative to the large lodges. It is near the quiet Lemala access route into the crater on the eastern rim, the same road used by guests at the nearby **Ngorongoro Sopa Lodge**. The 12 tents are set up in an acacia forest, and have gas heaters (essential for the chill), wood floors with rugs, solar lights and en suite flush loos and safari bladder showers. The mess tent is surprisingly well furnished given its location, with giant sofas, lamps and bookshelves. Escorted walks are available into the forest along the crater rim with the Maasai.

$$$$ Ngorongoro Crater Lodge
Reservations, Johannesburg, South Africa, T+27-11-809 4300www.craterlodge.com, www.andbeyond.com.
A lodge has been on this spot since 1934, but it was completely rebuilt in 1995, and the architecture and style is simply magnificent. It's the most luxurious lodge on the rim of the crater, very romantic and opulent with brocade sofas, gilt mirrors, chandeliers and wood-panelled walls. The 30 cottages are divided into 3 groups, each with their own lounge areas and butler service. With unobstructed views down into the crater even from the bathrooms, this is a special

place to stay. Very expensive from US$1000 per person, but fully inclusive of meals, drinks and game drives.

$$$$ Ngorongoro Wildlife Lodge
T027-254 4595, www.hotelsandlodges-tanzania.com.
With plunging views down on to the acacia forest on the floor of the crater, this large wood-and-stone lodge was the first to be built on the very rim in the 1970s. Today it has 80 comfortable rooms with balconies, some interconnect for families, bar with broad terrace outside and cosy log fires inside, TV room, library and restaurant serving either buffets or à la carte. Zebra can be seen on the lawns, and the surrounding trees are full of fairly tame birds.

$$$$-$$$ Ngorongoro Serena Safari Lodge
Reservations Arusha, T027-254 5555, www.serenahotels.com.
Stunningly perched on the rim of the crater, this long and low lodge is built from pebbles and camouflaged with indigenous vines. Each of the 75 rooms has a balcony with views and telescopes are provided on the main terrace. The centre of the public area is warmed by a roaring fire and lit by lanterns. Friendly staff, good food, and guided nature walks around the crater rim. A well-priced mid to upper range option from US$270 for a double.

$$$$-$$$ Ngorongoro Sopa Lodge
Reservations Arusha, T027-250 0630-9, www.sopa lodges.com.
Mid-range lodge with good Sopa standards, this occupies the highest point of the crater

rim (500 m) and the 92 rooms and split-level main building all enjoy uninterrupted views. Built and decorated in an African rondavaal design with lounges, restaurant and entertainment areas, and there's a swimming pool. Like the Lemala Ngorongoro Tented Camp, this is on the eastern rim and uses the quiet Lemala access route down into the crater itself; this does mean a little longer journey time to get to the lodge than to those on the southern rim.

$$$ Rhino Lodge
T0785-500 005, www.ngorongoro.cc.
Jointly owned by the governing body of the area's Maasai, this is the former home of the first conservationist to the area and part of the lodge's income goes directly to the Maasai communities. It's the only mid-budget option on the crater rim, although it's set back in the dense Ngorongoro forest and lacks the drop-dead views right into the crater. It offers good value, with 24 simply furnished Maasai-inspired rooms in terraced rows around an outside courtyard, all en suite with verandas. Restaurant and bar area with huge fireplaces, dinners are communal buffets followed by Maasai dancing. Rates start from US$135 per person full board.

National Park campsites

Simba Campsite
About 2 km from Crater Village.
A huge public campsite with showers, toilets and firewood, but facilities are basic and water supplies are irregular – make sure that you have sufficient drinking water to keep you going for the night and the game drive the next day. Given that you are camping at some elevation at the top of the crater, this place gets bitterly cold at night, so ensure you have a warm sleeping bag. Many budget safari companies use this site, and it gets very busy with tour groups, with up to 200 tents at any one time. The hot water runs out quickly – so don't expect to have a shower here. The advantage is the early start in the morning to get down into the crater, but in terms of facilities and comfort, quite frankly the campsites at Karatu are the better option. If in your own vehicle, there is no need to book. Just pay for camping (US$30 per person) along with park entry when you enter at the gate. In your own vehicle there is also the option of dropping into the lodges for a meal or drink.

Elsewhere in the Ngorongoro Conservation Area there are 5 special campsites (US$50, children (5-16) US$10), usually used by the safari companies going off the beaten track.

Olmoti and Empakaai craters

walking country

Olmoti and Empakaai are two other calderas in the Ngorongoro Highlands, which are located north and northeast of the Ngorongoro Crater respectively. Both are over 300-m high with grassy central bowls, but lack the rich wildlife found in the Ngorongoro Crater, although some animals such as zebra, buffalo, eland, hyena and monkeys may be spotted. The main attraction is the isolated walks among wonderful scenery with tremendous views. These walks are rarely included in organized safaris, but you can arrange a day visit from Ngorongoro Crater rim through a tour operator or one of the lodges which will organize the relevant armed rangers (necessary to walk where buffalo are present). These visits are usually also included in multi-day trekking itineraries in the highlands, accompanied by Maasai guides.

The access point to **Olmoti** is at the Maasai village of **Nainokanoka** (where there is a Special Campsite), 13 km north of the Lemala crater access road on the Ngorongoro Crater rim. From the road it's a 30-minute walk down to Olmoti's shallow crater floor, which is covered in grass and where the Munge River cuts through the southern wall and continues as a creek all the way into the Ngorongoro Crater where it fills Lake Magadi.

Empakaai is another 23 km northeast along the same road from Nainokanoka and Olmoti. From the rim are fantastic views north towards Ol Doinyo Lengai and Lake Natron, and on exceptionally clear days, Kilimanjaro can be seen in the far distance. There is a steeper trail here down from the road to the crater floor, which takes about 30 minutes to descend but more than an hour to climb back out. Roughly half of the crater floor is occupied by the alkaline **Lake Emakat**, which attracts good birdlife including pelicans, storks, ducks and kingfishers, while there are small patches of verdant evergreen forest in the southern part of the caldera.

Oldupai (Olduvai) Gorge

famous for its paleoanthropological relics

The Oldupai (Olduvai) Gorge is one of the most important paleoanthropological sites in the world, and has proved to be invaluable in our understanding of early human evolution.

It first aroused interest in the archaeological world as early as 1911, when a German, Professor Katurinkle, found some fossil bones while looking for butterflies in the gorge. This caused great interest in Europe and, in 1913, an expedition led by Professor Hans Reck was arranged. They stayed at Olduvai for three months and made a number of fossil finds. At a later expedition in 1933, Professor Reck was accompanied by two archaeologists, Dr Louis Leakey and his future wife, Mary. The Leakeys continued their work and, in July 1959, 26 years later, discovered 400 fragments of the skull *Australopithecus-Zinjanthropus boisei* – the 'nutcracker man' – who lived in the lower Pleistocene Age, around 1,750,000 BC. A year later the skull and bones of a young *Homo habilis* were found. The Leakeys asserted that around 1.8 to two million years ago two types of man existed in Tanzania: *Australopithecus-Zinjanthropus boisei* and *Homo habilis*. The earlier other two species, *Australopithecus africanus* and *arobustus*, had by then died out. They speculated that it was *Homo habilis*, a small, ape-like creature with the larger brain and his ability to use tools (also found at Olduvai), that gave rise to modern man– *Homo erectus* (about 1.2 million years ago) followed by *Homo sapiens* (17000 years ago). Prehistoric animal remains were also found in the area, and about 150 species of mammals have been identified. These include the enormous *Polorovis*, with a horn span 2 m, the *Dinotherium*, a huge, elephant-like creature with tusks that curved downwards, and the *Hipparion*, a three-toed, horse-like creature.

The reason these findings were discovered here is believed to be due to an eruption from a nearby volcano, now dormant. From the Ngorongoro Crater rim, the road descends out of the montane

> **Fact...**
> The name Olduvai is actually a misspelling of the Maasai word *oldupai*, which is a type of wild sisal that grows in the gorge. As such the name has been officially changed to the correct spelling of Oldupai Gorge by the Ngorongoro Conservation Area Authority, but you may well notice both names in written information.

forest zone into scrubby thorn bush with the Oldupai (Olduvai) Gorge reached about 25 km later. On the way, on the left, look out for two dormant volcano peaks; Lemakarot (3132 m) and Sadiman (2870 m). It is believed that an eruption of Sadiman some 3.6 million years ago covered the area in ash, thus sealing and preserving evidence of our hominid ancestors. As such this water-cut canyon, up to 90 m deep, has often been called the 'cradle of mankind'. Next to the excavation site there is a small **museum** ① *open until 1500, US$3*, which is to the right of the main road towards the Serengeti's Naabi Hill Gate (another 50 km or an hour's drive). All safari operators pull in here on the way past. It was built in the 1970s by the Leakeys, and now has a viewing platform overlooking the gorge, displays copies of some of the fossil finds, as well as a cast of the Laetoli Footprints (see page 93 for further information).

Listings Oldupai (Olduvai) Gorge

Where to stay

As well as the one permanent lodge and one camp in this region of the Ngorongoro Conservation Area, **Lemala** (reservations Arusha, T0736-210 966, www.lemalacamp. com) set up the 12-tent seasonal **Lemala Ndutu Tented Camp** from Dec to Mar.

$$$$ Ndutu Safari Lodge
On the southern shore of Lake Ndutu, reservations Arusha, T0736-501 045, www.ndutu.com.
Established in 1967 by professional hunter George Dove, Ndutu is one of the earliest permanent lodges in the Ngorongoro/ Serengeti area, although it's unfenced like a traditional tented camp. It's midway between the top of the crater and Seronera (90 km to both) and is in a good position for the migration in the calving season (Jan-Mar). Accommodation is in 34 solid stone cottages with verandas facing the

lake that extend in arcs from the central, open-sided bar, lounge and dining room. There's a curio shop, good food and an open fire is lit in the evening.

$$$$ Olduvai Camp
Just south of the Serengeti border, closest lodge to the Oldupai (Olduvai) Gorge (8 km), reservations Arusha, T0784-228 883, www. olduvai-camp.com.
In a lovely setting around a giant kopje, the highlight here are the Maasai guides from the villages immediately around the camp; you can go walking with them in the Ngorongoro Highlands. The 17 tents are of a modest size with thatched roofs and wooden floors, furnished with the basic essentials, en suite bathrooms have flush toilets and bladder showers. Thatched restaurant/bar and an open fire pit, and there's a platform right on top of the rocks with a telescope. Solar power and lanterns are provided at night.

Lake Nduto and Lake Masek

big cat country

In the western part of the Ngorongoro Conservation Area bordering the Serengeti, Lake Ndutu and Lake Masek form shallow basins where water accumulates from the nearby areas of slightly higher ground.

The water in both is extremely saline; too saline for consumption, but the lakes are situated in an area of shrub and woodland, surrounded by vast short-grass plains. This is often a good place for game drives during January to March, when the migration roams

ON THE ROAD
Ngorongoro's Maasai

When the region was established as the Ngorongoro Conservation Area in 1959, the Maasai had already occupied the land for some 200 years; their traditional way of life allowing them to live in harmony with the wildlife and the environment. As such the Ngorongoro Conservation Area was designated as a multi-use area providing protection status for wildlife while also permitting human habitation and the Maasai were not expelled; as was the case when other national parks were established in East Africa, including the Serengeti (in 1951). Today there are an estimated 43,000 Maasai pastoralists in the area, who graze their cattle, donkeys, goats and sheep. During the rainy seasons they move out on to the open plains; in the dry seasons they move into the woodland and highland regions. If they choose, the Maasai are permitted to take their animals into the crater for water and grazing, but not to live or farm there. Elsewhere in the Ngorongoro Conservation Area, they have the right to do as they wish.

this area during calving season and the big cats are regularly seen. You can explore this area on game drives from Ndutu Safari Lodge (see page 106), but seasonal tented camps set up on the Serengeti side, or north, of the lake and make use of the Ndutu airstrip, which is 1 km away from the Ndutu Safari Lodge.

Lake Eyasi
a forgotten lake and ancient peoples

This soda lake, one of several lakes on the floor of the Rift Valley, is sometimes referred to as the 'forgotten lake'. It is larger than Lakes Manyara or Natron and the Kidero Mountains tower to the south. Seasonal water levels vary greatly but it is relatively shallow even during the rainy season and has a mild saline content that attracts greater and lesser flamingos, sometimes in good numbers. It lies in a wild, scenic region offering an insight into the traditional way of life of the Wahadzabe and Datoga peoples.

Lake Eyasi mostly fills a graben, an elongated depression of the earth's crust that is commonly the site of volcanic and/or earthquake activity. The Mbari River runs through the swampy area to the northeast of the lake known locally as **Mangola Chini**, which attracts some hooved game, and flamingos, pelicans and plenty of other waders frequent the shallows. The northeastern region of the lake is a swampy area fringed by acacia and doum palm forests. Nearby are some freshwater springs and a small reservoir with tilapia fish. These springs are believed to run underground from Oldeani to emerge by the lakeshore. There are several kopjes (see box, page 115) close to the lake.

Two ancient peoples inhabit this area. The **Wahadzabe** people live near the shore and are estimated to have lived in this region for 10,000 years. They are hunter-gatherers, still live in nomadic groups, hunt with bows and arrows, and gather tubers, roots and fruits. These people are not closely genetically related to any other people, but their lifestyle is similar to the San (of the Kalahari) and the Dorobo (of Kenya). Their language resembles the click language associated with the San. Their hunting skills provide all their requirements – mostly eating small antelopes and primates. Their hunting bows are made with giraffe tendon 'strings', and they coat their spears and arrows with the poisonous sap of the desert rose. They live in communal camps that are temporary structures constructed in different locations depending on the season.

A tall, handsome people similar to the Maasai, the **Datoga** are pastoral herdsmen and cultivators who tend their cattle in the region between Lake Eyasi and Mount Hanang. They are also known as the Barabaig or Il-Man'ati (meaning the 'strong enemy' in the Maasai language), which probably derived from when, over 200 years ago, as the stronger Maasai moved into the Ngorongoro and Serengeti, the Datoga were pushed south. Cattle raids between the two are still not uncommon. They live in homesteads constructed of sticks and mud, and their compounds are surrounded by thornbush to deter nocturnal predators.

Visitors generally visit one of the Datoga villages or farms and walk with one of the local Wahadzabe groups to either go hunting with them or spend some time gathering honey, roots or seasonal fruits. It's about 50 km or a 1½-hour dusty and difficult drive from Karatu to Lake Eyasi – the turn-off is off the B144 east of town. The easiest way to arrive is to arrange transfers if you are overnighting at either of the two camps listed below, or, if staying in Karatu, most of the lodges there and the Ganako Karatu Cultural Tourism Programme (see page 99) can arrange day tours, or the tour operators in Arusha (see page 58) can also include Lake Eyasi in a longer safari itinerary of the Northern Circuit, and some of the longer multi-day Ngorongoro Highlands treks include this region.

Listings Lake Eyasi

Where to stay

$$$$ Kisima Ngeda Tented Camp
On the northeastern lakeshore, reservations Anasa Safari Collection, Arusha T027-254 8840, www.anasasafari.com.
There are 7 tents here right on the lakeshore, with thatched roofs, en suite stone baths, wooden furniture, electric lights and plenty of space. Activities include canoeing on the lake, walks, mountain biking and meeting the Wahadzabe people, and there's a swimming pool. Wholesome food includes vegetables grown in the local villages, dairy products from the Datoga people's cattle and tilapia fish from the lake. Far from luxurious, but the cultural experience is unique.

$$$ Tindiga Tented Camp
1.5 km from the eastern lakeshore, operated by Moivaro, reservations Arusha T027-250 6315, www.moivaro.com.
Located on a small hill overlooking the bush and local farms with some distant views across to the lake, this has 10 simple but comfortable tents with bathrooms, reliable hot water and electricity, and the dining and bar unit was constructed by the Datoga people themselves in the style of a typical homestead. All food comes straight from the local village market, and there's an attractive sunken fire pit and lounge area. Attentive staff organize all activities. The complaint here is the noisy water pump outside the camp, which provides water to the nearby onion fields.

Serengeti
National Park

The Serengeti supports the greatest concentration of plains game in Africa and for this it was granted the status of a World Heritage Site in 1978 and became an International Biosphere Reserve in 1981. Its far-reaching plains of endless grass, tinged with the twisted shadows of acacia trees, have made it the quintessential image of a wild and untarnished Africa. The park is the centre of the Serengeti Ecosystem – the combination of the Serengeti, the Ngorongoro Conservation Area, Kenya's Maasai Mara and several smaller game reserves. The system protects the largest single movement of wildlife on land – the annual wildebeest migration. This is a phenomenal sight: over a million wildebeest plus hundreds of thousands of gazelles and zebra – followed by their predators – embark on a 1000-km-long circular trek through unfenced Kenya and Tanzania in search of seasonal pasture and water. But the Serengeti also offers rewarding year-round adventure and wildlife experiences, with exceptional, high-density game-viewing as well as significant large predator-prey interactions.

Essential Serengeti National Park

Finding your feet

The Serengeti is divided into four regions. The **Central Serengeti** offers undeniably good game-viewing year round, but you need to be prepared for high numbers of tourists given that it is home to most of the park's permanent lodges; the **Western Corridor** – a funnel-shaped piece of land running from the Central Serengeti west to the park boundary near Lake Victoria, which sees a lot of action during June and July as the migration's route takes the herds across the Grumeti River; **Southern Serengeti** is home to the park's main entrance, Naabi Hill Gate, but is relatively free of tourists except between December and March when the migration passes through; the **Northern Serengeti** is described by some as the most scenic portion, where the Lobo grasslands are fed by permanent springs, and is where you'll find the migration between August and October attempting to cross the Mara River into Kenya's Maasai Mara.

Getting there

The park is served by eight airstrips: the Seronera airstrip serves Central Serengeti; the Grumeti, Fort Ikoma and Sasakwa airstrips service the Western Corridor; the Lobo and Kogatende airstrips provide access to the Northern Serengeti; and the Ndutu and Serengeti South airstrips serve the south and east. Scheduled and charter flights drop down at these airstrips in circuits from Arusha and Kilimanjaro airports with **Air Excel**, **Auric Air**, **Coastal Aviation**, **Flightlink**, **Regional Air** and **Tanganyika Flying Co (TFC)**. See page 157 for details.

By road, the Serengeti is usually approached from the Ngorongoro Conservation Area. From the top of the crater the spectacularly scenic road, with a splendid view of the Serengeti plains winds down the crater walls on to the grasslands below. Shortly before the Serengeti's boundary, there is the turning off to Olduvai Gorge where most safari companies stop. Then, entry is through the **Naabi Hill Gate** to the southeast of the park, where there is an information centre, shop and picnic site. From here it is 75 km to **Seronera**, the village in the heart of the Serengeti, which is 335 km from Arusha. Approaching from Mwanza or Musoma on the shore of Lake Victoria, take the road east and you will enter the Serengeti via the **Ndabaka Gate** in the west and through the Western Corridor to the Grumeti region. This road always requires 4WD and may be impassable in the rainy season. There is a third, less frequently used gate in the north, **Ikoma Gate**, which lies a few kilometres from Seronera. This also goes to Musoma but, again, is not a very good road.

Getting around

Most visitors to the park are usually on an organized safari from Arusha, or there are a few that can be arranged from Mwanza. Transfers to accommodation by either road or from the nearest airstrip will be included, as well as all game drives once there. It is possible to explore in your own vehicle, but the roads are quite rough and you can expect hard corrugations (especially the road from Naabi Hill Gate to Seronera, where there are deep ruts). In many regions of the park there is a fine top soil known locally as 'black cotton', which can get impossibly sticky and slippery in the wet. This is especially true of the Western Corridor. The dry season should not present too many problems, and at times the main roads and even some secondary roads are navigable in 2WD. The Park Headquarters are at Seronera where there is also a visitor's centre with an elevated walkway that leads you past informative displays about the park, a coffee shop and picnic site. There are also fuel pumps at Seronera; however it's essential to bring extra fuel in jerry cans if you are in the park for more than a day or two or intend to do a lot of game driving. Breakdown facilities are virtually non-existent, though the lodge/camp workshops might be able to assist with minor repairs (for a tip/fee).

Wildlife

Almost every species of African animal you would expect to see on safari lives on the Serengeti's plains, and for any visitor to Tanzania, seeing the annual migration is a highlight of visiting the country. The phenomena of over two million animals – wildebeest, gazelle and zebra – that move from the Serengeti when the dry season ends to the lush pastures in Kenya's Maasai Mara is one of nature's true spectacles.

Yet even when the migration has moved on, the Serengeti offers arguably some of the most scintillating game-viewing in Africa. It is believed to hold one of the largest populations of lion in Africa (around 3000) due in part to the abundance of prey species, and large prides are commonly seen. Leopards are most frequently detected resting in trees during the daytime along the Seronera River but they are present throughout the park with the population put at around 1000. Cheetahs are thought to number 1000-2000 and are fairly easy to spot in the flat grassland areas or at the kopjes, which they use as lookouts. The elephant population in Serengeti-Maasai Mara ecosystem is currently put at around 7500, while buffalo number more than 60,000. Then there are high densities of giraffe, eland, topi, impala, Thomson's and Grant's gazelle, waterbuck, hartebeest, dik-dik, klipspringer and warthog. Almost uniquely, all three African jackal species are present, as well as both the spotted and striped hyena and a host of more elusive small predators, ranging from the aardwolf to the serval. By 1992 the highly endangered wild dog was presumed extinct in the Serengeti, but the good news is that thanks to some relocations from the Maasai Mara and other regions over the last few years, there are now several packs of dogs in the western part of the park. Black rhino were once numerous on the Serengeti plains, but heavy poaching has reduced them to just a handful; these are now protected by armed anti-poaching rangers and their location is not usually disclosed. There are plenty of large crocodiles in the rivers (waiting knowingly for the migration to cross), and although there are hippos at most of the Serengeti's watering holes, nothing can compare to the Retina Hippo Pool where the Seronera and Orangi rivers converge; this deep puddle is home to more than 200. Baboons and vervet monkeys are prolific and are easily seen around the lodges and camps.

Birdlife is prolific with 500-plus species and include various species of kingfishers, sunbirds and rollers, ostrich, egrets, herons, storks, ibis, spoonbills and ducks. Birds of prey include Ruppell's vulture and the hooded vulture, several varieties of kestrels, eagles, goshawks and harriers.

When to go

The short October-November and long March-June rainy seasons notwithstanding, the Serengeti's temperate and mostly dry climate means there is great game-viewing all year round. The question of exactly when to go to really revolves around whether you want to see the migration. If so, then the best time to visit is usually from December to July, but the peak times of seeing high concentrations of wildebeest, zebra and gazelle and the associated predators on the move is June and July as they are returning to Kenya's Maasai Mara which they usually reach around August. With altitudes ranging from 920 m to 1850 m, average temperatures vary from 15°C to 28°C all year round, although evenings can be cool between June and October.

Park information

Tanzania National Parks (**TANAPA**), www.tanzaniaparks.com, www.serengeti.org, 0600-1900, US$60, children (5-16) US$20, foreign-registered vehicle US$40, Tanzanian-registered vehicle TSh20,000.

Serengeti National Park

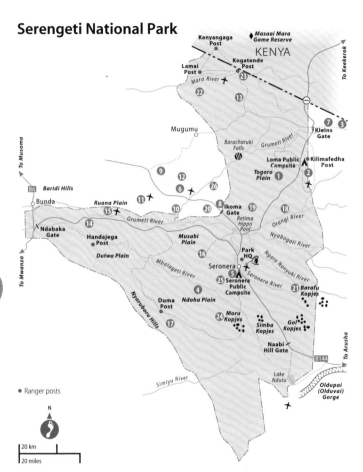

KENYA

Masaai Mara Game Reserve

Kenyanga Post
Kogatende Post **23**
Lamai Post
Mara River **22**
13

To Keekerok

Mugumu

Baracharuki Falls

Grumeti River

Kleins Gate **7** **3**

Kilimafedha Post
Loma Public Campsite **2**
Togoro Plain **1**

To Musoma

Baridi Hills **B6**

Bunda

Ruana Plain
15
9 **12**
6 **26**

Grumeti River
Ndabaka Gate
14 **11**
Handajega Post
Dutwa Plain

10
Ikoma Gate **8** **20** **19** **18**
Retima Hippo Pool
Orangi River

Musabi Plain
16
Mbalageti River
Park HQ
Seronera
Seronera River
Nyabogati River

Ngare Nanyuki River

4
Ndoha Plain
25 Seronera Public Campsite
21 Barafu Kopjes

24 Moru Kopjes
Duma Post
17

Simba Kopjes
Gol Kopjes

Nyaruboru Hills

Naabi Hill Gate
B144

To Mwanza

To Arusha

Simiyu River

Lake Ndutu
Oldupai (Olduvai) Gorge

● Ranger posts

N

20 km
20 miles

Where to stay 🛏
Buffalo Luxury Camp **3**
Faru Faru Lodge **10**
Four Seasons Safari Lodge Serengeti **19**
Grumeti Migration Camp **6**
Grumeti Serengeti Tented Camp **15**

Ikoma Tented Camp **8**
Ikoma Safari Camp **12**
Kirawira Serena Camp **14**
Klein's Camp **7**
Lemala Ewanjan Tented Camp **25**
Lemala Kuria Hills Lodge **13**
Lobo Wildlife Lodge **2**

Mapito Tented Camp **20**
Mbuzi Mawe Serena Camp **18**
Namiri Plains **21**
Sabora Tented Camp **11**
Sanctuary Kusini **17**
Sayari Camp **23**
Serengeti Bushtops **22**

Serengeti Migration Camp **1**
Serengeti Pioneer Camp **24**
Serengeti Serena Safari Lodge **16**
Serengeti Simba Lodge **26**
Serengeti Sopa Lodge **4**
Seronera Wildlife Lodge **5**
Singita Sasakwa Lodge **9**

BACKGROUND
Serengeti National Park

The name Serengeti is derived from the Maasai word '*siringet*' meaning 'extended area' or 'endless plains'. A thick layer of ash blown from volcanoes in the Ngorongoro Highlands covered the landscape between three and four million years ago, preserved traces of early man, and enriched the soil that supports the grassy plains. Much of the Serengeti was once known to outsiders as Maasailand, and the Maasai had been grazing their livestock on the open plains for around 200 years when the first European explorers visited the area – the first was German geographer and explorer Dr Oscar Baumann who arrived in 1892. However, a rinderpest epidemic and drought, also during the 1890s, greatly reduced the numbers of the Maasai and their herds, and the area became uninhabited by humans but teemed with wild animals. The hunting of lion made the wild animal population so scarce, however, that the British decided to make a partial game reserve in 1921, which was extended again in 1929. These actions, and because the woodlands had tsetse flies carrying trypanosomiasis (sleeping sickness) preventing any significant human settlement in the area, meant the Serengeti National Park was established in 1951. The few remaining Maasai were relocated to the Ngorongoro Highlands, a move that still elicits controversy today. Today, at 14,763 sq km, the Serengeti is Tanzania's second largest national park after the Selous Game Reserve in the south of the country. It rises from 920 to 1850 m above sea level and its landscape varies from the long and short grass plains in the south, the central savannah, the more hilly wooded areas in the north and the extensive woodland in the Western Corridor. One of the park's most endearing and enduring physical features are the kopjes (see page 115) – isolated rocky hills or inselbergs made of seemingly piles of boulders, which rise abruptly from the virtually level 'endless plains'.

Routes

a protected area slightly larger than Montenegro

Short Grass Plains

If you are approaching the Serengeti from the southeast (from the Ngorongoro Conservation Area), **Lake Ndutu**, fringed by acacia woodland, lies southeast of the main road (see page 106). Next you will reach the Short Grass Plains. The flat landscape is broken by the **Gol Mountains** to the right and by kopjes (see box, page 115). The grass here remains short during both the wet and dry seasons. There is no permanent water supply in this region as a result of the nature of the soil. However, during the rains, water collects in hollows and depressions until it dries up at the end of the wet season. It is then that the animals begin to move on. The **Southern Plains** provide nutritious grasses for the wildebeest and, when the short rains come in November, these mammals move south to feed. In February-March, 90% of female wildebeest give birth and the plains are filled with young calves.

Long Grass Plains

Naabi Hill Gate marks the end of the Short Grass and beginning of the Long Grass Plains. Dotted across the plains are kopjes, and the ones you might visit include the **Moru Kopjes** in the south of the park to the left of the main road heading north. You may be lucky enough to see the Verreaux eagle, which sometimes nests here. The Moru Kopjes have a cave with Maasai paintings on the wall and a rock called **Gong Rock** after the sound it makes when struck with a stone. Also on the left of the road before reaching Seronera, the **Simba Kopjes**, as their name suggests, are often a hideout for lions.

Tip...
Naabi Hill Gate is about a two-hour drive from the top of the Ngorongoro Crater; four hours from Lake Manyara; 6½ hours from Tarangire; and around eight hours from Arusha. The drive from Naabi Hill Gate to Seronera takes around 1½ hours.

Passing through the Long Grass Plains in the wet season from around December to May is an incredible experience. All around, stretching into the distance, are huge numbers of wildebeest, Thompson's gazelle, zebra, etc.

Seronera Valley

It's about 1½-hour drive from Naabi Hill Gate to the village of Seronera in the middle of the park, set in the Seronera Valley, which forms an important transition zone between the southern grasslands and the northern woodlands. In the approach to Seronera the number of trees increases, particularly the thorny acacia trees. Here is the park headquarters with a visitor's centre, a fuel station, the Seronera airstrip, the Seronera Wildlife Lodge (see page 118) and the public campsites. Seronara is the best area to visit if you can only manage a short safari. The area is criss-crossed by rivers and, as a result, this is game-viewing country year-round. You can expect to see buffalo, impala, lion, hippo and elephant. If you are lucky, you might see leopard in the branches of the trees lining the Seronera River.

North of Seronera

About 5 km north of Seronera the track splits. To the left it goes to the **Western Corridor**, and to the right it goes to **Banagi**, where it splits again to go northeast to the **Lobo area** and beyond to the Mara River, and northwest to **Ikoma Gate**. Banagi was the site of the original Game Department Headquarters before it became a national park, and to the north of here the land is mainly rolling plains of both grassland and woodland with a few hilly areas and rocky outcrops. Just to the west of Bangagi, off the main track to Ikoma Gate, is the **Retima Hippo Pool**, which is about 20 km north of Seronera.

Lobo Northern Woodland

In the northeast section of the park is the Lobo Northern Woodland. Wildlife remains in this area throughout the year, including during the dry season. The area is characterized by rocky hills and outcrops, where pythons sunbathe, and woodlands frequented by elephant fringing the rivers. Further north is the **Mara River**, with riverine forest bordering its banks. This is one of the rivers that claims many wildebeest lives every year during the migration. You will see both hippo and crocodile along the riverbanks.

Tip...
Around Seronera look out for the smaller predators – banded mongoose, side-striped jackal, serval and bat-eared fox. The name Seronera is probably derived from the Maasai word '*siron*' (bat-eared fox) and Seronera means 'the place of the bat-eared foxes'.

Grumeti Region

If you take the left-hand track where the road splits north of Seronera, you will follow the **Western Corridor** into the Grumeti region. The best time to follow this track is in the dry season (June-October) when the road is at its best and the migrating animals

ON THE ROAD

The kopjes of the Serengeti

Sticking out like rocky islands in a sea of grass, these interesting geological formations are made up of ancient granite that has been left behind as the surrounding soil structures have been broken down by centuries of erosion and weathering. Aside from providing a scenic contrast to the surrounding grasslands, they play an important role in the ecology of the Serengeti plains, providing habitats for many different animals from rock hyraxes (a small guinea pig-like creature whose closest relation is actually the elephant) to cheetah. They sustain a variety of plants, insects, birds, lizards and snakes, caves for dwelling, and the hollows in the rock surfaces provide catchments for rainwater. They also offer a superb vantage point for Serengeti's predators; the elevated boulders are perfect places to warm up in the morning or evening sun and survey the plains for food.

have reached the area. Part of the road follows, on your right, the **Grumeti River**, fringed by lush riverine forest, home to the black-and-white colobus monkey. On the banks of the river you will also see huge crocodiles basking in the sun.

Listings Serengeti National Park map p112

Where to stay

Inside the park

Rates for the lodges and camps in the Serengeti vary widely over the course of the year – sometimes by a few hundred dollars – and are determined by the season. Prices take a substantial hike during peak times when the migration is expected to pass through but are reduced by as much as 50% during the long rains, especially in Apr-May, when some of the smaller camps close altogether.

$$$$ Four Seasons Safari Lodge Serengeti
About 20 km north of the Retima Hippo Pool, reservations Arusha T0768-981 981, www.fourseasons.com/serengeti.
This is the Four Seasons hotel group's only safari lodge, and has 77 a/c suites and villas with DSTV, Wi-Fi and minibars and all the other amenities you would expect; some even have their own plunge pools. That said, its safari appeal in the large fenced property is lacking – it is after all a 5-star hotel in the

bush – but will appeal to those who like luxury hotels and to families (children over the age of 8). Facilities include an infinity pool with views over the plains, a gym, spa, library, wine cellar, several bars and a restaurant, and the whole architecturally impressive stone-and-thatch complex is centred on 2 very active waterholes.

$$$$ Grumeti Serengeti Tented Camp
Western Corridor, 93 km west of Seronera and 50 km east of Lake Victoria, reservations Johannesburg, South Africa, T+27-(0)11-809 4300, www.andbeyond.com.
Overlooks a tributary of the Grumeti River that teems with hippo and crocodile. Central bar/dining area near the river, swimming pool, 10 charming, custom-made tents raised on platforms with stylishly colourful decor. Fantastic service and a great location, especially during the migration from late May to early Jul.

$$$$ Kirawira Serena Camp
Western Corridor, reservations Arusha, T027-254 5555, www.serenahotels.com.

This smart tented camp is the most luxurious of the Serena's stable of safari properties, and lies 90 km from Seronera in the Western Corridor. All the 25 tents have Edwardian decor of writing desks, brass lamps and 4-poster beds, while the central public tent is adorned with exquisite antiques, including an old gramophone, and the swimming pool overlooks the plains.

$$$$ Lemala Ewanjan Tented Camp
In the Seronera Valley, resrvations Arusha T0736-210 966, www.lemalacamp.com.
Within the game-rich Seronera Valley, but situated up a dead-end track so as not to be disturbed by other game-viewing vehicles in this busy part of the park. 12 comfortable tents, 1 is for families, and the mess tent is beautifully decorated with leather sofas, chandeliers, rugs and chests, and in the evening there's a campfire. It's a 35-min drive from the Seronera airstrip.

$$$$ Lemala Kuria Hills Lodge
In the north of the park, in the Wogakuria Hills, reservations Arusha T0736-210 966, www.lemalacamp.com.
This is about a 30-min drive from the Mara River and has a slick and contemporary design and is the most luxurious in the Lemala stable. It is cleverly built around a kopje with boulders dominating the public areas, and there are superb views of the plains from the bar, lounge and dining area. The spacious 15 glass-fronted rooms have canvas walls and their own plunge pools and free-standing bath. Swimming pool, and massages available.

$$$$ Namiri Plains
In the east, reservations Asilia Africa, Arusha T0736-500 515, www.asiliaafrica.com.
Opened in 2014, this new camp from **Asilia Africa** is in a wonderfully remote area (more than 1½-hr drive from the Seronera airstrip), which for 20 years was closed to the public for cheetah research – as such it's good cheetah country and sightings are common, and lion and leopard are frequently seen languishing on the kopjes in this region.

8 elegant tents with outdoor showers and sweeping views of the plains, a comfortable mess tent, and outdoor lounge and fire-pit under giant acacias. **Asilia Africa** also sets up its mobile camps (see box, page 117), the Dunia Camp, Kimondo Camp, Ubuntu Migration Camp and Olakira Migration Camp, each at 2-3 locations across the Serengeti to follow the migration.

$$$$ Sanctuary Kusini
At the Hambi ya Mwaki-Nyeb Kopjes in the southwest, near the border with the Maswa Game Reserve, reservations Sanctuary Retreats, Arusha T027-250 9817, www.sanctuaryretreats.com.
Well off the usual tourist track and the only permanent camp in this remote region, it is also a good place to witness the calving season from mid-Dec. It is situated in an outcrop of kopjes, offering superb views, with 12 stylish tents, 1 of which is a honeymoon suite. Hospitable camp managers arrange sundowners on cushions up on the kopjes and candlelit dinners each evening. There's also a library and lounge.

$$$$ Sayari Camp
In the far north of the Serengeti, near the Kenyan border, reservations Asilia Africa, Arusha T0736-500 515, www.asiliaafrica.com.
Formerly a mobile camp that followed the migration, this is now a permanent tented camp and one of the few in this remote region just south of the Mara River, with 15 luxurious and comfortable tents, the mess tent has a bar, lounge, library and restaurant centred around a campfire, and there's an infinity swimming pool and spa, attentive service. **Asilia Africa** also runs a number of mobile camps (see above and box, page 117).

$$$$ Serengeti Bushtops
Northern Serengeti, about 20 km south of the Mara River, reservations Mombasa, Kenya T+254 (0)20-213 7862, www.bushtopscamps.com.
One of the few permanent camps in this region – although plenty of mobile camps

As well as the choices of permanent accommodation in the Serengeti, a number of safari companies also set up seasonal semi-permanent tented camps in good spots to see the migration. Sometimes these are termed as 'mobile' camps, meaning they are temporarily erected for a few weeks; they do not move location every night, but they may move once or twice within the migration's season. There are scores of them to choose from and are usually small and very comfortable, often luxurious, perhaps with 8-12 tents that have en suite bathrooms with flush loos and 'bladder' safari showers (these are filled with hot water heated on the campfire), and lighting provided by solar power. Plus there will be a 'mess' tent for dining and drinks, and vehicles for airstrip transfers and game drives. A great option if you want a bush experience but one that comes with home comforts. Tour operators in Arusha (see page 58) can book these as part of a safari itinerary, or check out the options with the following companies:

Ang'ata Camps & Safaris, *Arusha T0786-025 352, www.angatacamps.com.*
Asilia Africa, *Arusha T0736-500 515, www.asiliaafrica.com.*
Kirurumu Under Canvas, *Arusha T027-250 2417, www.kirurumu.net.*
Nasikia Camps, *Arusha T0732-930 833, www.nasikiacamps.com.*
Nomad Tanzania, *Arusha T0787-595 908, www.nomad-tanzania.com.*

Sanctuary Retreats, *Arusha T027-250 9817, www.sanctuaryretreats.com.*
Serengeti Savannah Camps, *Arusha T027-254 7066, www.serengetisavannah camps.com.*
Tanganyika Wilderness Camps, *Arusha T0736-502 471, www.tanganyika wildernesscamps.com.*
Tanzania Wilderness Camps, *Arusha T027-254 3068, www.tanzania wildernesscamps.com.*

set up here when the migration is preparing to cross the Mara River – Bushtops has 12 tents, 2 are linked to accommodate families, with vast wooden decks overlooking the plains, all positioned to watch the sunset, and attractively decorated in a contemporary style. Restaurant, library/ bar, campfire and lovely stone and wooden deck swimming pool area.

$$$$ Serengeti Migration Camp
Built within the rocks of a kopje in the Ndassiata Hills near Lobo, overlooking the Grumeti River, reservations through the Elewana Collection, Arusha T0754-250 630, www.elewanacollection.com.
Luxury tented camp which provides excellent views of the migration in the Lobo

area, with 20 richly decorated tents include a secluded honeymoon suite and a family tent sleeping 6; each one is surrounded by a 360° veranda, and there are many secluded vantage points linked by timber walkways, bridges and viewing platforms. There's a swimming pool, bar and restaurant.

$$$$ Serengeti Pioneer Camp
In south central Serengeti near Moru Kopjes, reservations Elewana Collection, Arusha, T027-250 0630, www.elewanacollection.com.
This smart tented camp has an early explorer theme with leather chairs, storage trunks and copper basins as sinks, and each of the 12 well-spaced tents has a decanter of sherry. Well-located for the Moru Kopjes and surrounding plains, and the makuti thatched

lounge sits on top of a rocky outcrop and offers commanding views. Often booked though the Elewana Collection as part of a 2-camp safari with the Serengeti Migration Camp to the north.

$$$$-$$$ Lobo Wildlife Lodge
Northeast of Seronera in the Lobo area, reservations Arusha, T027-254 4595, www.hotelsandlodges-tanzania.com.
Only 28 km from the Maasai Mara in Kenya, this 4-storey stone-and-timber lodge with 75 rooms, some of them adjoining for families, is well-camouflaged among clusters of large boulders; the swimming pool and bar are both dug into the rock. From its elevated position, there are sweeping views over the savannah and there's an active waterhole, as well as a buffet restaurant, TV room and curio shop.

$$$$-$$$ Mbuzi Mawe Serena Camp
In the northeast of the park, about 45 km from Seronera, reservations Arusha, T027-254 5555, www.serenahotels.com.
Built around rocky kopjes, Mbuzi Mawe means 'the place of the klipsringer' in Kiswahili and you'll see several of them skipping up the rocks here, no longer shy of people. It's a charming, understated camp with 16 tents stylishly decorated with private verandas, a relaxing bar and restaurant, a fire-pit and stone terrace, and friendly staff.

$$$$-$$$ Serengeti Serena Safari Lodge
20 km north of Seronera, reservations Arusha T027-254 5555, www.serenahotels.com.
Another quality Serena property and good mid-range large lodge option in an idyllic central location with superb views towards the Western Corridor. Set high overlooking the plains, the lodge is constructed to reflect the design of an African village. Each of the a/c 66 rooms is a domed, stone-walled and thatched rondavel, with wooden balcony, natural stone bathrooms, and carved furniture. Also has a spa and infinity pool with views over the plains.

$$$$-$$$ Serengeti Sopa Lodge
In the Nyarboro Hills north of Moru Kopjes, reservations Arusha T027-250 0630, www.sopalodges.com.
A good value offering from the Sopa group decorated in an African-village theme with murals, giant pots and thatch. There are 69 rooms and 4 suites, excellent views of the Serengeti plains through double-storey window walls in all public areas, multi-level buffet restaurant and lounges, swimming pool, gift shop and TV room.

$$$$-$$$ Seronera Wildlife Lodge
At Seronera, reservations Arusha T027-254 4595, www.hotelsand lodges-tanzania.com.
This large mid-range lodge really is at the heart of the Serengeti, and it's only a short drive from the Seronera airstrip and the launch site for the balloon, and more importantly has good game-viewing year round. The public areas are very cleverly built into a rocky kopje, as is the swimming pool (making it look like an attractive natural pool). There are 75 decent-sized rooms, restaurant, shop, bar and viewing platform at the top of the kopje.

Camping

TANAPA
Dodoma (A104) road, Arusha, T027-250 3471, www.tanzaniaparks.com.

Seronera Campsite
There are a string of 6 public campsites at Seronera – **Dik-dik, Nyani, Tumbili, Nguchiro, Pimbi** and **Ngiri** – and not surprisingly are collectively called Seronera Campsite. Each has a thatched cooking area/ shelter, cold showers, toilets and camping and vehicle pitches demarcated with small stones. The water supply however is frequently disrupted by thirsty elephants so the showers do not always work. These are used by the budget camping safari operators, and if you are self-driving, you need to be totally self-sufficient including bringing food and drinking water. It is not

necessary to pre-book; you simply pay for camping when you enter the park: US$30; children (5-16) US$5. They are all are unfenced, and are regularly visited by hyenas and baboons scavenging for scraps, and lions have also been known to wander through; ensure that you stay in your tent at night and pack up your vehicle when going on a game drive. It is possible to visit (suitably dressed) the bars and restaurant at the **Seronera Wildlife Lodge** in the evening, as driving around the immediate vicinity of Seronera is permitted until 2200.

Lobo Public Campsite
Lobo Public Campsite is located in the Lobo area at the base of a kopje and has the same facilities. As it's not far from the Lobo Wildlife Lodge, again you may be able to visit for a drink or meal. There are also dozens of special campsites (US$50, children (5-16) US$10), spread around the park (no facilities at all, just cleared spaces in the bush), and they are often used by the camping safari tour operators, or they are booked exclusively by the safari companies for their seasonal mobile camps.

Outside the park
The lodges and camps outside the national park boundaries are able to offer additional night drives and game walks, which are not permitted within the Serengeti. Standard park entry fees apply to go game driving within the park, and/or if you are reaching these camps from within the park.

$$$$ Buffalo Luxury Camp
On a private concession area on the northeastern boundary of the park, 5 km from Kleins Gate, reservations through Intimate Places Tanzania, Arusha T0732-971 771, www.intimate-places.com.
This comfortable camp has 15 unusual split-level tents, with a raised sleeping area towards the back and a lower lounge with leather chairs and a veranda at the front. Solid wooden floors throughout and surprisingly spacious tiled bathrooms with bathtubs as well as showers. The main brick and canvas building has the lounge with fireplace, bar/library and terrace restaurant with views over the Loliondo Hills.

$$$$ Grumeti Migration Camp
In the Grumeti Wildlife Reserve concession on the northwestern boundary of the park, 14 km from Ikoma Gate, reservations Arusha T027-275 2999, www.ecolodgeafrica.com.
This concession is one of a handful of buffer zones put in place in recent years to provide a series of corridors for the migration and this camp lies not far north of the Grumeti River. It has 20 tents with verandas, some are triples and quads but no children under 7, and the central area has the restaurant, bar and fireplace, and the neat swimming pool is surrounded by a flagstone sun-bathing and viewing deck overlooking savannah woodland.

$$$$ Klein's Camp
On a private concession on the northeastern boundary of the park, 2.6 km from Kleins Gate, reservations Johannesburg, South Africa, T+27-(0)11-809 4300, www.andbeyond.com.
Named after the American big game hunter, Al Klein, who in 1926 built his base camp in this valley. The 10,000 ha private concession is located on the Kuka Hills between the Serengeti and farmland, which forms a natural buffer zone for the animals and overlooks a wildlife corridor linking the Serengeti and the Maasai Mara. 10 super-luxury stone-and-thatch cottages, the dining room and bar are in separate rondavels with commanding views of the Grumeti River Valley, and there's a swimming pool.

$$$$ Singita Sasakwa Lodge
Sabora Tented Camp and Faru Faru Lodge, these 3 lodges are located in a 350,000 ha exclusive-use Grumeti Reserves north of the Grumeti River and Ikoma Gate, reservations, Cape Town, South Africa, T+27 (0)21-683 3424, www.singita.com.

ON THE ROAD
Balloon safaris

Seeing the Serengeti from a hot-air balloon is one of the highlights of many people's safaris. In fact some may say the experience is essential if you're doing all transfers to the park by road, less so if you're flying in or out by plane. If you can afford it, of course. At US$540 per person it's not cheap, but floating above the vast plains tinted pink by the rising sun, while the herds gallop below, is a memorable experience. There are three launch sites: near the Seronera River in Central Serengeti, Southern Serengeti and the Western Corridor. Balloon flights launch at dawn and last approximately an hour. They are followed by a bush breakfast with a glass of fizz while the silk is stowed away. Pickups from the lodges are around 0500; you can expect to be back around 0945 (the excursion effectively is an alternative to an early morning game drive). All the lodges and camps and tour operators can book the balloon excursion, or contact Serengeti Balloon Safaris, Arusha T027-254 8967, www.balloonsafaris.com.

Owned by **Singita**, one of Africa's top safari brands with many lodges in southern Africa, the options here are the epitome of luxury. **Sasakwa** has been built in the style of an Edwardian manor house and has 9 luxury cottages and a 4-bedroomed house (with separate staff quarters), each with fireplace, private infinity pool and deck with telescope. It is set on a hill with stunning views over the main migration route in the Western Corridor. Facilities include a gym and yoga room, spa, tennis courts and they have their own an equestrian centre. **Sabora** is a classic tented camp reminiscent of the 1920s safari style and has 6 tents and a swimming pool, and **Faru Faru** is a beautifully designed contemporary stone-and-thatch lodge constructed around 2 rim-flow swimming pools with 9 suites and 1 villa. Both are located further down the hill on the plains.

$$$$-$$$ Mapito Tented Camp
5 km from Ikoma Gate, reservations Arusha T0732-975 210, www.mapito-camp-serengeti.com.
This relaxing and well-priced camp has 15 large en suite tents that can sleep up to 4 with small stone patios, rustic wooden furniture, hot water bucket outside showers and solar-powered electricity. The lounge, bar and restaurant is in an impressive and unusual double-storey timber-and-canvas structure with a giant thatched roof.

$$$$-$$$ Serengeti Simba Lodge
Just outside Ikoma Gate, reservations Arusha T027-275 3001, www.simbaportfolio.com.
Set on the hill overlooking the distant Grumeti River, the 15 'tents' have solid stone foundations and thatched roofs but canvas walls, and have outdoor showers and are decorated with local fabrics and hard wood furniture. There's also a 6 room stone house; the rooms can be occupied individually or the whole house can be taken for a group. The double-volume main building has the lounge, bar, dining room, viewing deck, swimming pool with sun deck and campfire area.

$$$ Ikoma Tented Camp
2 km from Ikoma Gate, reservations Arusha, T027-250 6135, www.moivaro.com.
This camp has the concession for the area and works in close collaboration with the local Maasai villages. It is comfortable, secluded and sheltered in a grove of acacia trees, with 31 spacious tents and a bar and dining area under thatch around a central fire-pit. Simpler and slightly cheaper than some of the more luxurious tented camps above.

There's also a campsite here (**$**) with hot showers and a thatched kitchen area or you can eat at the restaurant; very useful for self-drivers coming from the Musoma direction.

$$$ Ikoma Safari Camp
10 km from Ikoma Gate T0713-350 601, www.ikomasafaricamp.com.
A fairly simple but good value camp with accommodation in 8 wooden thatched cottages (not tents) with panelled walls and a slightly raised deck, 3 of which can sleep 4, en suite with solar-powered hot water. Open dining area under thatch with tables covered with Maasai blankets, which adds to the rustic and unpretentious atmosphere. Although it's some way from the gate, from US$120 per person per night full board, this is one of the cheapest places in the Ikoma region.

Maasai Mara National Reserve

In the southwest region of Kenya, the Maasai Mara National Reserve is an equally exciting safari destination as the bordering Serengeti National Park in Tanzania. It is part of the contiguous Serengeti ecosystem and teems with the same species of wildlife, and in similar numbers, and is where the wildebeest migration can be found in season. Covering 1510 sq km, the Mara scenery is wonderful, with vast savannah plains covered with gently rolling grassland and scrub-bush of acacias and thorn trees. The Mara River runs from north to south through the park and then turns westwards to Lake Victoria.

The wildlife

The reserve is home to good-sized populations of predators – lion, cheetah, leopard and hyena – and the same herbivores seen in the Serengeti, and the migrating wildebeest, zebra and gazelle have usually arrived in the Mara by August. Sometimes thousands of animals will amass on the banks of the Mara River, waiting for an opportunity to cross. Eventually they will choose a crossing point, usually a fairly placid stretch of water without too much predator-concealing vegetation on the far side, and in places, the riverbanks have been worn down considerably after centuries of crossings. First one, then another and then the whole frenetic herd leap into the water. Most make it to the other side, but occasionally they will choose seemingly illogical (or suicidal) places and drown in their hundreds, or are taken by the enormous Mara crocodiles. Once the Mara's new grass has been eaten, the animals retrace their long journey south in around late October and November.

The reserve

The Maasai Mara is not a national park but a game reserve, and is not managed by the Kenya Wildlife Services (KWS), who are the custodian of Kenya's other national parks. It is divided into an inner and outer section. The inner section – the Mara Triangle between the Mara River and the Oloololo Escarpment – is administered by the Trans-Mara County Council and has no human habitation apart from the lodges. The outer section – or the rest of the national reserve, namely the Musiara sector in the north and the Sekenani sector in the centre and east – is administered by the Narok County Council, and is where the Maasai graze their herds and coexist with the wildlife (like they do in the Ngorongoro Conservation Area). The game, however, does not recognize these designated boundaries and an even larger region, known as the 'dispersal area', extends north and east of the reserve, where the Maasai live with their stock, and where many of the lodges and camps are in conservancies on Maasai group ranches (usually meaning they contribute financially to the Maasai in exchange for use of their land).

Getting there

To get to the Maasai Mara from Tanzania you will need to go through Nairobi. There are nine airstrips in the Maasai Mara and flights from Nairobi take between 45 minutes and 1¼ hours; like in the Serengeti, they run in circuits and may touch down a few times. By road the Mara is 275 km southwest of Nairobi (five to six hours). The main access to the reserve is through the Maasai trading town of Narok, 143 km to the west of Nairobi on the smooth tarred B3 road. From Narok, there is no one clear route and various access roads go to the gates of the reserve – Sekenani, Talek, Ololaimutiek, Musiara and Oloololo gates – with tracks veering off to the conservancies.

Park information

Daily 0630-1900, US$80, children (3-18) US$45, under threes free, vehicle US$4 (less than six seats), US$10 (six to 12 seats); entry is per 24 hours or part thereof. Fees are taken at the gates or airstrips and are paid in US$ cash (although the Mara Triangle entry points of Oloololo Gate and Serena Airstrip also accept Visa cards). If you are on an organized safari or lodge package, entry fees will be part of the price. For more information visit www.maratriangle.org and www.maasaimara.com.

Where to stay

$$$$ **Kichwa Tembo Camp & Bateleur Camp**, *Oloololo Game Ranch, reservations South Africa T+27 (0)11 8094300, www.and beyond.com*. These long-term favourite luxury camps are superbly located on the west bank of the Mara River. Kichwa Tembo has 40 Hemingway-style safari tents, some for families, garden with hammocks and a stunning infinity swimming pool. Bateleur has a romantic 'Out of Africa' early explorer theme with 18 tented suites and a pool. Both are at the base of the Oloololo Escarpment and offer broad views of the plains.

$$$$ **Naboisho Camp**, *Naboisho Conservancy, T020-232 4904, www.asilia africa.com*. With excellent guides, attention to detail and service, the 8 large tents here have a contemporary chic feel and extras like outdoor showers and hosted dining is in a comfortable mess tent.

$$$$ **Saruni Camp**, *Mara North Conservancy, T020-218 0497, www.saruni mara.com*. Overlooking a game-filled valley, this intimate and stylish camp has just 6 large and very elegant cottages and 2 family villas furnished with colonial antiques and Persian carpets. Mara North is an exclusive wildlife concession, where night drives and bush walks are permitted, and there are excellent Maasai guides.

$$$$-$$$ **Mara Intrepids & Mara Explorer**, *in the National Reserve, T020-444 6651, www.heritage-eastafrica.com*. These 2 sister camps are on the forested banks of the Talek River. A good family option, Intrepids has 30 tents with 4-poster beds, a game-viewing tower to climb, and a kids' adventure club. Explorer is more upmarket (and is unfenced)

and has 10 tents geared to couples with outside claw-foot baths, lovely riverside lounge/dining area, and guests can swim at the pool at Intrepids.

$$$$-$$$ **Mara Serena Safari Lodge**, *in the Mara Triangle, T0732-123 333, www.serena hotels.com*. Well-designed safari lodge on top of a hill with 74 boma-style rooms with balconies and superb view over the Mara River and plains beyond, restaurant overlooking a waterhole, swimming pool, wildlife films, Maasai dancing. A mid-range option with good Serena standards and good value out of migration season.

$$$$-$$$ **Sarova Mara Game Camp**, *in the National Reserve, T050-222 386, www.sarova hotels.com*. This popular mid-range and well-run place is easily accessible as its only 2 km inside Sekenani Gate. There are 70 comfortable tents, some for families, and has good facilities like a swimming pool set in spacious gardens, buffet restaurant and central lounge/bar areas with fireplaces. The surrounding plains see plenty of animal action.

$$-$ **Mara Explorers Camp & Backpackers**, *3 km before Sekenani Gate to the National Reserve, T0706-856 216, www.mara explorers.com*. One of the best of a collection of budget options outside Sekenani Gate, this friendly spot can be reached by taxi from Narok and can organize all game drives into the reserve itself, or opt for a safari package from Nairobi. There are wooden and reed cottages, walk-in tents with camp beds, plus dorm beds and a campsite, long-drop toilets and warm bush showers, and decent meals in a thatched boma.

Moshi
& Mount
Kilimanjaro

Moshi is the first staging post on the way to climbing Mount Kilimanjaro. Reaching the 'Roof of Africa' is one of the continent's greatest challenges, and also provides an adventurous contrast to game-viewing. Despite its altitude, even inexperienced climbers can climb it, provided they are reasonably fit and allow themselves sufficient time to acclimatize to the elevation. It is in fact the tallest mountain in the world that can be walked up. Trekking expeditions depart from Moshi into Kilimanjaro National Park early each morning and the air of excited trepidation is tangible among climbers. Moshi itself is a vibrant, colourful town and a pleasant place to spend a few days organizing your trip. It is a little more laid back than Arusha, has less of a hustly element, and it's easy to stroll around the markets, peek into shops and spend a lazy afternoon on the terrace of a coffee shop. Moshi is set in a fertile volcanic area and is well fed by streams off the mountain, ideal for growing Arabica coffee, the most profitable local export. The lower slopes of Kilimanjaro are blanketed with a peaceful patchwork of small-scale farms and villages, and you can walk through the banana and coffee plantations, and learn about coffee production from the local Chagga people. Hikes in this area are ideal for acclimatization before climbing Kilimanjaro, while admiring the imposing beauty of the mountain above.

Moshi
& around

Moshi is a neat town with a certain air of prosperity thanks to it serving as 'base-camp' and is always busy with climbers preparing (and recovering) in the hotels, and many of the townsfolk are employed as guides, porters and cooks. The two peaks of this shimmering snow-capped mountain can be seen from all over the town and it dominates the skyline except when the cloud descends and hides it from view. Moshi means 'smoke' – perhaps either a reference to the giant volcano that once smoked or the regular smoke-like cloud. The fertile foothills of Kilimanjaro provide plenty of other opportunities for worthwhile day trips including foothill walks, birdwatching and observing rural Africa.

Moshi

Moshi lies on the east–west A23 road connecting Arusha and Voi in Kenya and just to the east of Moshi is the junction with the B1 north–south road to Dar es Salaam. It is a busy town of just under 200,000 people, with the former European and administrative areas clustered around the clock tower, and the main commercial area southwest of the market. Despite being an attractive town, there are few places worth visiting in Moshi itself, and many visitors stay here just long enough to arrange their trek up the mountain and to enjoy a hot shower when they get back. The limited sights include the (non-operating) **railway station** southeast of the clock tower, a two-storey structure from the German period, with pleasing low arches, a gabled roof with Mangalore tiles and arched windows on the first floor. On the corner of Station Road and Ghalla Road is a fine **Indian shop building** dating from the colonial period, with wide curved steps leading up to the veranda, tapering fluted stone columns and a cupola adorning the roof. To the north of town on the roundabout marking the junction with the Dar–Arusha road is the **Askari Monument**, a soldier with a rifle, that commemorates African members of the British Carrier Corps who lost their lives in the two World Wars.

Essential Moshi and around

Finding your feet

Moshi is 80 km east of Arusha on the A23. **Kilimanjaro International Airport**, 55 km west of Moshi, off the A23/Arusha road, T027-255 4252, www.kilimanjaro airport.co.tz, is well served by domestic flights and some international flights. See Practicalities for further information. A taxi from the airport should cost around US$50 to Moshi, or you can arrange transfers with one of the hotels or tour operators. There are numerous buses in all directions from Moshi, and it is a pickup/dropoff terminus for the many daily buses between Dar and Arusha. It is also served by the daily Nairobi–Arusha–Moshi shuttle buses, which also call in at Kilimanjaro International Airport on their way past. There is a steady stream of *dala-dalas* that cover the 27 km between Moshi and Marangu.

Time required

You need a day in Moshi to get prepared or recover from the climb, but you could easily spend another day exploring the surrounding area.

Materuni and Kuringe Waterfalls

Tanzania Cultural Tourism Programme office or the Tanzanian Tourist Information Centre, both on Boma Rd in Arusha, see page 59, www.tanzaniaculturaltourism.co.tz, or any of the hotels or tour operators in Moshi can organize a 4- to 6-hr trip for around US$40-60 per person depending on the size of the group including a picnic lunch.

On the lower slopes of Kilimanjaro, Materuni is a Chagga coffee village lying at an altitude of 1800 m. From here a 45-minute upward hike through coffee, banana and avocado 'shambas', the Kiswahili word for farms, to 2500 m (demanding, and hiking boots are recommended) takes you to the very impressive Kuringe Waterfalls. Surrounded by cliffs, this is one of the tallest in the area where crystal clear glacier water falls in a 70-m curtain into its basin. You can swim but obviously it's somewhat chilly given that it's the snowmelt from the mountain. The excursion includes a visit to a small coffee farm to learn about how coffee is grown, harvested and processed locally, and you can try your own hand at roasting and preparing a fresh cup of coffee in the local Chagga way. There may also be a demonstration on making banana wine (administer with care). If you don't want to go on

Moshi

an organized tour, to get to Materuni under your own steam, the village is 15 km or a 30-minute drive directly north of Moshi – go past the **Keys Hotel** on Uru Road. *Dala-dalas* go part way to the outskirts of town and then get a *piki-piki*.

Machame

Machame, 25 km northwest of Moshi (the road to the village turns off the Moshi–Arusha road (A23) 12 km west of Moshi), is the start of the Machame Route up Kilimanjaro (see page 150). It is tougher than the Marangu Route but is considered one of the most beautiful trails up. Machame itself lies in a fertile valley of farmland on the lower slopes of the mountain; the park gate is 4 km beyond the village. There are only a couple of accommodation options here, but climb operators will transport you to the park gate from Moshi.

West Kilimanjaro

The road running in a northerly direction from Boma ya Ng'ombe, 27 km west of Moshi on the Moshi–Arusha road (A23), passes through Sanya Juu and Engare Nairobi to reach the village of **Ol Molog**, about 70 km north of the main road and on the northern side of the mountain very close to the border with Kenya. This was the main area for European farming in northern Tanzania prior to Independence. After Independence most estates were

Where to stay 🛏
AMEG Lodge Kilimanjaro **11**
Bristol Cottages **7**
Hibiscus B&B **5**
Karibu Hostel **9**
Keys **14**
Kilemakyaro Mountain
  Lodge **15**
Kilimanjaro Crane **2**
Kindoroko **8**
Leopard **18**
Mountain Inn **16**
Mt Kilimanjaro View
  Lodge **4**
Parkview Inn **1**
Rafiki Backpackers **10**

Sal Salinero **12**
Springlands **3**
YMCA **13**

Restaurants 🍴
Aroma Coffee House **3**
Chrisburger **1**
The Coffee Shop **7**
Deli Chez **6**
El Rancho **5**
Fifi's **2**
Indoitaliano **9**
Kaliwa **4**
Tanzania Coffee Lounge **10**

BACKGROUND
Coffee-producing country

While various ethnic groups such as the Chagga and Pare have lived on the lowers slopes of Kilimanjaro for centuries, and historically the Maasai used the region as a retreat when drought afflicted the barren plains below, Moshi doesn't have a long formal history. Germany established a military camp in Moshi (which they called Neu-Moschi) in 1893, but it was coffee that established this typical Tanzanian market town. The region, particularly fertile due to the volcanic soils and melt-water streams fed by the snow running off the mountain, is where the Chagga people grow Arabica coffee.

The name Arabica is derived from Arabia, as the crop is also grown in Yemen on the Arabian Peninsula. It is also commonly called 'mountain coffee' as it flourishes at altitudes of 1000-2500 m. As such, the lower slopes of Kilimanjaro are blanketed with low coffee bushes, grown here among taller banana palms for shade. The first coffee grown in Tanzania was planted at the Kilema Roman Catholic Mission in 1898 in what is now Marangu and later on by Germany settlers. The local Chagga people at first were not permitted to plant coffee themselves and instead worked on the settlers' plantations. But this all changed after the First World War when the Germans retreated from Tanganyika, and, by 1925, growth on the Chagga farms was steady and more than 100 tonnes were being produced each year. The Chagga people are particularly enterprising and in 1929 formed the **Kilimanjaro Native Cooperative Union** (KNCH, www.kncutanzania.com) to collect and market the crop themselves, and to compete on equal terms in world markets with European growers. KNCH flourished in the 1950s and 1960s and drove much of the development of the Kilimanjaro region, with Moshi developing into a prosperous town. In 1977 KNCH was nationalized by the government but became independent again in 1984. Today it is considered one of the oldest cooperatives in Africa. It presently collects coffee from 92 villages and represents over 60,000 small-scale farmers, and trades about 12% of all the coffee grown in Tanzania. KNCU also works closely with 'Fair Trade' initiatives.

Not surprisingly the **Tanzania Coffee Board** (www.coffeeboard.or.tz), the regulator on all matters pertaining to production, coffee grading and marketing, is also based in Moshi and holds a weekly auction in season (harvesting is from July to December) to international buyers. Interestingly, only about 7% of coffee grown in Tanzania is consumed in the country; simply because Tanzanians are traditionally chai (tea) drinkers. Today's Moshi also benefits from its role of 'base-camp' for ascents of Kilimanjaro – many of the local people are employed in the tourism industry – and the local economy also thrives on service industries given that it is on a transport route via the B1 road from the port in Dar es Salaam.

nationalized. These days, while pockets of farmland still exist, most of the plains in this region are used by wildlife on a migratory route between **Arusha National Park** and Kenya's Amboseli National Park. In the dry season up to 600 elephant use this corridor, and it's an important calving area for zebra, wildebeest, and Grant's and Thompson's gazelles. In addition to its diverse habitats and wildlife communities, West Kilimanjaro is home to a number of Maasai communities that depend on cattle grazing. There are a couple of lodges in this region (see Where to stay, page 135).

Marangu

Marangu, 11 km north of Himo and 27 km east of Moshi on the A23 road to the Kenya border, is a busy little village that most people visit only to attempt the climb on the Marangu Route to the summit of Kilimanjaro lying just 5 km south of the entrance gate to the Mount Kilimanjaro National Park. However, Marangu is also an excellent base for hiking, birdwatching and observing rural Africa in the foothills of the mountain, and the main tracks in the region radiate from the village and forest boundary through the cultivated belt of coffee and bananas. There are several waterfalls within a short walk of the village and, indeed, in the Chagga language, Marangu means 'a place with too many streams' in reference to the profusion of waterways running off the mountain. For full details of climbing Kilimanjaro, see page 144.

Chagga Live Museum ⓘ *In the grounds of the Kilimanjaro Mountain Resort (see below). Daily 1000-1700, US$3.* This is a mock-up of a traditional Chagga homestead where guides demonstrate the use of traditional Chagga tools and farming implements, some drums and a 'bugle' made of kudu horns, and introduce you to the goats and cows in the pen outside. Nearby there are the remains of some Chagga 'caves' to look at, and climb down into thanks to a wooden ladder. They are in fact tunnels typically built beneath a house to protect livestock and women from Maasai raids. Historically, in times of drought, the Maasai would migrate up the lower slopes of Kilimanjaro in search of food and water, and given that it is said that the Maasai believe that all the cattle in the world are theirs by right, they would steal from the Chagga and in some cases reputedly took the women too. The guides explain this conflict while you visit the caves.

Foothill walks ⓘ *Tanzania Cultural Tourism Programme office, or the Tanzanian Tourist Information Centre, both on Boma Rd in Arusha, see page 44, www.tanzaniaculturaltourism. co.tz.* The **Marangu/Mamba Cultural Tourism Programme** arranges guided walks through the attractive scenery of the valleys near Marangu and Mamba. **Mamba** is a small village, 3 km from Marangu. From here you can also visit caves where women and children hid during ancient Maasai-Chagga wars or see a blacksmith at work, using traditional methods to make Maasai spears and tools. From Marangu there is an easy walk up Ngangu Hill. You can also visit a traditional Chagga home and visit the home and memorial of the late Yohano Lawro, a local man who accompanied Dr Hans Meyer and Ludwig Purtscheller on the first recorded climb of Mount Kilimanjaro in 1889. He is reputed to have guided Kilimanjaro climbs until he was 70 and lived to the age of 115. Profits from the programme are used to improve local primary schools. Any of the Marangu hotels can organize guides from the programme.

Lake Chala

52 km east of Moshi off the A23 towards the Holili-Taveta border with Kenya. 10 km after the B1 (to Dar es Salam) junction and 6 km before Holili is the turn off to the north, from where it's roughly another 15 km on a rough gravel road to the lakeshore and camp.

This picturesque, undetermined deep-water crater lake straddles the border with Kenya. About 4 sq km, it is totally clear, with 100-m-high steep and vegetated walls, and it is filled and drained by underground streams fed by the waters running off

Kilimanjaro. It is a tranquil, beautiful place to explore on foot and, aside from plenty of fish, there are also monitor lizards, baboons, monkeys and numerous birds, especially raptors. Bring good walking shoes, as it's a steep ascent down to the lake itself. **Lake Chala Safari Camp** (see Where to stay, below) is a peaceful overnight retreat and there is a tented camp as well as campsites, and you may glimpse the sun reflecting off the snow at the top of Kilimanjaro at dusk. It also makes a doable day trip from Moshi for swimming and exploring and lunch at the **Caldera Restaurant**, built right on the edge of the crater cliffs. If you don't have transport, the Moshi tour operators can organize a vehicle for around US$80 on the pretence of a 'guided tour' but it's just as easy and cheaper to negotiate it yourself with a taxi.

Listings Moshi and around *map p128*

Where to stay

Most of the hotels in Moshi and Marangu offer arrangements to climb Kili, or at the least will recommend a tour operator. They all offer a base from which to begin your climb, and there is an excellent choice of mid-range and budget places where you will enjoy the 'camaraderie' of other excited (or afterwards weary) trekkers. Ensure that the hotel will store your luggage safely while you are on the mountain. Facilities to consider include hot water and a comfortable bed, and of course cold beer and a good hot meal on your return from the climb. Some establishments also offer saunas and massages. Almost all hotels can organize transfers from Kilimanjaro International Airport for about US$40-50.

Moshi

$$$ Kilemakyaro Mountain Lodge
7 km from Moshi, take the Sokoine road out of town, T0763-777 400, www.kilimanjarosafari.com.
Set in a 240-ha coffee plantation at an altitude of 1450 m above Moshi, a stay here will be a big help to climbers with acclimatization. The reception, bar and dining room are in the main house, a restored 1880s farmhouse, while the 20 rooms are in chalets dotted throughout the lovely palm-filled garden, which has a swimming pool. They can arrange climbs

of Kilimanjaro and also Meru, day trips to Arusha National Park (see page 69) and picnics at local waterfalls.

$$$ Sal Salinero Hotel
Lema Rd, Shantytown, T0758-555 554, www.salsalinerohotel.com.
A little pricier than the alternatives (from US$120) but a quiet option with good standards and rooms in neat modern villas in manicured gardens, with mini-bar, tea and coffee making facilities, DSTV and Wi-Fi. The furnishings however are quite old-fashioned for such a new place. Great pool area in park-like grounds, and the **Leopard bar and Choma Grill**.

$$ AMEG Lodge Kilimanjaro
Off Lema Rd, near the Moshi International School, Shantytown, T0754-058 268, www.ameglodge.com.
A modern if somewhat characterless lodge set in 1.5 ha of garden. 20 rooms with smart tiled en suite bathrooms and lovely bright contemporary furniture, DSTV, phone and fan. Swimming pool and pool bar, the **Peppers Restaurant** serves both Western and Indian dishes, gym, Wi-Fi and business centre.

> **Tip...**
> The Marangu hotels are better located on the lower slopes of Kilimanjaro but are considerably more expensive than those in Moshi.

$$ Bristol Cottages
98 Rindi Lane, T027-275 5083,
www.bristolcottages.com.
Within walking distance of the bus stand,
this is set in a pretty garden compound with
parking and, although furnishings are a
little old fashioned, it is spotlessly clean and
adequate. The 8 cottages, including 3 family
ones, are spacious and have a/c, DSTV,
reliable hot water and Wi-Fi, and there are
another 13 more basic and cheaper rooms in
the main building. The pleasant restaurant
and bar serves continental and Indian food
and can organize packed lunches.

$$ Eastpoint Hotel
*Corner of Swahili and Somalia sts, T0255-
688 200 200, www.eastpointhotel.net.*
Hotel in a modern block with views of
Kilimanjaro and Moshi town. Spacious
rooms (single/double/triple US$65/75/90)
and rooftop restaurant serving local and
international cuisines.

$$ Kilimanjaro Crane
Kaunda St, T027-275 1114,
www.kilimanjarocranehotels.com.
Opposite **Nakumatt Supermarket**, with
30 simple but tired rooms with mosquito
nets and DSTV. Facilities include swimming
pool, sauna, gym, gardens, good views, bar
and restaurant. Unremarkable but well-
priced: single/double/triple US$50/60/75.

$$ Leopard Hotel
Market St, T027-275 0884,
www.leopardhotel.com.
This centrally located hotel has 48 spotless
but cramped rooms in a 4-storey block,
with balconies, a/c, DSTV and tiled en
suite bathrooms, half of which have a
view of Kilimanjaro. Restaurant downstairs
with reasonable food and quick service,
a bar with nice views on the roof, friendly
management but has fewer facilities or
amenities than the other places. Doubles
from US$60.

$$ Mountain Inn
*Taifa Rd, 5 km from Moshi on the road
to Marangu, T0716-26 4 427, www.
mountaininn.co.tz.*
This is the base for **Shah Tours**, see What to
do, below, a quality operator for Kilimanjaro
climbs. 24 basic but comfortable rooms,
some are triples, a dining room with a
veranda, set meals and an à la carte menu,
Indian food at the pool bar and restaurant
(see page 137), lush gardens, swimming
pool, sauna and Wi-Fi. Doubles from US$65.

$$ Parkview Inn
Aga Khan Rd, T027-275 0711, www.pvim.com.
Local business hotel with little character but
nevertheless will appeal to those wanting

something modern and has spacious tiled rooms, DSTV, a/c, Wi-Fi, secure parking in a compound, spotless swimming pool and a restaurant serving continental and Indian food and can make up lunch boxes to takeaway.

$$ Springlands Hotel
Tembo Rd, Pasua area towards the industrial area, T027-275 3581, www.zara.co.tz/springlands.htm.
Set in large, attractive gardens, this place offers all sorts of treats that are ideal to recover from a Kili climb. 37 rooms, restaurant, bar, swimming pool, TV room, Wi-Fi, massages, sauna, manicures and pedicures, bicycle hire. Doubles are from US$72 with a generous breakfast. Base for **Zara Tours**, see What to do, below, a recommended operator for climbs. Also offer 'day rooms' for those returning from the climb to freshen up. US$36.

$$-$ Keys Hotel – Uru Road
Uru Rd, just north of the town centre, T027-275 2250, www.keys-hotel-tours.com.
This hotel functions primarily as a base for budget climb operations. Accommodation is in 20 rooms in the main building and 15 garden cottages, which have DSTV and a/c, or 30 economy huts, some with 3 beds. There is a restaurant, bar, Wi-Fi and swimming pool. The location itself is not particularly interesting and it's probably not as pleasant as some of the more rural locations; it is, nevertheless, a firm favourite with budget travellers. Doubles are from US$60 with breakfast, and camping is available in the grounds for US$8 per person. They also run **Keys Hotel – Mbokomu Road**, which is nearby and is usually referred to as the 'Keys Annex', with another 48 budget rooms, some with a/c, balcony and mountain views, and identical facilities including a swimming pool.

$$-$ Mt Kilimanjaro View Lodge
16 km from Moshi, follow the unpaved road out of town north of the YMCA or arrange a pick up, T0758-014 342,
www.mtkilimanjaroviewlodge.com.
A country retreat in the Kilimanjaro foothills, with great views and accommodation in colourful stone and thatch Chagga huts with bathrooms and home-made chunky wooden furniture. You can also camp (US$10 per person). There's a restaurant and bar serving authentic African food, jacuzzi, lots of local walks to nearby waterfalls and, in the evenings, traditional dancing and storytelling. An excellent opportunity to interact with the local Chagga people. Doubles from US$90, and they'll pick up 1-3 people from Moshi for US$45, and from **Kilimanjaro International Airport** for US$90.

$ The Hibiscus B&B
Paris St, 1.5 km northwest of the centre on the opposite side of the A23, T0766-312516, www.thehibiscusmoshi.com.
A friendly B&B in an old 1950s colonial house in a peaceful residential area, 12 fairly simple but neat en suite rooms with splashes of colour, some at the front have balconies. Continental breakfast included, dinner on request (US$10), pleasant garden and Wi-Fi, and can stroll into town from here. Doubles from US$30.

$ Honey Badger Lodge
6 km east of town off the Moshi–Arusha road (A23), T0767-551 190, www.honeybadgerlodge.com.
A refreshing rural alternative to the town hotels, set in a grassy walled compound with 14 rooms in cottages accommodating 1-5 people and a good option for groups of friends and families, reliable solar-powered hot water, pleasant *makuti* thatch bar and swimming pool in the gardens where you also camp, there's a restaurant and you can self-cater in the kitchen. They can organize massages, drumming lessons and village walks. Doubles from US$42.

$ Karibu Hostel
Nsilo Kwai St, off the Moshi–Arusha road (A23), T0774-500 884, www.karibuhostel.com.
Run by the NGO Born to Learn (www.

borntolearn.eu) that provides education to mostly street kids and also finds them sponsors to put them into schools, this hostel offers accommodation to both budget travellers to Moshi and volunteer teachers for the programme. There are 4-bed dorm rooms (US$11), good shared bathrooms with hot showers, TV lounge, pleasant garden full of mango trees, kitchen and meals are available, and there's a car park. It's less than 1.5 km west of the clock tower in town, so an easy walk.

$ Kindoroko Hotel
Mawenzi Rd, close to the Central Market, T027-275 4054, www.kindorokohotels.com.
One of the best budget options in the middle of town, very organized and friendly and fantastically decorated. 46 rooms, which are on the small side but have DSTV, some also have fridges, and bathrooms have plenty of hot water. Rates include a hot breakfast. Downstairs is a restaurant and bar, internet café and tour booking office for Kindoroko Tours for climbs, safaris and a good selection of day trips, upstairs is the rooftop restaurant and bar with excellent views of Kili. A great place to meet other travellers even if you are not staying here. Single/double/triple US$25/35/50.

$ Rafiki Backpackers
Uru Rd; from the A23 to the east of town follow signs past Keys Hotel, T0758-555 554, www.rafikibackpackers.com.
A neat set up in a colourful suburban house with single/twin/double rooms with mosquito nets, fans and shared bathrooms, plus 4-8 bed dorms (from US$12), and camping (US$10). Shared kitchen, laundry, reliable hot water, Wi-Fi, simple cold breakfasts are provided and there is a bar and restaurant across the road. You can walk into town from here (about 25 mins) and it's a good source of local information and can arrange mountain climbs and local day tours in the region.

$ YMCA
Kibo Rd, on the corner of the Moshi–Arusha road (A23), T027-275 2923, ymcatanzania@gmail.com.
Facilities include gym, shop, several tour desks, bar, restaurant, Wi-Fi and Olympic-sized swimming pool (non-guests can use the pool for US$2.50). Mostly used by local people, this has 60 bare rooms with communal showers with hot water. Nevertheless, it's secure and clean with spotless sheets and mosquito nets and rates are from US$10 per person. It's a short stroll to the clocktower in town proper.

Machame

$$$ Kaliwa Lodge
25 km from Moshi in Machame village, T0762-620707, www.kaliwalodge.com.
Beautiful setting near Machame Gate and run by a German couple, this is one of the nicest hotels in the region and not badly priced from US$170 for a double. The service is excellent, the 12 rooms stylish and very comfortable with white linen, splashes of primary colours, French doors and patios, the food tasty and there are superb views of Kili from the terrace. The modern concrete buildings are architecturally interesting and blend well into the mature gardens. A good choice for a rural retreat even if not climbing the mountain.

$$$ Protea Hotel Aishi
25 km from Moshi in Machame village, T027-275 6941, www.proteahotels.com.
This is one of the nicest hotels in the region, run by South African chain **Protea**, and is an ideal base to conquer Kili on the Machame Route (see page 150). The 30 rooms are set in well-kept gardens, and there's a restaurant, coffee shop, bar, heated swimming pool and gym. The hotel arranges mountain climbing, safaris and also nature trails in the area and rents out mountain bikes.

West Kilimanjaro

$$$$ Kambi ya Tembo
Reservations Arusha, T0767-333 223,
www.tanganyikawildernesscamps.com.
A traditional tented camp set on a 600-sq-km
private concession, with 14 spacious tents
and good views of either the mountain
or across the Kenya border towards the
Amboseli Plains. There's a rustic semi-
open-air restaurant and bar, picnics can
be arranged and activities include game
drives and walks with the Maasai.

$$$$ Ndarakwai Ranch
Reservations Arusha, T027-250 2713,
www.ndarakwai.com.
Set on a private conservancy, the 16 tents
here are spacious and are tastefully and
individually furnished, set under thatch roofs
and spreading branches of acacia trees.
Excellent home-cooked food, the views of
Kilimanjaro are superb, and there is game in
this region. Game drives, night drives, walks

with the Maasai, and there's a treehouse
overlooking a waterhole. A conservancy
fee of US$45 per day is charged on top of
the rates.

Marangu

$$$ Marangu Hotel
5 km back from Marangu towards Moshi,
T0717-408 615, www.maranguhotel.com.
Long-established, family-owned and run
country-style hotel, warm and friendly
atmosphere, self-contained cottages with
private baths and showers, hot water, set in
10 acres of gardens offering stunning views
of Kilimanjaro, swimming pool, croquet lawn,
one of the original operators of Kilimanjaro
climbs – they organized the first ones in 1932.
Can arrange treks on all the routes. Also has
a pretty campsite and will safely look after
vehicles for overlanders doing the climb.
Partnered with the **Kilimanjaro Porters
Assistance Project** (see box, page 148).

$$$-$$ Kilimanjaro Mountain Resort
2 km from Marangu Village and 3 km before the park gate, T0754-693461, www.kilimountresort.com.
Reasonable mid-range option with 42 rooms with balconies, kettles and DSTV set in picturesque gardens complete with duck pond, swimming pool and mountain views, good restaurant and bar with W-Fi and terrace in a large domed, thatched mock-up of a Chagga hut, coffee shop serving freshly brewed Arabica coffee, gym and they can organize climbs. The **Chagga Live Museum** is here (see page 130).

$$ Babylon Lodge
500 m from the post office on Jarakea Rd, T027-275 6355, www.babylonlodge.com.
Cheerful, clean and comfortable, sited in well-kept gardens, built into the hillside, all 25 slightly small rooms have DSTV and private facilities, and there's Wi-Fi in the lobby, a bar and restaurant and a swimming pool with sun deck. Reasonable value from US$70 for a double.

$$ Nakara Hotel
3 km from Marangu village and 2 km before the park gate, T0784-605 728, www.nakarahotels.com.
Old German building with 17 old-fashioned but adequate rooms, Wi-Fi, restaurant, cheery bar and fine gardens featuring banana trees and coffee bushes, but it lacks other facilities, such as a swimming pool. Climbs can be organized. Doubles from US$60 and you can also negotiate to camp.

Lake Chala
Camping

$$-$ Lake Chala Safari Camp
52 km east of Moshi off the A23 towards the Holili-Taveta border with Kenya, T0753-641087, www.lakechalasafaricamp.com.
Picturesque and remote spot with spacious tented rooms with wooden floors and verandas, good bathrooms and set well apart from each other. Plus there are 6 secluded

camping sites under acacia trees, could be grassy if it has rained, with a stone ablution block with flush loos and hot showers provided by a wood-burning stove, kitchen area with picnic tables, fireplace and grills (US$10 per person, and you can hire a tent and bedding for US$20 per person). The outstandingly positioned thatched **Caldera Restaurant** clings to the edge of the crater-lake cliff and overlooks the entire lake and Kilimanjaro on a clear day. The menu offers snacks and main meals such as chicken and fish and there's a fully stocked bar.

Restaurants

Moshi
The best restaurants are in the hotels. For Indian food and pizzas (an odd combination that seems to be very popular in Moshi), try the **Kilimanjaro Crane** and catch the sunset from the rooftop bar. Budget travellers should head for the restaurant at the **Kindoroko Hotel**, and again there are Kili views from the rooftop. There are several places around town where you can try the locally grown Arabica coffee.

$$ El Rancho
Off Lema Rd, Shantytown, T027-275 5115. Tue-Sun 1230-2300.
Despite its odd vaguely Mexican name, this serves northern Indian food, good choice for vegetarians, very authentic and a full range of curries, each dish is prepared from scratch so it can take a while, so be prepared to wait with appetizers and drinks. Has a full bar known for its large selection of whisky, covered veranda and tables on the lawn, and a walled car park.

$$ La Fuente Gardens
1 Kilimanjaro Rd, T0686-807 711. Tue-Sat 0900-2100.
Now this is a Mexican restaurant and quite a surprise in Moshi set in a circa-1960s house in pleasant gardens with a children's playground. Authentic dishes, such as enchiladas and nachos, are fresh

and tasty with beef, pork, chicken and vegetarian varieties. Portions are large too, and there's an additional breakfast menu until 1100. To get here follow Kilimanjaro Rd from the YMCA roundabout on the Moshi–Arusha road (A23) right to the end near the golf course.

$$-$ Indoitaliano
New St, T027-275 2195. Open 1200-2230.
A wide selection of Indian and Italian food, with main dishes, such as pizza or mutton curry with naan bread, for around US$10. The outside veranda is popular and gets very busy from around 1900, when you may have to wait for a table. A good choice of imported wine is on offer and plenty of cold beer too.

$$-$ Kaliwa
Arusha Rd, on the corner of Uhuru Park, T0762-620 707. Open 1100-2300.
A pleasant and relaxed semi-open restaurant under thatch and run by the same German owners as Kaliwa Lodge in Machame (see Where to stay above), this offers a good try at Thai food (green curry, pad thai and the like) although it's not very spicy. Also freshly squeezed juices, different coffees, German-style cakes, a bar with cocktails and Wi-Fi. It's 400 m northwest of Market St.

$$-$ Mountain Inn
6 km from Moshi on the road to Marangu, see Where to stay, above. Open 0700-2300.
Probably the best of the restaurants in the out-of-town hotels, there's a formal dining room with veranda but the better option is the pool bar and restaurant; non-guests can swim. The long menu includes continental, Chinese and Indian dishes and snacks, such as sandwiches and salads, bar with DSTV, and a *nyama choma* grill at the weekends.

$ Deli Chez
Kilima St, T027-275 1144. Wed-Mon 1000-2200.
Popular white-tiled restaurant with a/c and decorated with mirrors and plants. The comprehensive (and very long) menu offers

everything from local dishes, burgers and sandwiches to Indian and Chinese food, plus coffee, milkshakes and ice cream desserts. No alcohol, though. Try and get a seat on the upstairs balcony for views of Kili on a clear day, and quite conversely, the *dala-dala* and bus stands opposite.

Cafés

Aroma Coffee House
Boma Rd, T027-275 134. Open 0800-1800.
Pleasant café selling a good range of coffee from the region, including creamy cappuccinos and lattes and iced coffee, plus a good choice of teas, snacks and ice cream. There are a couple of wooden tables outside on the street.

Chrisburger
Kibo Rd, close to the clock tower, T027-275 0419. Mon-Sat 0830-1530.
Local spot popular with guides and porters returning from Kili trips for something hot to eat, and has a small veranda at the front. Sells snacks such as samosas, fried sausages, whole chicken and fish and chips, and of course burgers (the Chrisburger itself has an additional fried egg and cheese), plus good fruit juice, cold sodas and beers. However, the kitchen closes mid-afternoon.

The Coffee Shop
Kilima St, T027-275 2707. Mon-Fri 0800-1900, Sat 0800-1630.
Lovely food using fresh farm produce such as home-made jam, yoghurt, cheese and tea. Healthy breakfasts, and light meals include omelettes, soup and quiche, and the cakes are delicious. Garden to sit in at the back and Wi-Fi. Outlet of St Margaret's Anglican Church.

Fifi's
Rindi Lane, T0789-666 878, www. fifistanzania.com. Open 0800-2200.
The 2nd branch of this popular Arusha coffee shop, the menu's the same and again it's always buzzing thanks to the excellent coffees and free Wi-Fi. A huge choice of

breakfasts – try the French toast stuffed with caramelized bananas – plus pastries, muffins and sandwiches, and burgers, steaks, stuffed chicken breast and nachos for lunch and dinner. There are cheaper places to get a coffee, but the lattes with spices such as cinnamon, cardamom and cloves are quite delicious.

Tanzania Coffee Lounge
Chagga St, opposite the fruit and vegetable market, T027-275 1006. Mon-Sat 0800-2000, Sun 0800-1800.
A Western-style café serving good coffees, milkshakes, juices, beers, muffins, bagels, waffles and cakes. Also has internet terminals and Wi-Fi. In a walled compound but a few outside tables under umbrellas.

Union Café
Corner of Arusha and Selous rds, T0767-834500. Open 0700-2200.
Set in an old 1939 corner shop, this is run by the Kilimanjaro Native Co-Operative Union (KNCU), Africa's oldest co-operative that represents more than 60,000 small-holder coffee farmers around the mountain (see also box, page 129). Profits from the café go back into the farming communities. Naturally great coffee (cappuccinos, lattes, Americanos etc) is roasted on the premises (the aroma is lovely) and there's a long menu of anything from Mexican and pizza, to salads and cakes. A good place to meet other travellers, free Wi-Fi and tables outside on the veranda. You can also buy coffee beans.

Shopping

Moshi
Central Market, *Market St. Daily 0800-1800.* Hemmed in by Market St and Chagga St, Moshi's main market is a lively if somewhat dilapidated place, which sells just about everything. It's a good place to have a wander and look for souvenirs although you will be pestered by people trying to take you to their stall or trying to earn a commission by taking you to somebody else's.

Tip...
Local fabrics such as *kangas* and *kitenge* are a popular purchase and these can be made into clothes by the market's tailors within 24 hours.

Memorial Market, *Off the Moshi–Arusha road (A23) 5 km west of town, behind the Highway Supermarket. Daily 0800-1700.* This sprawling market on what used to be a football field sells second-hand clothes (*mitumba* in Kiswahili, see box, opposite), so come here in the event you need more warm clothes for the Kili climb, or just to get some excellent bargains of clothes made in the US, Canada and Europe. Many well-known labels can be found and it's considered one of the largest of its kind in Tanzania. Tue, Fri and Sat are the busiest as this is when the 'bales' arrive from the port in Dar es Salaam – look for the auction section of the market where vendors bid for the bales. It's a maze of crudely built stalls, and at first is seemingly random and chaotic, but there is method behind the madness, and stalls selling similar items cluster together in 'departments' for men, women and children – shirts, jeans, jackets, hats, dresses, shoes, etc. Some are organized with washed clothes on hangers; others are simply a pile of unsorted clothes on a tarpaulin on the ground. It's a lot of fun, but as with all markets don't take anything valuable with you and watch out for pickpocketing.
Nakumatt, *Station Rd, T0712-298 198, www.nakumatt.net. Mon-Sat 0830-2200, Sun 1000-2100.* Moshi's largest supermarket, this branch of Kenyan supermarket chain Nakumatt is so well stocked; people from over the border in Taveta come here for supplies.
Shah Industries, *Karakana St in the industrial area to the west of town. T0754-851 393. Mon-Sat 0800-1700.* Established in 1971, this family company has a policy of giving employment to disadvantaged people, especially the

ON THE ROAD

Mitumba

On any visit to East Africa will you will fail not to notice the amount of second-hand clothes for sale in open markets and from street side stalls. In Kiswahili, it's called *mitumba*, a word meaning 'bale or bundle', as the clothes arrive and are sold to retailers in bales, and it's believed the name became part of the language in the 1980s when western countries began sending second-hand clothes to Africa as part of charitable initiatives Today the tightly packed bales are brought to East Africa by a number of importers who mostly get their stock from charity shops or buy end of line stock from the clothing manufacturers. It's big business and a proper industry and not only provides affordable clothing but employs an estimated three million people across the region as importers, transport providers, wholesalers and market traders. A common criticism is that some Americans and Europeans think they are making charitable donations to the poor. Not so – clothes are donated to be sold in charity shops to raise an income for the charity, and it's no different from selling the clothes to the *mitumba* industry as the income is still raised. It's trade-aid if you like. Another criticism is that it dama0ges the local textile industries. True to a certain extent but in East Africa cotton is a marginal crop, and while clothing manufacturers produce school and work uniforms, they cannot keep up with meeting the needs of burgeoning populations. It is now so popular the East African governments charge VAT and a hefty import duty on the bales. For anyone who is curious about how your donations of clothes reach Africa, then visit a *mitumba* market, and you may pick up some bargains yourself. Rather predictably, because women buy many more new clothes and wear them for a less length time than men, they also discard more clothes as well, and women's *mitumba* is often in very good condition.

disabled, and produces high-quality crafts, such as wood carvings, leatherwork, batiks and furniture. Visitors are welcome to wander around the factory and meet and watch the people at work, and prices for the likes of leather bags, wallets and belts are very good.

What to do

Tour operators

It is cheaper to book tours for Kilimanjaro from Moshi than it is from either Arusha or Marangu. Like booking an organized safari in Arusha for the game parks (see box, page 58), give yourself a day or 2 in Moshi to talk to a couple of the tour operators that arrange Kilimanjaro climbs. Find one that you like and does not apply to much pressure.

Ignore the touts on the street. You may find, if it is quiet, that the tour companies will get together and put clients on the same tour to make up numbers. All tour operators below offer Kili climbs on most of the routes and most additionally offer climbs of Mount Meru, as well as multi-day safaris to the Northern Circuit parks, such as the Serengeti, Ngorogoro, Manyara, etc, which can be organized before or to follow on from your climb. This is a far from comprehensive list. A good place to start looking for a registered tour operator is on the **Tanzania Association of Tour Operators**' website (www.tatotz.org). Most of the hotels also organize climbs, and packages usually include a night's accommodation before and after the climb. The **Keys** (see page 133), **Marangu Hotel** (see page 135), **Mountain Inn** (see page 132)

Kilimanjaro Marathon

The Kilimanjaro Marathon is held in Moshi at the end of February/beginning March and runs on a 42.2-km route around the town and in the foothills of the mountain. The route is at an altitude of 800 to 1100 m and passes along a stretch of the Moshi–Dar road before crossing a landscape of banana plantations and smallholder farms, with Africa's highest mountain as a backdrop. It's open to professionals, many of whom are famed Tanzanian, Kenyan and Ethiopian long-distance runners, as well as amateurs. Established in 2002, it now attracts some 6500 runners for the full- and half-marathon and the 5-km fun run. Visit www.kilimanjaromarathon.com.

An additional event is the Kili(man)jaro Adventure Challenge, which is a six-day climb to the top of Kili (this part is not raced), a two-day/90-km mountain bike race around the mountain, followed by the marathon. Visit www.kilimanjaro-man.com.

and **Springlands Hotel** (see page 133) have excellent long-established reputations. For an idea of costs for an organized climb, see page 73. Additionally the tour operators and hotels offer day tours (US$40-60) around Moshi; mostly to the foothills for walks and visits to Chagga villages and coffee farms.

Akaro Tours & Travel, *ground floor of NSSF House on Old Moshi Rd*, T027-275 2986, www.akarotours.com.

Kilimanjaro Travel Services, *Rindi Lane*, T027-275 2124, www.kilimanjarotravels-tz.com.

Kindoroko Tours, *at Kindoroka Hotel*, *see page 134*, T027-254 5712, www.kindorokotour.com.

Mauly Tours & Safaris, *Boma Rd, opposite Exim Bank*, T027-275 0730, www.maulytours.com.

MJ Safaris, *CCM Building, Taifa Rd*, T027-754 478117, www.mjsafaris.com.

Moshi Expedition & Mountaineering (MEM), *Station Rd, opposite Nakumatt*, T027-275 4234, www.memafrica.com.

Shah Tours, *Sekoutoure Rd, Shantytown* (with base at the Mountain Inn Hotel, see page 132), T027-275 2370, www.shah-tours.com, www.kilimanjaro-shah.com.

Snow Cap Tanzania Tours, *CCM Building, Taifa Rd*, T027-275 4826, www.snowcap.co.tz.

Summit Expeditions & Nomadic Experience, *based in Marangu*, T027-275 3233, www.nomadicexperience.com.

Trans-Kibo Travels, *YMCA Building*, T027-275 2207, www.transkibo.com.

Zara Tours, *at Springlands Hotel, see page 133*, T0754-451000, www.zaratours.com, www.kilimanjaro.co.tz.

Transport

Air

Kilimanjaro International Airport is 55 km west of Moshi, off the A23/Arusha road, T027-255 4252, www.kilimanjaroairport.co.tz. It has a full range of facilities including restaurants, cafés and shops, plus ATMs and bureaux de change, and is well served by domestic flights and some international airlines. For details of these, see page 157. A taxi from the airport costs an official flat rate of US$50 to **Moshi** (45 mins); try and share one with other airline passengers into town to bring the price down. A taxi to the airport from Moshi may well cost less, depending on your negotiation skills. Alternatively you can pre-arrange transfers with one of the hotels or tour operators which vary in price depending on how many in the group from US$20-40 per person. The Nairobi–Arusha–Moshi shuttle services also

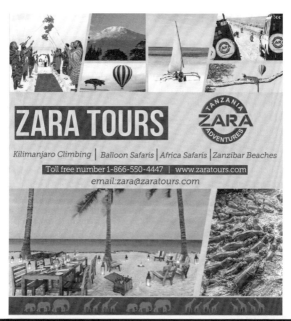

ON THE ROAD
Short hikes on the slopes of Kilimanjaro

The Marangu Route on Kilimanjaro is the only route up the mountain where short hikes are permitted. Not to be confused with walks in the foothills of the mountain (see pages 127-130), the climbing operators can arrange day hike higher up within the Kilimanjaro National Park's boundaries. Geared to people who do not want to make the full multi-day ascent to the summit, this goes from Marangu Gate (1800 m) up to Mandara Hut (2743 m) – an elevation of 915 m. The path goes through the thick and lush rainforest zone, full of birds and various species of monkeys, and you may well meet climbers descending from the top. A picnic lunch is taken at Mandara Hut and there's time to take a short walk to the Maudi Crater, from where there are views east to Taveta in Kenya. Park fees apply for the day and a certified Kilimanjaro guide is required; expect to pay around US$160 all in.

stop in at the airport on request (see box page 127).

Bus and *dala-dala*
Moshi is 80 km east of Arusha on the A23, and 580 km northwest of Dar es Salaam. The main bus and *dala-dala* stands are in the middle of town hemmed by Market and Mawenzi rds.

Local buses and *dala-dala* to nearby destinations such as **Marangu** and **Arusha** cost little more than US$3-4. Those who organize a Kili climb in Moshi will be transferred to the park gates by their tour operator.

Long-distance buses are not permitted to travel at night, so except for those going to nearby destinations, departures are early in the morning. Buses to **Dar es Salaam** depart at least every 15 mins between 0600 and 1100 (8½ hrs; US$15), and may well

Tip...
Pickpocketing is rife around the bus and *dala-dala* stands – protect your belongings. On arrival, it's best just to jump straight into a taxi as soon as you get off the bus. The hustlers, who try to get people on to their buses, can be particularly annoying too.

have come from Arusha first. They offer a complementary bottle of soda or water, and they stop for 30 mins-1 hr for lunch at a petrol station (usually in Mombo or Korogwe) where there's a canteen-like restaurant, takeaway, shop etc. If you are getting off the bus take everything with you – although main luggage is locked securely beneath the bus, it's not unheard of for things to go missing from overhead shelves inside.

There are numerous bus companies at Moshi, and they have kiosks around the bus stand. For the Arusha–Moshi–Dar route, **Dar Express** (Old Moshi Rd, T0744-286 847) and **Kilimanjaro Express** (also known as KLM Express; Rengua Rd, T0715-213231) are recommended for their relatively new a/c buses. Usefully they both have offices near the clocktower too. To get from Moshi to Dar and then get the last afternoon ferry across to **Zanzibar** in 1 day, you need to leave on one of the 1st buses – it's a good idea to book the day before to ensure a seat and confirm departure time.

To Kenya Mombasa is 305 km from Moshi via the Holili-Taveta border, 40 km east of Moshi on the A23. From Taveta, the road goes on to Voi in Kenya where it joins the main Nairobi-Mombasa road (A109). It is possible to get a bus from Moshi to Mombasa (approximately US$13-15; 7-8 hrs);

however there are few direct services and you may well have to change in Voi. This is easy enough and Nairobi-Mombasa buses come into Voi all day.

Nairobi is 349 km from Moshi. There are several shuttle services to **Nairobi** via Arusha and the Namanga border (see Practicalities), which leave Moshi at around 0630 and 1100 daily and take 5-6 hrs, US$40, and can be booked through hotels or tour operators. These will pick-up/drop-off at hotels and also pull into **Kilimanjaro International Airport** on request. The cheaper alternative would be to *dala-dala* 'hop' from Moshi to Arusha to Namanga to Nairobi, which could take a full day.

Kilimanjaro
National Park

In *The Snows of Kilimanjaro*, Ernest Hemingway described the mountain: "as wide as all the world, great, high, and unbelievably white in the sun, was the square top of Kilimanjaro." It is one of the most impressive sights in Africa, visible from as far away as Tsavo National Park in Kenya. Just 80 km east of the eastern branch of the Rift Valley, it is Africa's highest mountain, with snow-capped peaks rising from a relatively flat plain, the largest free-standing mountain worldwide, measuring 80 km by 40 km, and one of Earth's highest dormant volcanoes. At lower altitudes, the mountain is covered in lush rainforest, which gives way to scrub – there is no bamboo zone on Kilimanjaro – followed by alpine moorland until you get to the icefields. Try to see it in the early morning before the clouds mask it, although it often makes an appearance just before dusk too.

Getting to the top
it is all in the acclimatization

About 35,000 climbers attempt to get to the top of Kilimanjaro each year. The altitude at Marangu Gate is 1829 m and at Kibo/Uhuru Peak 5895 m – that's a long way up. Officially anyone aged over 10 may attempt the climb, while the oldest person to date was 85. However, despite it being a massive personal challenge and a once-in-a-lifetime experience, it is not easy. The number of people who attempt the climb but do not make it to the top can be as much as 40%. And there is no obvious distinction between those that do succeed and those that don't – a super fit athlete in their 20s is just as likely to fail as an elderly person in their 80s is to reach the summit. Everyone's body has its own unique way with dealing with altitude, and altitude sickness is not selective. The important things to remember are to come prepared and to take it slowly – if you have the chance, spend an extra day halfway up to give you the chance to acclimatize.

ON THE ROAD

Seven Summits

As the highest in Africa, Mount Kilimanjaro is one of the 'Seven Summits' – the highest mountains on each of the seven continents. Today it's possible to summit all of them, and this mountaineering challenge was first achieved in 1985.

Mount Everest – Asia – first ascent 1953 – 8848 m
Aconcagua – South America – first ascent 1897 – 6961 m
Mount McKinley – North America – first ascent 1913 – 6194 m
Mount Kilimanjaro – Africa – first ascent 1889 – 5895 m
Mount Elbrus – Europe – first ascent 1874 – 5642 m
Mount Vinson – Antarctica – first ascent 1966 – 4892 m
Mount Kosciuszko – Australia – first ascent 1840 – 2228 m

There are several routes up the mountain: Machame, Umbwe and Marangu approach from the south; Shira, Lemosho and the Northern Circuit from the northwest; and Rongai from the northeast. The Mweka Route is used for descent only. The three most popular are described in full here. The Marangu Route is often nicknamed the 'Coca-Cola' route, and the reason is the false assumption that it is easier (it's not – and in fact has the lowest success rate of reaching the summit). The name actually comes from when historically Coca-Cola used to be bought along the way in tea huts. The Machame Route is often dubbed the 'Whiskey' route, in response to the (mis-titled) 'Coca-Cola' route because it is steeper than Marangu and therefore more demanding. In reality it has a better success rate than Marangu and is also today the most heavily trafficked route on Kilimanjaro. Selecting a route is one of the most important decisions you have to make, but at the same time there is no single 'best' one. It depends on several factors including the time and money you have, previous experience and fitness, the time of the year, and personal preference.

Marangu Route

least scenic, gentlest gradient

This is probably the least scenic of the routes but it is the gentlest climb and has a crop of hotels at the beginning in Marangu and hutted accommodation on the way up. It is therefore popular, and is often the recommended route for older persons or younger people who are not in peak physical condition, but by no means is it any easier in terms of success rate for reaching the summit. The huts sleep up to about 60 and mattresses and pillows are supplied, but sleeping bags are still required. There are communal dining halls and basic washrooms, ranging from flushing toilets and running water at the lower huts to long drop toilets and buckets of water at Kibo Hut.

Day 1

The national park gate (1830 m) is about 5 km north of the village of **Marangu**, along a road where most of the hotels are located. From here to the first night's stop at **Mandara Hut** (2700 m) is a walk of three to four hours. It is through *shambas* – small farms growing coffee – as well as some lush rainforest, and is an enjoyable walk, although it can be quite muddy.

Essential Kilimanjaro National Park

Finding your feet

Regular *dala-dalas* travel from the bus stand in Moshi the 30 km to the village of Machame (for the Machame Route) and the 27 km to Marangu (for the Marangu Route). They each take about 45 minutes and cost around US$3. Those who organize a Kili climb in Moshi will be transferred to these, and the park gates on the other routes, by their tour operator. The hotels in Machame and Marangu will also be able to arrange an airport pickup from **Kilimanjaro International Airport**.

When to go

Kilimanjaro can be climbed throughout the year, but the best times are from July to October and from December to February, which coincide with the driest months in Tanzania when there is also less cloud cover. However these are the times when the mountain is busiest. It is worth avoiding the two rainy seasons from late March to mid-May and November. The shoulder seasons of December, March and June are quieter, but there's more of a gamble with the weather and cloud cover is greater.

Park information

Anyone planning to climb Mount Kilimanjaro is advised to buy *Kilimanjaro: The Trekking Guide to Africa's Highest Mountain*, by Henry Steadman (Trailblazer Guides), which is full of practical information and covers preparing and equipping for the climb; much of the book's information is also available on Henry's website, www. climbmountkilimanjaro.com. There are plenty of maps on the market, many of which now list GPS coordinates, and other locally produced maps and coffee-table books are available in both Moshi and Arusha. The tour operators that offer climbs have comprehensive information on their websites, as does the **Tanzania National Parks Authority** (**TANAPA**), www.tanzaniaparks.com.

Acclimatization and altitude sickness

It is normal to feel a little breathless and unenergetic at high altitude, but above 3000 m changes in air density and oxygen levels begin to impact and can lead to altitude sickness (also known as Acute Mountain Sickness or AMS). Susceptibility to these changes is very difficult to predict and there is little or no correlation with AMS and factors such as gender, age, fitness, experience etc. In short, some people get it and some people don't. What is known however is that going too high too fast is the key cause, and other contributing factors are dehydration and over exertion at altitude. Acclimatization is therefore essential; the process by which the body becomes accustomed to the lower availability of oxygen before progressing higher. All of the routes up Kilimanjaro factor in an extra acclimatization day half way up to do just that, and it is highly recommended if time and money allow. It will greatly increase your chances of reaching the summit. If you are unlucky, common AMS symptoms include bad headache, dizziness, loss of appetite, nausea, vomiting and severe fatigue. More extreme conditions include acute pulmonary oedema and/or cerebral oedema – intense headache, hallucinations, confusion, disorientation and staggering gait. Once AMS symptoms occur, acclimatization is not possible, and it is critical to descend immediately to below the point where the symptoms began – after a rest, this is usually enough for them to subside. If the symptoms are mild, the treatment is rest, painkillers (preferably not aspirin-based) for the headaches and anti-sickness pills for vomiting. If conditions are very severe, sufferers will be escorted down the mountain to receive medical attention. The drug Acetazolamide or Diamox have been proved to be effective at mitigating AMS and should be taken before the ascent. But the most effective prevention is time; take it slowly and the body will adapt to high altitude.

Organized tours

It is compulsory to go on an organized trek with a tour operator on all routes, who will supply not only guides but porters and relevant equipment (for Moshi tour operators, see page 139). The Marangu Route is the only one that uses hutted dorm accommodation. On the other routes, even though the campsites are sometimes called huts, this actually refers to the green shacks used by the guides and porters. Trekkers are accommodated in tents carried and set up by the porters.

Equipment

Being well equipped will increase your chances of reaching the summit. In particular, be sure you have a warm sleeping bag, insulated sleeping mat, warm rainproof jacket, thermal underwear, gloves, wool hat, sunglasses or snow goggles, sun cream, large water bottle and first-aid kit. As regards clothing, it is important to wear layers as they provide better insulation than bulkier items, and sturdy, waterproof hiking boots should be well worn-in. Other essential items include a small daypack for things you'll need during the day – porters carry your main pack but tend to go on ahead by some distance – a head torch and spare batteries (essential for the final midnight ascent), toilet roll, and you may want to consider a light weight trekking pole. Energy snacks are also a good idea.

Costs

Climbing Mount Kilimanjaro is an expensive business, although everyone who makes it to the summit agrees that it is well worth it. The total cost charged by a tour operator includes park, camping and hut fees for Mount Kilimanjaro National Park (for both the trekker and the associated costs for guides and porters), salaries, 20% VAT, 10% commission if booking through a third party travel agent, transport to the start of the trail, food and the costs of equipment. The absolute cheapest is around US$1430 for the five-day Marangu Route, but it is highly recommended to add on an acclimatization day; US$335 on this route. The six-day (camping) Machame, Rongai, Umbwe, Shira and Lemosho routes start from US$1675, with the extra acclimatization day, US$210. The nine-day Northern Circuit Route starts from US$2500. With all of them, discounts may apply if you book a group of more than six people together. Tips excluded.

ON THE ROAD

Tipping on Kilimanjaro

When climbing to the top of Kilimanjaro, your trekking team could be made up of about 12 people: the head guide; the assistant guides (those members of the team that accompany you along with the head guide on the final leg to Uhuru Peak are considered as assistant guides); the cook; and porters that carry your gear (some porters have extra jobs such as toilet cleaner, camp crew and waiter). Tipping is more or less mandatory, as a way of supplementing the low incomes of people who essentially have a remarkably physically demanding job. Porters in particular are very poorly paid and cannot always afford the right equipment/clothes needed on the mountain. Remarkably, while you slog on up carrying just a day pack and a camera and wearing a warm waterproof jacket, it is these people that pass you by carrying luggage, gas bottles, chairs, full jerry cans of water and anything else needed for a comfortable hike. And they often go up and down Kili time after time in inadequate shoes and clothing fit only for the base of the mountain where they live.

A good tour operator will have a fair tipping procedure in place or at least will be able to give advice. But generally, you should budget between 10-15% of your total cost of your climb for tips – depending on how much you paid, this could be US$175-280 for a six- to seven-day trek. If you are climbing in a small group, you should contribute more per person to the kitty. However if you feel your climb was particularly difficult or a certain person went out of his way to help you, or, on the flipside the staff were surly or weren't as helpful as they should have been, then this should reflect in the amount you tip.

Always try to come to an agreement with other members of the group about what each of you are paying and put the tip into a common kitty. Ordinarily this is presented to the head guide at the gate when leaving the Kilimanjaro National Park, who divides it among the team. It is not necessary to tip all the staff individually; indeed doing so will remove the guide's prerogative to reward workers that only he knows have worked especially hard, often behind the scenes away from the attention of climbers. Tips can be paid in US$ or TSh cash – but remember that the forex bureaux in Moshi charge for exchanging so the team will benefit more by receiving TSh.

For more information about tipping on Kilimanjaro (and why you should do it), and for recommendations of responsible tour operators, visit the website for the **Kilimanjaro Porters Assistance Project**, www.kiliporters.org, who are committed to improving the working conditions of porters on Kili, including programmes to collect and lend them suitable equipment. Something else to consider is that you won't need much 'stuff' on the mountain – you'll be wearing most of it anyway – and porters are limited to 20 kg of trekkers' packs and 5 kg of their own things. Kili is a hard slog for anyone – imagine what it's like climbing it over and over again with 25 kg on your back? Keep it light and leave the bulk of your luggage at a hotel. Finally, if you're never going to climb a big mountain again, think about making gifts of your specialist clothing and gear to your trekking team; it is after all these people who were responsible for your welfare on the mountain and (hopefully) got you to the top safely.

On the walk you can admire the moss and lichens and the vines and flowers, including orchids. You may also spot blue monkeys (they have become very used to people), and with a bit of luck black-and-white colobus monkeys. If you have the energy, the 15-minute walk to **Maundi Crater** will be rewarded with good views up to Mawenzi Peak.

Day 2
The second day will start off as a steep walk through the last of the rainforest and out into tussock grassland, giant heather and then on to the moorlands, crossing several ravines on the way. There are occasional clearings through which you will get wonderful views of Mawenzi and Moshi far below. You will probably see some of the exceptional vegetation that is found on Kilimanjaro, including the giant lobelia, Kilimanjaro's 'everlasting flowers', and other uncommon alpine plants. The walk to **Horombo Hut** (3720 m) is about 14 km,

Kilimanjaro National Park

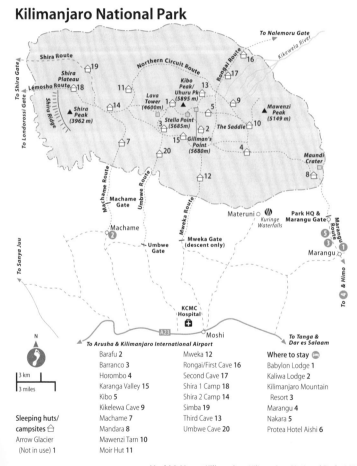

Sleeping huts/
campsites ⌂
Arrow Glacier
(Not in use) 1

Barafu **2**	Mweka **12**
Barranco **3**	Rongai/First Cave **16**
Horombo **4**	Second Cave **17**
Karanga Valley **15**	Shira 1 Camp **18**
Kibo **5**	Shira 2 Camp **14**
Kikelewa Cave **9**	Simba **19**
Machame **7**	Third Cave **13**
Mandara **8**	Umbwe Cave **20**
Mawenzi Tarn **10**	
Moir Hut **11**	

Where to stay 🛏
Babylon Lodge **1**
Kaliwa Lodge **2**
Kilimanjaro Mountain
  Resort **3**
Marangu **4**
Nakara **5**
Protea Hotel Aishi **6**

with an altitude gain of about 1000 m, and will take you five to seven hours. An extra day for acclimatization is spent here, and, if you are doing this, there are a number of short walks in the area but remember to move slowly, drink plenty of water and get lots of sleep.

Day 3/4
On the next day you will climb to the **Kibo Hut** (4703 m), 13 km from Horombo. The vegetation thins to grass and heather and eventually to bare scree. The most direct route is a climb of six to seven hours up the valley behind Horombo to **Last Water** (4200 m), which is indeed the last chance to collect water, and your porters will do so. From here it is up and on to the **Saddle**, a wide, fairly flat U-shaped barren desert between the two peaks of Mawenzi and Kibo. This landscape can be quite dramatic, open and windswept, with big clouds rolling across it, and you'll be looking at Kibo the whole time. But while the path across the Saddle isn't steep, the lack of oxygen by this point makes the hike an effort. **Kibo Hut** is also used by climbers on the Rongai Route, and from here the ascent path is the same.

Day 4/5
On ascent day, in order to be at the summit at sunrise, and before the cloud comes down, you will have to get up at about midnight. This final five-hour climb is steep, but due to the many switchbacks the path itself isn't that bad, but it can be slippery and you must take it slowly. You'll pass **Williams Point** (a big rock that marks

Tip...
On the evening before the ascent to the summit (departure will be around midnight), pack your day pack: rain gear, if you aren't wearing it already, gloves, hats etc, fresh batteries in your head torch and camera, and plenty of water.

the 5000 m line), and **Hans Meyer Cave** (5150 m). With any luck you will be on the crater rim at **Gillman's Point** (5680 m) as sun rises and it is a wonderful sight. From here you have to decide whether you want to keep going another two or three hours to get to **Kibo/Uhuru Peak** (5895 m). The walk around the crater rim is only an extra 200 m but at this altitude it is a strenuous 200 m. The descent on the Marangu Route is the same back down and from the summit you will return to **Horombo Hut** the same day (about six hours), and the next day (**Day 5/6**) return to Marangu, where you will be presented with a certificate. Those on the Rongai Route will also follow the Marangu Route back down.

Machame Route
pretty route, steeper gradient

The Machame Route is nowadays as popular, if not more, as Marangu and is considered by many to be the most attractive of the routes up Kilimanjaro and goes through a variety of habitats. The Shira and Lemosho routes join it from the west too. It is however a steeper trek, with more ups and downs, and is better suited to the more physically fit people with some hiking experience. However, it offers much better acclimatization than Marangu and thus a better success rate. The disadvantage is that at times 'traffic' is heavy. As with the other routes except Machame, it's a camping route.

Day 1
From the village to the first huts takes about nine hours, and an early start is required. From the park gate a clear track climbs gently along a ridge that is between the Weru Weru and Makoa streams. It is about 7 km to the edge of the rainforest; named for a reason

BACKGROUND
Kilimanjaro National Park

Formation

Kilimanjaro was formed about one million years ago by a series of volcanic movements along the Great Rift Valley. Until this point, the area was a flat plain at about 600 to 900 m above sea level. About 750,000 years ago volcanic activity forced three points above 4800 m – Shira, Kibo/Uhuru and Mawenzi. Some 250,000 years later Shira became inactive and collapsed into itself forming the crater. Kibo and Mawenzi continued their volcanic activity, and it was their lava flow that forms the 11-km saddle between the two peaks. When Mawenzi died out, its northeast wall collapsed in a huge explosion creating a massive gorge. The last major eruptions occurred about 200 years ago; Kibo now lies dormant but not extinct. Although Kibo appears to be a snow-clad dome, it contains a caldera 2.5 km across and 180 m deep at the deepest point in the south. Within the depression is an inner ash cone that rises to within 60 m of the summit height and is evidence of former volcanic activity. On the southern slopes the glaciers reach down to about 4200 m, while on the north slopes they only descend a little below the summit.

Vegetation and wildlife

Kilimanjaro has well-defined altitudinal vegetation zones. From the base to the summit these are: plateau, semi-arid scrub; cultivated, well-watered southern slopes; dense cloud forest; open moorland; alpine desert; moss and lichen. The lower slopes are home to elephant, buffalo, leopard, monkey and eland. Birdlife includes the enormous lammergeyer, the scarlet-tufted malachite sunbird, as well as various species of starlings, sunbirds, the silvery-cheeked hornbill and the rufous-breasted sparrowhawk.

History

When, in 1848, the first reports by the German missionary Johannes Rebmann of a snow-capped mountain on the equator arrived in Europe, the idea was ridiculed by the Royal Geographical Society of Britain. In 1889 the report was confirmed by the German geographer Hans Meyer and the Austrian alpine mountaineer Ludwig Purtscheller, who climbed Kibo and managed to reach the snows on Kilimanjaro's summit. At the centenary of this climb in 1989, their Tanzanian guide was still alive and 115 years old. Mawenzi was first climbed by the German Fritz Klute in 1912.

The mountain was originally in a part of British East Africa (now Kenya). However, the mountain was 'given' by Queen Victoria as a gift to her cousin, and so the border was moved and the mountain included within German Tanganyika. This is why if you look at a map of the border between Tanzania and Kenya, Tanzania juts into Kenya to include Kilimanjaro on the otherwise dead straight border drawn up by the colonialists. The national park was established in 1973 and covers an area of 756 sq km.

as this side of Kilimanjaro gets the most rain and even if it's dry in the morning, chances are there will be a shower in the afternoon (rain gear is essential from Day 1). But the forest is quite beautiful and moss and lichen dangle from the branches of the tall trees. It is then four to five hours up to the **Machame Huts** (3000 m), where you camp. The forest has opened up, and if you're lucky you may get a first glimpse of Kibo Peak above.

ON THE ROAD
The meaning of Kilimanjaro

Since the earliest explorers visited East Africa, people have been intrigued by the name Kilimanjaro and its meaning. The Chagga people do not have a name for the whole mountain, just the two peaks: *Kibo* (or *kipoo*) means 'spotted' and refers to the rock that can be seen standing out against the snow on this peak; *Mawenzi* (or *Kimawenze*) means 'having a broken top' and again describes its appearance.

Most theories as to the origin of the name Kilimanjaro for the whole mountain break the word down into two elements: *kilima* and *njaro*. In Swahili the word for mountain is *mlima*, while *kilima* means hill – so it is possible that an early European visitor incorrectly used kilima because of its similarity to the two Chagga words *Kibo* and *Kimawenzi*.

The explorer Krapf said that the Swahili of the coast knew it as *Kilimanjaro* 'mountain of greatness', but he does not explain why. He also suggests it could mean 'mountain of caravans' (*kilima* – mountain, *jaro* – caravans), but while *kilima* is a Swahili word, *jaro* is a Chagga word. Other observers have suggested that *njaro* once meant 'whiteness' and therefore this was the 'mountain of whiteness'. Alternatively, *njaro* could be the name of an evil spirit, or a demon. The first-known European to climb Mount Kilimanjaro mentions 'Njaro, the guardian spirit of the mountain', and there are many stories in Chagga folklore about spirits living here – though there is no evidence of a spirit called Njaro, either from the Chagga or from the coastal peoples.

Another explanation suggests that the mountain was known as 'mountain of water', because of the Maasai word *njore* for springs or water and because all the rivers in the area rose from here. However, this theory does not explain the use of the Swahili word for 'hill' rather than 'mountain', and also assumes that a Swahili word and a Maasai word have been put together.

The final explanation is from a Kichagga term *kilelema* meaning that 'which has become difficult or impossible' or 'which has defeated'. Njaro can be derived from the Kichagga words *njaare*, a bird, or else *jyaro*, a caravan. Thus the mountain became *kilemanjaare*, *kilemajyaro* or *kilelemanjaare*, meaning that which defeats or is impossible for the bird or the caravan. This theory has the advantage of being composed entirely of Chagga elements.

It seems possible either that this was the name given to the mountain by the Chagga themselves, or by people passing through the area, who heard the Chagga say *kilemanjaare* or *kilemajyaro*, meaning that the mountain was impossible to climb. Over time the name was standardized to Kilimanjaro.

Day 2

From the Machame Huts the route goes across the valley, over a stream, then up a steep ridge for three to four hours. The path then goes west and drops into the river gorge before climbing more gradually up the other side and on to the moorland of the **Shira Plateau** to join the Shira Route near the **Shira Hut** (3800 m). This takes about five hours. From the Shira Plateau you will get some magnificent views of Kibo/Uhuru Peak and the Western Breach. The area is home to a variety of game including buffalo, and the taller vegetation has all but disappeared and the scenery is starting to look barren. The campsite at the

Shira Hut is also used by people on the Shira Route. You cover little distance on this day but about 1800 m in altitude and most people will start to feel the effects.

Day 3
The Machame Huts mark where the montane forest gives way to the giant heathers of the moorland zone. Today is a long day of six to eight hours, and from the Shira Plateau, you continue to the east up a ridge, and then the direction changes to the southeast towards the **Lava Tower** (4600 m), which includes scrambling over scree, rocks and snow fields – tough at times. From here you go down again into the beautiful Barranco Valley to the **Barranco Hut** (3963 m). This is the overnight camp and although you end the day at the same elevation as when you started, this day is very important for acclimatization. This is without a doubt the most spectacular campsite of this route, with fantastic views of Kibo and the first of the southern glaciers.

Day 4
Whether trekkers reached the Barranco Hut via the Machame, Shira or Lemosho routes, from this point onwards all climbers follow the same route. First thing in the morning, you will tackle the **Barranco Wall**, which is over volcanic scree and exposed and you will need use your hands to steady yourself, but you can pretty much walk all the way to the top, which takes about an hour and a half. From here it's another couple of hours through several small, sheltered valleys until you reach **Karanga Valley** campsite. (On the day six of the climb, Karanga is a lunch stop, but on the seven-day climb, an extra night is spent here for acclimatization and to take the time to eat, rest and have an early night.) From Karanga you meet the junction with the Mweka Route (the descent route) and continue on up to the **Barafu Hut**, which has an other-worldly feel to it, perched on an exposed ridge in a bleak and barren landscape but offers views of the summit from many different angles.

Day 5/6
Ascent day, and departure from Barafu Hut will be between midnight and 0200. Again the final push takes about five hours and the path begins by going between the Rebmann and Ratzel glaciers, before going up over heavy scree to **Stella Point** (5685m) on the crater rim. The scree is lose and you keep sliding back down, and this is the most mentally and physically challenging portion of the trek, and again it is still important to go extremely slowly. But at Stella Point you may well be rewarded with a magificant sunrise. From here, you may encounter snow on the traverse of the crater rim to **Kibo/Uhuru Peak** (5895 m), but the advantage of the Machame route over Marangu is that it only takes 45 minutes as opposed to a couple of hours. The descent is straight down to the junction with the Mweka Route, and after four to six hours from the summit you reach the Mweka Hut campsite in the upper forest, stopping at Barafu for lunch.

Day 6/7
The next day the descent continues down to Mweka Gate (three to four hours) where you receive your certificate. At lower elevations, again it can be wet and muddy.

Tip...
Take all the time you need – one step at a time – and don't let anyone pressure you into moving faster than you feel comfortable with. It doesn't matter if you reach Uhuru Peak or even the crater rim in time for sunrise. It only matters that you reach it, and that you will be able to get back down safely. You cannot move too slowly on Kilimanjaro.

Climbing Kilimanjaro on the Rongai Route used to guarantee an isolated trek away from the masses, but in recent years has seen a surge in popularity. But still, it's much quieter than Machame or Marangu and has an excellent success rate. Additionally, as it is the only route that approaches from the north, the northern side of Kilimanjaro is drier and you are unlikely to have to slosh through mud and rain on the first two days. Also, and given that the descent is on the Marangu Route on the southern side, you get to see both sides of the mountain. It is however more expensive as there is the extra couple of hours to drive to the gate.

Day 1

Your first day on Kilimanjaro starts with a two- to three-hour transfer to the village and gate of Nalemoru (1950 m). This route used to start from Rongai on the Kenyan border (hence its name), but was moved to Nalemoru near Loitokitok. The first day on the Rongai Route leads initially through cypress plantations and patches of montane forest with plenty of birds and monkeys. You soon reach the Rongai (or First Cave) campsite (2830 m). Don't be disheartened if you see this camp teeming with climbers and staff, because from here the Rongai Route has several variations.

Day 2/3

Until lunchtime on Day 2 all groups follow the same path, through moorland covered in heather, on an increasingly steep trail to **Second Cave** campsite (3450 m). Depending on which way they are going and how many days the trek is, some will have lunch here and continue, while others will camp. The groups on five-day treks will head for the **Third Cave** campsite (3875 m), from where they will walk to **Kibo Hut** (4700 m) the next day to join the Marangu Route. Those on the six-day treks without the Mawenzi detour may spend a night here, the next night at Third Cave, and then continue on to Kibo Hut. Others will go on a route that swings southeast towards **Mawenzi** and allows for extra acclimatization. Going this way, the path crosses heathland with the occasional rocky section with great views towards Mawenzi and the eastern glaciers of Kibo. On a clear day you might see Amboseli National Park in Kenya. The Kikelewa Cave campsite (3600 m) is in a valley below the Saddle.

Day 4 onwards

Still continuing on the Mawenzi detour, the route becomes increasingly steeper and the last of the vegetation disappears too, but the hike doesn't take long and you may well have reached the **Mawenzi Tarn** campsite (4315 m) by lunchtime, from where there are several short walks to help acclimatisation. Mawenzi Tarn is one of the most spectacular campsites on the mountain right under Mawenzi Peak and next to a tiny lake. From here, you head towards Kibo Hut, first climbing over a small ridge, then on a comfortable path along the northern side of The Saddle. At Kibo Hut you re-join the other groups and the Marangu Route trekkers for the final ascent. All the Rongai variations descend down the Marangu Route.

Shira and Lemosho routes

Both the Shira and Lemosho routes start on the northwestern side of Kilimanjaro and cross the Shira Plateau before joining the Machame Route near Lava Tower. Usually seven days, they involve extra transport costs so are therefore more expensive. On the plus side they are quieter, with varied and quite beautiful scenery and have good summit success rates.

Again there are variations – in fact the Shira Route is nearly identical to the Lemosho Route. Shira was the original and Lemosho is the improved variation. **Lemosho** starts at Londorossi Gate and treks through the rainforest zone to Shira 1 Camp, while the **Shira Route** bypasses this walk by using a 4WD to transport climbers to Shira Gate. These climbers would then spend the first day on the mountain beginning their hike at 3600 m and spend their first night at the same elevation at Simba campsite. This high altitude may well not suite everyone (and is ill-advised if coming from sea level), and trekkers using Shira should be confident of their ability to acclimatize, but it does shorten the trek by a day. Both routes merge and then join the Machame Route for the final ascent, and descent is via the Mweka Route.

Northern Circuit Route

Northern Circuit Route is the newest, and many say, most exciting route on Kilimanjaro, which follows the Lemosho Route to start with, but instead of following the southern traverse, takes the mountain around the quiet, rarely visited northern slopes. This vantage point offers great views out across the plains that stretch out across the Kenyan border. After crossing the Shira Plateau, it heads north and circles clockwise from Moir Hut to Buffalo Camp to Third Cave, before summiting from the east the same as the Rongai Route. Usually a nine-day climb, the Northern Circuit is the longest in terms of distance and given that more time is spent above 4000 m, acclimatization is excellent, resulting in the highest summit success rates of all routes on Kilimanjaro. Descent is made via the Mweka route.

Umbwe Route

The six- or seven-day Umbwe Route is a short, steep and direct route, and is considered to be the most challenging way up because of its sharp rise in altitude in the first couple of days – from Umbwe Gate (1600 m), to Umbwe Cave campsite (2850 m), to Barranco Hut campsite (3963 m). Although traffic on this route is very low, so are the chances of success. Historically the route utilized the steep Western Breach and Arrow's Glacier path to the summit, but because of difficulty and safety risks, instead the Umbwe Route now joins the Machame Route at Barranco, again descending via the Mweka Route.

Practicalities

Getting there

Air

Tanzania has three international airports: **Kilimanjaro International Airport** (KIA), which is halfway between Arusha and Moshi, about 40 km from each (see box, page 44); Dar es Salaam's **Julius Nyerere International Airport** (JNIA), which is 13 km southwest of the city centre along Nyerere Road; and **Zanzibar International**

> **Tip...**
> When flying to Tanzania from the north, getting a window seat is definitely a good idea as, cloud permitting, you may be lucky enough to glimpse the gleaming top of Mount Kilimanjaro.

Airport (ZAN), 4 km southeast of Stone Town. Most travellers to the Northern Circuit and Kilimanjaro arrive at Kilimanjaro International Airport. Other options are to fly into Dar es Salaam and get a bus up to Moshi (8½ hours) or Arusha (10 hours), or you take a flight from Dar es Salaam to Kilimanjaro (one hour 10 minutes). If you are going to Zanzibar before or after your Northern Circuit safari or Kilimanjaro climb, the option is going to Dar es Salaam and connecting to the island by ferry or another short flight. Finally an alternative access point to the Northern Circuit (given that Arusha is only 273 km to the south) is to fly into Nairobi in Kenya (see box, page 158). Nairobi is served by many more airlines than both Kilimanjaro and Dar es Salaam, so competitively priced fares can be found. Further airport information can be found on the **Tanzania Airports Authority** website, www.taa.go.tz.

TRAVEL TIP
Packing for a trip to Tanzania

Before you leave home, send yourself an email to a web-based account with details of airline tickets, passport, driving licence, credit cards and travel insurance numbers. Be sure that someone at home also has access to this information.

A good rule of thumb when packing is to take half the clothes you think you'll need and double the money. Laundry services are generally cheap and speedy in Tanzania and you shouldn't need to bring too many clothes. A backpack or travelpack (a hybrid backpack/suitcase) rather than a rigid suitcase covers most eventualities and survives the rigours of a variety of modes of travel. A lock for your luggage is strongly advised – there are cases of pilfering by airport baggage handlers the world over. Light cotton clothing is best, with a fleece or woollen clothing for early mornings and evenings. A light rain jacket is required if you're travelling in the rainy seasons. Also pack something to change into at dusk – long sleeves and trousers (particularly light coloured) help ward off mosquitoes, which are at their most active in the evening. During the day you will need a hat, sunglasses and high-factor suncream, and binoculars and cameras are safari essentials. Footwear should be airy because of the heat: sandals or canvas trainers are ideal. Trekkers will need comfortable walking boots and ones that have been worn in if you are climbing Kilimanjaro. Those going on camping safaris will need a sleeping bag, towel and torch, and budget travellers may want to bring a sleeping sheet in case the sheets don't look too clean in a budget hotel.

TRAVEL TIP

Flying to Nairobi

Nairobi is the busiest air transport hub for East Africa, and international and domestic flights touch down at **Jomo Kenyatta International Airport**, T+254 (0)20-661 1000, www.kaa.go.ke, which is 15 km southeast of the city off the Mombasa Road. A disastrous fire in 2013 destroyed much of the original airport, and presently a fully functioning but temporary building is being used for arrivals and departures. A new terminal with a capacity of 20 million passengers, the single largest terminal in Africa, is currently under construction and completion is expected in 2016. For now, facilities include cafés and snack bars, banks, forex bureaux and ATMs, a left luggage facility, hotel booking, tour operator and car hire desks, and duty free and souvenir shops. There are taxis outside; Nairobi hotels can pre-organize transfers, and the shuttle buses that go via the Namanga land border to Arusha (six hours) and Moshi (7½ hours) will pick up and drop off at the airport (see page 44). You can also fly from Jomo Kenyatta to Kilimanjaro International Airport (one hour).

Nairobi's second airport is **Wilson Airport**, T+254 (0)20-603 260, www.kenya airports.com, which is 4 km south of the city off Langata Road. This is used for domestic scheduled and charter flights by the light aircraft airlines; most of which do circuits of the safari destinations in Kenya such as the Maasai Mara National Reserve. Also from Wilson, **Air Kenya** and **Safarilink** both have direct flights to Kilimanjaro International Airport (55 minutes).

From Europe

There are no direct flights to either **Kilimanjaro International Airport** or Dar es Salaam's **Julius Nyerere International Airport** from the UK. Flying time to either is a minimum of 11 hours and there will be at least one change of planes. Some of the international airlines serving Tanzania touch down at both Kilimanjaro and Dar on the same flight. The options to Kilimanjaro are combinations of **British Airways** or **Kenya Airways** from London to Nairobi and then **Precision Air** or **Kenya Airways** to Kilimanjaro; **KLM** via Amsterdam; **Lufthansa** via Frankfurt, **Turkish Airlines** via Istanbul; **Ethiopian Airlines** via Addis Ababa; or **Qatar Airways** via Doha. The options to Dar are **Kenya Airways** via Nairobi; **Turkish Airlines** via Istanbul; **Egypt Air** via Cairo; **Swissair** via Zurich and Nairobi; **KLM** via Amsterdam; **Emirates** via Dubai, **Ethiopian Airlines** via Addis Ababa; and **Etihad Airways** via Abu Dhabi.

Tip...
Jet lag is not an issue when flying from Europe to Tanzania as there is only a minimal time difference.

From North America

There are no direct flights from the USA or Canada to Tanzania and routes go via Europe or the Middle East, which means there may be two changes of plane. However there are a couple of exceptions: **KLM** fly from New York to Kilimanjaro with just one stop in Amsterdam, and **Ethiopian Airlines** fly from Toronto to Kilimanjaro with just one stop in Addis Ababa. To get to Dar es Salaam, another alternative from going via Europe or the Middle East is with **Delta Airlines** who have a code-share agreement with **South African Airways** and flights go from Atlanta and New York to Johannesburg, from where **South African Airways** fly to Dar (see below).

From Australia and New Zealand

There are no direct flights from Australia and New Zealand to Tanzania, but a number of indirect routes go via Kenya, the Middle East, Asia or South Africa. **Qantas** and **South African Airways** fly between Australia and Johannesburg; **Singapore Airlines** fly between Australia and New Zealand and Johannesburg via Singapore; and **Malaysia Air** fly between Australia and New Zealand and Johannesburg via Kuala Lumpur. From Johannesburg there are connections to Dar es Salaam with **South African Airways** and **Fast Jet**, Nairobi with **South African Airways** and **Kenya Airways**, but none to Kilimanjaro so there'll be another change in Dar or Nairobi.

From Africa and the Middle East

The following airlines fly to Nairobi: **Egyptair** via Cairo, **Emirates** via Dubai, **Ethiopian Airlines** via Addis Ababa, **Etihad Airways** via Abu Dhabi, **Qatar Airways** via Doha and **South African Airways** via Johannesburg. Many of these also have flights to Europe/North America, so a connection in the hub cities of these airlines is the option.

Airlines

British Airways, www.britishairways.com.
Delta, www.delta.com.
Egypt Air, www.egyptair.com.
Emirates, www.emirates.com.
Etihad Airways, www.etihad.com.
Ethiopian Airlines, www.ethiopian airlines.com.
Fast Jet, www.fastjet.com.
Kenya Airways, www.kenya-airways.com.
KLM, www.klm.com.

Lufthansa, www.lufthansa.com.
Malaysia Airlines, www.malaysia airlines.com.
Precision Air, www.precisionairtz.com.
Qantas, www.qantas.com.au.
Qatar Airways, www.qatarairways.com.
Singapore Airlines, www.singaporeair.com.
South African Airways, www.flysaa.com.
Swissair, www.swissair.com.
Turkish Airlines, www.turkishairlines.com.

Road

The main road crossing is at Namanga (Kenya), about halfway along the A104 road between Nairobi and Arusha. As this border receives thousands of tourists on safari each week en route between the Kenyan and Tanzanian parks, it is reasonably quick and efficient. There are regular shuttle buses (see box, page 44) connecting Nairobi with Arusha (six hours) and Moshi (7½ hours). A cheaper alternative is to do the journey in stages by taking a minibus (matatu in Kenya) from the matatu stage on the corner of River Road and Ronald Ngala Road in downtown Nairobi to Namanga, crossing the border on foot, and then catching another minibus (dala-dala in Tanzania) to Arusha. This will take a little longer than the shuttle, and will cost half the price, but the minibuses only leave when full and not to a timetable and there will be a problem of the vehicles accommodating luggage (it might have to go on your knees).

If you are coming from southern Kenya, local buses and dala-dalas frequent the quieter border crossing at Taveta, between Voi in Kenya and Moshi.

> **Tip...**
> Single-entry and transit visas for both Tanzania and Kenya are available at the borders (see page 179 for details).

ON THE ROAD

24 hours in Nairobi

Nairobi, capital of Kenya, is a lively, cosmopolitan and bustling city. It does, like many African cities, have its frenetic markets, alarming *matatu* drivers, potholed roads and shanty towns, but it's also a fast-developing modern and prosperous city and also features its fair share of gleaming skyscrapers, glitzy shopping malls and affluent leafy suburbs.

Nairobi is the base for safaris into the parks in Kenya's share of the Rift Valley, which includes the Maasai Mara National Reserve (see page 122), but if you find yourself here with 24 hours or so to spare, it is worth sticking around to visit some of Nairobi's interesting sights that explore both its colonial past and Kenya's wildlife and cultural heritage.

Sights

Nairobi National Museum ① *Museum Hill, T020-374 1424, www.museums.or.ke, daily 0830-1730, US$12, children (under 16) US$6).* This impressive museum presents an overview of Kenya's culture and natural history, and exhibits of archaeological findings made so famous by the work of the Leakeys.

Nairobi Railway Museum ① *Near the railway station, daily 0800-1645, US$6, children (under 16) US$3).* This is the best place to come and learn the history of the Uganda Railway, which effectively founded the colony of Kenya.

The Norfolk Hotel ① *Harry Thuku Rd, T020-226 5555, www.fairmont.com/norfolk-hotel-nairobi.* The elegant Tea Room offers a sumptuous afternoon high tea, but if time has gotten the better of you, not to worry. You get a taste of Kenya's lingering colonial atmosphere at the Lord Delamere Terrace, which opened in 1904. The bar is an ideal place for a Tusker, Kenya's favourite beer, or a gin and tonic. The Tatu Restaurant (*T020-226 5000, daily 1800-2300*) here is also highly acclaimed and offers a long menu from Indian cuisine to seafood flown up from Kenya's coast.

David Sheldrick Wildlife Trust ① *Access via the Mbagathi Gate of Nairobi National Park, Magadi Rd, T020-230 1396, www.sheldrickwildlifetrust.org, daily 1100-1200, minimum contribution US$5.* Early next morning head out to this remarkable refuge for lost, abandoned and orphaned elephants rescued in Kenya's parks and reserves. For one hour each morning, visitors can watch the keepers bring out the baby elephants into an enclosure for a bath or a play and to guzzle milk out of giant bottles. An endearing experience and the guides explain some basics of elephant behaviour.

Karen Blixen Museum ① *Karen Rd, T020-800 2139, www.museums.or.ke, daily 0930-1800, US$12, children (under 16) US$6.* Further west from Langata, the leafy suburb of Karen is named after Karen Blixen, the Danish baroness who as Isak Dinesen wrote *Out of Africa*. This was her home on her coffee plantation from 1914 to 1931 – in the book she wrote, "I had a farm in Africa, at the foot of the Ngong Hills …" The rooms are decorated in the original style.

Nairobi Safari Walk ⓘ *Langata Rd, T020-600 0800, www.kws.org, daily 0900-1730, US$25, children (3-18) US$15).* For a great introduction to the animals you're likely to see on safari visit come here to the main gate of the Nairobi National Park. Here you can follow a 1.5-km suspended boardwalk through indigenous trees and over some well-designed enclosures. Residents include lion, cheetah, leopard, hyena, hippo and a number of antelope. If time allows, a couple of hours game-driving in the 117-sq-km Nairobi National Park (US$50, children (3-18) US$25) will be well-rewarding in terms of seeing a good selection of animals and birds, although being so close to the city it doesn't have the wild atmosphere of the parks that you will visit on a longer safari.

Carnivore ⓘ *Langata Rd, T020-514 1300; www.tamarind.co.ke/carnivore, lunch 1200-1430, dinner 1900-2230.* The restaurant on most tourists' Nairobi must-do list is this flame-lit palace devoted to barbecued meat grilled on Maasai spears over a huge charcoal fire. It is gut-busting affair (there are vegetarian options too) and a fun night out: it's also home to bars and dance floors, and a Carnivore speciality is a *dawa* – vodka, crushed ice, sugar and lime served with a stick coated with honey; dawa means 'medicine' in Kiswahili.

Where to stay

$$$$ Hemingway's Nairobi
Mbagathi Ridge, Karen, T020-229 5013, www.hemingways-nairobi.com.
A modern and stylish 45-room boutique hotel set on a large plantation-style property in Karen with views of the Ngong Hills. Impeccable service including personal butlers, heated swimming pool, restaurant and spa.

$$$$ The Norfolk Hotel
Harry Thuku Rd, city centre, T020-226 5555, www.fairmont.com/norfolk-hotel-nairobi.
This world-famous luxury hotel was built in 1904 and is steeped in colonial history. Most of the 165 rooms are in cottages in the delightful tropical gardens, and there are several restaurants and bars, a heated swimming pool and spa.

$$$$-$$$ Tribe Hotel
Limuru Rd, Gigiri, T020-720 0000, www.tribe-hotel.com.
Adjacent to the Village Market shopping mall, this contemporary hotel has chic decor with African touches, 142 well-equipped rooms, some have free-standing baths, restaurant serving continental cuisine, rooftop bar and spa.

$$$ Fairview Hotel
Bishops Rd, city centre, T020-288 1000, www.clhg.com.
A popular, friendly and centrally located mid-range option set in lovely, flowering and surprisingly peaceful gardens. It has more than 100 rooms, a large swimming pool and courtyard restaurant, and also runs the simpler but cheaper Town Lodge Upper Hill on the same property.

$$$-$ Wildebeest Eco Camp
151 Mokoyeti Road West, Langata, T020-272 7991, www.wildebeestecocamp.com.
Something for most budgets here from smart garden cottages and walk-in, en suite safari tents, simpler tents that share bathrooms, dorm rooms and a grassy campsite. Restaurant/bar, family-friendly and good location for the Langata attractions.

TRAVEL TIP
Overland tours

Overland truck multi-week tours are a popular and hassle-free way of exploring East Africa and most itineraries visit many of Tanzania's places of interest by road. It's a great adventure, and lots of fun for the camaraderie and company, but be aware it's group and participatory travel and you'll have to help with making camp and preparing meals etc. The standard route most tours take is from Nairobi on a two-week loop via some of the Kenya's national parks into Uganda, to go chimpanzee and mountain gorilla tracking, before returning to Nairobi to head south to Tanzania's Northern Circuit parks. The route then continues to Dar es Salaam, for an excursion to Zanzibar, and then on through Malawi and Zambia to Victoria Falls. Another three weeks takes you from there to Cape Town in South Africa via Botswana and Namibia. The itinerary also runs in reverse from Cape Town to Nairobi. There are several overland companies with departures almost weekly from Nairobi, Livingstone/Victoria Falls and Cape Town. If you're flying into Kilimanjaro or Dar es Salaam airports, there is also the option of joining one of these circuits from there.

Overland operators

Acacia Africa, www.acacia-africa.com.
Africa Travel Co, www.africatravelco.com.
African Trails, www.africantrails.co.uk.
Dragoman, www.dragoman.com.
Exodus, www.exodus.co.uk.
G Adventures, www.gadventures.com.

Gecko's Grassroots Adventures, www.geckosadventures.com.
Intrepid, www.intrepidtravel.com.
Oasis Overland, www.oasisoverland.co.uk.
Tucan Travel, www.tucantravel.com.

Car

If you are driving, border crossings between Tanzania and its neighbours is straightforward as long as your vehicle's paperwork is in order. For all cars you must have a vehicle registration document (if it's not in the name of the driver, a letter of authorization is also required), and a driving licence printed in English with a photograph. You will be required to get a Temporary Import Permit or TIP from the customs desk at the border, and (if you don't already have it) take out third-party insurance for Tanzania from one of the insurance companies who have kiosks at the border. For a foreign-registered vehicle, you will also need a Carnet de Passage en Douanes, which is an international customs document that allows you to temporarily import a vehicle duty-free and is issued by a body in your own country (such as the RAC in the UK). Most car hire companies will not allow you to take a rented vehicle out of Tanzania, but some may consider it if you only want to go to Kenya (the same goes for hiring a car in Kenya and only going to Tanzania). See page 166 for information about hiring a car in Tanzania.

Shuttle buses

Shuttle buses run daily between Kenya and Tanzania: Nairobi (city centre)–Nairobi Jomo Kenyatta International Airport–Arusha (via the Namanga border post)–Kilimanjaro International Airport–Moshi. The operators utilize 20- to 30-seat buses with comfortable individual seating, and drivers assist passengers during the border crossings. There is an early morning and an early afternoon departure. Expect to pay about US$30 for

Nairobi to Arusha, US$40 for Nairobi to Moshi, US$15 for Arusha to Moshi, and US$20 from Kilimanjaro International Airport to Arusha or Moshi. The journey time from Nairobi to Arusha is six hours and it's another 1½ hours to Moshi via the airport. The company websites have booking facilities, timetables, prices and information about where to meet the buses, and they can also be booked at the company town offices, or through hotels or local tour operators.

AA Luxury Shuttle Bus
www.aashuttles.com.
East Africa Shuttles
www.eastafricashuttles.com.
Nairobi Arusha Shuttle Transport Company www.nairobiarushashuttle.com.

Regional Luxury Shuttle
www.regionalluxuryshuttle.com.
The Riverside Shuttle
www.riverside-shuttle.com.

Getting around

Air

There are a number of airlines that offer extensive air coverage of the country and more than 60 airports and airstrips managed by the **Tanzania Airports Authority** (www.taa.go.tz). Regular daily flights connect the major towns and cities and the safari destinations, all of which can be reached within a couple of hours' flying time from each other. There's a fair amount of competition, so flights can be affordable. Many of these airlines run services in circuits, and flights may involve intermediate stops as the plane drops passengers at different airstrips on each circuit and may often return on the same route. For example, a flight to the Serengeti may actually 'drop down' at several safari lodges. The smaller airlines will only fly with the required minimum of passengers, although sometimes this is only two people. All tickets can be booked online, through a tour operator or can be bought directly from the airline town offices or desks at the airports.

> **Tip...**
> On the smaller aircraft that fly to the safari destinations, the baggage allowance is 15 kg in 'soft' bags and not hard suitcases. Extra luggage can be left at hotels in Arusha and Moshi, or your tour operator will be able to make arrangements to store bags.

Airlines

Air Excel, Arusha Airport, Dodoma (A104) Rd, Arusha, T027-254 8429, www.airexcelonline. com. Flights to/from Arusha, Kilimanjaro, Lake Manyara, the Serengeti and Zanzibar.

Air Tanzania, Dar, T022-117 5 00, www. airtanzania.co.tz. Flights to/from Dar, Arusha, Kilimanjaro, Mbeya, Mwanza, Mtwara, Tabora, Kigoma and Zanzibar.

Auric Air, TFA Shopping Centre (see page 57), Sokoine Rd, Arusha, T0688-723 274, www.auricair.com. Flights to/ from Dar es Salaam, Arusha, Bukoba, Iringa, Lake Manyara, Mafia Island, Mbeya, Mwanza and the Serengeti.

Coastal Aviation, Dar es Salaam, T022-284 260 2430, Arusha Airport, T0785-500 004, www.coastal.co.tz. Flights to/from Dar, Arusha, Dodoma, Kilwa, Tarangire, Mafia Island, Lake Manyara, Mwanza, Pemba, Ruaha, Selous, the Serengeti, Tanga and Zanzibar, plus Nairobi's Wilson Airport in Kenya.

Fast Jet, Corridor Springs Hotel, Ingira Rd, Arusha, Kaunda St, Moshi; both T0784-

108 900, www.fastjet.com. Flights to/ from Dar, Kilimanjaro, Mwanza, Mbeya and Zanzibar. Regionally there are flights between Dar and Lusaka in Zambia, Lilongwe in Malawi, Harare and Victoria Falls in Zimbabwe, Johannesburg in South Africa, Nairobi's Jomo Kenyatta International Airport in Kenya and Entebbe in Uganda. Also flies between Kilimanjaro and Nairobi.

Flightlink, Dar, T022-211 3820, www. flightlinkaircharters.com. Flights to/from Dar, Arusha, Dodoma, Lake Manyara, the Serengeti, Selous, Pemba and Zanzibar.

Precision Air, Boma Rd, Arusha, T027-7 25 45489, KNCU Building, Old Moshi Rd, Moshi, T027-2 753495, www.precisionairtz.com. Flights to/from Arusha, Dar, Kilimanjaro, Mwanza, Bukoba, Mtwara and Zanzibar, plus Nairobi's Jomo Kenyatta International Airport in Kenya.

Regional Air, Sable Square, off the Dodoma (A104) Rd, just beyond Arusha Airport, Arusha, T0784-285 753, www. regionaltanzania.com. Flights to/from

Dar, Arusha, Kilimanjaro, Lake Manyara, the Serengeti and Zanzibar.
Tanganyika Flying Co. (TFC), Arusha Airport, Dodoma (A104) Rd, Arusha, T0785-931 200, www.flytfconline.com. Flights to/from Dar, Arusha, Kilimanjaro, Lake Manyara, the Serengeti and Zanzibar, plus Nairobi's Wilson Airport in Kenya.
ZanAir, Zanzibar, T024-223 3670, www.zanair.com. Flights to/from Dar es Salaam, Arusha, Pemba, Saadani, Selous and Zanzibar.

Air charter

Several companies offer small planes for charter, especially on the routes between the parks and islands making them no different to the scheduled flights above. The advantage is by booking the whole plane, you can decide on departure times and it works out economical for groups of four to six people. **Air Excel, Auric Air, Flightlink, Regional Air** and **Tanganyika Flying Co (TFC)** (see above) can organize charters. Also try **Kilimanjaro Aero Club**, Moshi (T0784-276 430, www.kilimanjaroaeroclub.com), or **Zantas Air** (Arusha Airport, Dodoma (A104) Road, Arusha, T0688-434 343, www.zantasair.com).

Road

Boda-bodas

The use of *boda-bodas* (bicycle taxis) started in the 1960s/1970s and they are now a ubiquitous form of East African transport. These days bicycle *boda-bodas* have largely been replaced by mopeds or more powerful motorbikes depending on the terrain. In Tanzania these are also called *piki-pikis*. They can be flagged down in the street and are useful for short journeys, but bear in mind they have a very poor safety record and accidents are common – always ensure the driver gives you a spare crash helmet. Agree the price before getting on.

Buses and dala-dalas (minibuses)

There is an efficient network of privately run buses across the country. Larger non-stop buses cover the longer distances, and minibuses (*dala-dalas*) cover the shorter routes between the small towns and villages and stop along the way to pick up and drop people off. If you have problems finding the right vehicle, just ask around and someone will direct you. Most buses and *dala-dalas* will only leave when full; you can join an almost full vehicle and leave promptly, or wait in a half empty one for an hour or two on a less busy route. On the main long-distance bus routes it is sometimes also possible to book ahead at a kiosk at the bus station – known as bus 'stage' or 'stand' in Tanzania. *Dala-dalas* are also the most popular form of urban transport. They follow routes along the main roads in the towns and cities (most have a sign indicating their route and destination on the front) and can be flagged down on the street for short journeys in the direction you are going (fares are around US$0.40 for a short hop). By law, all public service vehicles have to be speed governed at 80 kph, standing is not permitted and everyone gets their own seat with a seat belt. However, these rules are often flaunted and overcrowding and reckless and fast driving can occur – do not continue in a vehicle if you are not comfortable. Petty theft can be a problem on vehicles and at stands/stages – keep an eye on your belongings and keep any valuables out of sight.

Car

Driving is on the left side of the road. The key roads are in good condition, and there has been considerable road building going on in Tanzania in recent years. The best roads are the tarmac ones from Dar es Salaam to Zambia and Malawi, Dar es Salaam to Arusha, Arusha to the Ngorongoro Crater and the road from Arusha to the Kenyan border at Namanga. Away from the main highways, however, most of the minor roads are unmade gravel with potholes, and road conditions in Tanzania's parks and reserves are extremely rough; dusty in the dry season and muddy in the wet season. Fuel is available along the main highways and towns, but in remote areas petrol stations will not accept credit cards or have an ATM, so carry enough cash. If you're going way off the beaten track, consider taking a couple of jerry cans of extra fuel. Also ensure the vehicle has a jack and possibly take a shovel to dig it out of mud or sand.

Tip...
A 4WD, or at the very least a vehicle with high clearance, is essential for driving around the national parks and game reserves.

Car hire Most people visit the national parks on an organized safari, but if you're confident about driving in Tanzania, there is also the option to hire a car, or hire a car with driver, which most car hire companies can organize. Renting a car has certain advantages over public transport, particularly if you intend visiting any of the remoter regions of the country, or there are at least four of you to share the costs. To hire a car you generally need to be over 23, have a full driving licence (it does not have to be an international licence, your home country one will do as long as it's got a photograph – with an English translation if necessary) and a credit card. Always take out the collision damage waiver premium as even the smallest accident can be very expensive. Costs vary between the different car hire companies and are from around US$70-80 per day for a normal saloon car; US$100-120 for a minibus; and US$140-170 for a 4WD. Deals can be made for more than seven days' car hire. It is important to shop around and ask the companies what is and what is not included in the rates and what the provisions are in the event of a breakdown. Things to consider include whether you take out a limited mileage package or unlimited mileage depending on how you many kilometres you think you will drive. Finally, 20% VAT is added to all costs. On safari you will have to pay the park entrance fees for the car (see box, page 82), which are considerably cheaper for Tanzanian-registered vehicles than foreign-registered ones, as well as for the driver if you have one; again resident park entry fees are much less than non-residents. See individual transport sections for car hire company details. In Arusha, tour operators will be able to organize car hire on your behalf.

Tip...
If you break down, it is common practice in East Africa to place a bundle of leaves 50 m or so before and behind the vehicle to warn oncoming motorists. Also slow down if you see this – a broken down vehicle may be blocking the road ahead.

Hitchhiking

In the Western sense (standing beside the road and requesting a free ride) hitchhiking is not an option. However, truck drivers and many private motorists will often carry you if you pay and, on that basis, if you are stuck where there is no public transport you can approach likely vehicles. Nevertheless, it is not generally recommended and women alone should be especially wary of hitchhiking.

Taxis

Hotels and town centre locations are well served by taxis, some good and some very run down but serviceable. Hotel staff, even at the smallest locations, will rustle up a taxi even when there is not one waiting outside. If you find a taxi driver you like, get their mobile phone number. Taxis don't have meters, so you should establish the fare (*bei gani?* – how much?) before you set off. Prices are generally fair, as drivers simply won't take you if you offer a fare that's too low. A common practice is for a driver to set off and *then* go and get petrol using part of your fare to pay for it, so often the first part of a journey is spent sitting in a petrol station. Also be aware that taxi drivers never seem to have change, so try and accumulate some small notes for taxi rides.

Maps

The best map and travel guide store in the UK is **Stanfords** (12-14 Long Acre, Covent Garden, London WC2E 9LP, T0207-836 1321, and 29 Corn Street, Bristol, BS1 1HT, T0117-929 9966, www.stanfords.co.uk). That said the *Michelin Map of Africa: Central and South* (www.michelintravel.com), covers Tanzania in detail. In South Africa, **Map Studio** (T+27 (0)21-460 5400, www.mapstudio.co.za), produces a wide range of maps covering much of Africa, which are available to buy online. In Tanzania you can pick up locally produced maps of the most popular parks, such as the Serengeti, in book and gift shops and some of the lodges stock them.

Essentials A-Z

Accident and emergency

Police, fire and ambulance T112.

Bargaining

While most prices in shops are set, the exception are curio shops where a little good natured bargaining is possible, especially if it's quiet or you are buying a number of things. Bargaining is very much expected in the street markets, whether you are buying an apple or a Maasai blanket. Generally traders will attempt to overcharge tourists who are unaware of local prices. Start lower than you would expect to pay, be polite and good humoured and, if the final price doesn't suit – walk away. You may be called back for more negotiation if your final price was too high, or the trader may let you go, in which case your price was too low. Ask about the prices of taxis, excursions, souvenirs and so on at your hotel.

Children

Tanzania has great appeal for families: animals and safaris are very exciting for children, especially when they catch their first glimpse of an elephant or lion. However, small kids may get bored driving around a hot game park or national park all day if there is no animal activity. It's a good idea to get children enthused by providing them with checklists for animals and birds and perhaps giving them their own binoculars and cameras. Also think about the long hours inside the vehicle sharing little room with other people; noisy and bickering children can annoy your travel mates and scare the animals away. Most tour operators use minibuses for safaris so consider taking one for yourself or share it with another family.

In the parks, there are considerable reductions to entry fees for children under 16, and under 5s go free. Children also get significant discounts for accommodation and while adjoining rooms aren't common, putting extra beds into rooms is. Some safari lodges are completely child-friendly and will be fenced to stop animals coming into the property and children wandering around in the bush, while at some smaller unfenced tented camps children are not permitted at all.

Disposable nappies, formula milk powders and puréed foods are only available in major cities and they are expensive, so you may want consider bringing enough of these with you. It is important to remember that children have an increased risk of gastro-enteritis, malaria and sunburn and are more likely to develop complications, so care must be taken to minimize risks. See Health, below, for more details.

Customs and duty free

The official customs allowance for visitors over 18 years includes 200 cigarettes, 50 cigars, 250 g of tobacco, 2 litres of wine, 1 litre of spirits, 50 ml of perfume and 250 ml of eau de toilette. There is no duty on any equipment for your own use (such as laptops or cameras). Once in Tanzania, be careful about accepting any wildlife-derived object from villagers and guides. Any souvenir made from an endangered species is prohibited. If you were to buy such items, you should always consider the environmental and social impact of your purchase, and it cannot be taken out of Tanzania. Attempts to smuggle controlled products can result in confiscation, fines and imprisonment under the **Convention on Trade in Endangered Species** (**CITES**), www.cites.org.

Disabled travellers

There are few specific facilities for disabled people in Tanzania; wheelchairs are not accommodated on public road transport, the towns have very uneven pavements and few accommodation options (with the exception of the more modern upmarket hotels) have rooms with disabled facilities so the best option for a visit is on an organized tour or in a rented vehicle. Safaris should not pose too much of a problem for wheelchair-bound travellers given that most of the time is spent in the vehicle, and many of the safari lodges have rooms that are accessible on the ground floor. Also consider a camping or tented safari, which provides easy access to a tent at ground level. Most tour operators are accommodating and should be able to make special arrangements for disabled travellers. Contact the **Tanzania Association of Tour Operators** (**TATO**), www.tatotz.org, and ask if they can make a recommendation. Tanzanians themselves will do their very best to help, and being disabled should not deter you from visiting Tanzania.

Tip...
Climbing Mount Kilimanjaro is not completely out of bounds for wheelchair uses and specialist treks can be organized utilizing all-terrain wheelchairs and extra porters.

Electricity

230 volts AC at 50 Hz. Square 3-pin British-type sockets. Travellers with round-pin plugs will require adaptors. Hotels usually have 2-pin round sockets for razors, phones etc. Some hotels and businesses have back-up generators in case of power cuts, which are more common at the end of the dry seasons. The more remote places off the national grid only use generators, which applies to many of the safari lodges and tented camps in the parks and reserves, some of which also generate their power from solar panels. On safari, expect the power to be only on for a few hours in the early morning and from dusk until about 2200 or 2300 – torches and lanterns are provided at other times and the management of lodges and camps will advise when you can charge devices etc.

Embassies and consulates

For a list of Tanzanian embassies and consulates abroad, see http://embassy.goabroad.com.

Gay and lesbian travellers

Homosexuality is illegal in Tanzania and is considered a criminal offence, so discretion is advised. However, there is a general toleration by ordinary people of discreet behaviour, especially by those in the tourism industry. There are no specific gay clubs or bars.

Health

See your GP or travel clinic at least 6 weeks before departure for general advice on travel risks, malaria and vaccinations. Make sure you have travel insurance, get a dental check, know your own blood group and, if you suffer from a long-term condition such as diabetes or epilepsy, make sure someone knows or that you have a Medic Alert bracelet/necklace (www.medicalert.org.uk). If you wear glasses, take a copy of your prescription.

Vaccinations

Confirm that your primary courses and boosters are up to date (diphtheria, typhoid, polio and tetanus). Vaccinations commonly recommended for travel in Tanzania are yellow fever, hepatitis A and B, meningitis and rabies, especially if staying for long periods in remote areas. Note: Travellers from non-endemic countries travelling to Tanzania do not require a yellow fever vaccination certificate. However, travellers from non-endemic countries that travel through Tanzania will be asked to show the certificate after departing Tanzania and arriving at other destinations, which include all land borders in Tanzania and very possibly your home country – so it's essential that you get a certificate for any visit to Tanzania.

Health risks
Altitude sickness
Above 3000 m, changes in air density and oxygen levels begin to impact and can lead to altitude sickness (also known as Acute Mountain Sickness or AMS). There are 2 places in Tanzania where this may occur – Mounts Meru and Kilimanjaro. The best way of preventing AMS is a relatively slow ascent when trekking to high altitude and spending some time walking at medium altitude, to acclimatize to the rarefied air. For more information see page 146.

Cholera
There are occasional outbreaks of cholera in the more impoverished rural areas of the country. The main symptoms of cholera are profuse watery diarrhoea and vomiting, which may lead to severe dehydration. However, most travellers are at extremely low risk of infection, and the disease rarely shows symptoms in healthy well-nourished people. The cholera vaccine, Dukoral, is only recommended for certain high-risk individuals such as health professionals or volunteers.

Diarrhoea
Diarrhoea can refer either to loose stools or an increased frequency of bowel movement, both of which can be a nuisance, but symptoms should be relatively short lived. Adults can use an antidiarrhoeal medication to control the symptoms but only for up to 24 hrs. In addition, keep well hydrated by drinking plenty of fluids and eat bland foods. Oral rehydration sachets taken after each loose stool are a useful way to keep well hydrated. These should always be used when treating children and the elderly. Bacterial traveller's diarrhoea is the most common form; if there are no signs of improvement,

the diarrhoea is likely to be viral and not bacterial and antibiotics may be required. Also seek medical help if there is blood in the stools and/or fever.

The standard advice to prevent problems is to be careful with water and ice for drinking. If you have any doubts then boil the water or filter and treat it. Food can also transmit disease. Be wary of salads (what were they washed in, who handled them), re-heated foods or food that has been left out in the sun having been cooked earlier in the day. There is a simple adage that says wash it, peel it, boil it or forget it. Also be wary of unpasteurized dairy products as these can transmit a range of diseases.

Hepatitis
Hepatitis means inflammation of the liver. Viral causes of the disease can be acquired anywhere in the world. The most obvious symptom is a yellowing of your skin or the whites of your eyes. However, prior to this all that you may notice is itching and tiredness. Pre-travel hepatitis A vaccine is the best bet. Hepatitis B (for which there is a vaccine) is spread through blood and unprotected sexual intercourse: both of these can be avoided.

HIV
Africa has the highest infection rate of HIV in the world. Efforts to stem the rate of infection have had limited success, as many of the factors that need addressing such as social change, poverty and gender inequalities are long-term processes. Visitors should be aware of the dangers of infection from unprotected sex and always use a condom. If you have to have medical treatment, ensure any equipment used is taken from a sealed pack or is freshly sterilized. If you have to have a blood transfusion, ask for screened blood.

Malaria
Malaria is present in almost all of Tanzania and prophylactics should be taken. Take

expert advice before you leave home, and ensure you finish the recommended course of anti-malarials even if means taking them after you have arrived home. It can start as something just resembling an attack of flu. You may feel tired, lethargic, headachy, feverish, or, more seriously, develop fits, followed by coma and then death. Have a low index of suspicion because it is very easy to write off vague symptoms, which may actually be malaria. If you have a temperature, go to a doctor as soon as you can and ask for a malaria test. On your return home, if you suffer any of these symptoms, get tested as soon as possible.

To prevent mosquito bites wear clothes that cover arms and legs and use effective insect repellents. Repellents containing 30-50% DEET (Di-ethyltoluamide) are recommended; lemon eucalyptus (Mosiguard) is a reasonable alternative. Rooms with a/c or fans also help ward off mosquitoes at night.

Rabies

Avoid dogs and monkeys that are behaving strangely. If you are bitten by a domestic or wild animal, do not leave things to chance: scrub the wound with soap and water and/or disinfectant, try to at least determine the animal's ownership, and seek medical assistance at once. The course of treatment depends on whether you have already been satisfactorily vaccinated against rabies.

Schistosomiasis (bilharzia)

Bilharzia is a disease carried by parasitic snails living in fresh water; it occurs in most of the freshwater lakes of Tanzania, including Lake Victoria and Lake Tanganyika, and can be contracted from a single swim or wade. Symptoms can appear within a few weeks and for many months afterwards. These include fever, diarrhoea, abdominal pain and spleen or liver enlargement. A single drug cures this disease, so get yourself checked out as soon as possible if you have any of these symptoms. Broad advice is that the

parasite is not present in fast-moving water, so avoid any stagnant water or still reedy shores, and don't wade or swim too close to villages where people who may be infected use the water to bathe or wash clothes. Chlorinated swimming pools are fine.

Sun

Protect yourself adequately against the sun. Apply a high-factor sunscreen (greater than SPF15) and also make sure it screens against UVB. Prevent heat exhaustion and heatstroke by drinking enough fluids throughout the day (your urine will be pale if you are drinking enough). Symptoms of heat exhaustion and heatstroke include dizziness, tiredness and headache. Use rehydration salts mixed with water to replenish fluids and salts and find somewhere cool and shady to recover. If you suspect heatstroke rather than heat exhaustion, you need to cool the body down quickly (cold showers are particularly effective).

If you get sick

There are private hospitals in Arusha and Moshi, which have 24-hr emergency departments and pharmacies, and have a high standard of healthcare. In other areas of Tanzania, facilities range from government hospitals to rural clinics, but these can be poorly equipped and under staffed. For extreme emergencies or surgery, visitors with adequate health insurance will be transferred to a private hospital in Nairobi (Kenya), which has the best medical facilities in East Africa. If you are planning to travel in more isolated areas, consider the **Flying Doctors' Society of Africa**, based at Wilson Airport in Nairobi, Kenya, T+254 (0)20-699 3000, www.amref.org. For an annual tourist fee of US$50, it offers free evacuation by air to a medical centre or hospital, and the service covers Tanzania. This may be worth considering if you are visiting remote regions, but not if visiting the more popular parks as adequate provision is made in the case of an emergency. The income goes back

TRAVEL TIP
Bites and stings

There are a few insects and small creatures in Tanzania that, if you are unlucky, may bite or sting you. These rarely cause any more problems than mild irritation and can be relieved by cool baths, antihistamine tablets or mild corticosteroid creams. However, if bites and stings fester they can become infected and you may have to progress to antiseptic or antibiotic cream or, even better, powder, which are all available locally in Tanzania. If the redness around the infection spreads or you develop a fever, a course of antibiotics may be required.

Ticks These usually attach themselves to the lower parts of the body, often after walking in areas of long damp grass or where cattle have grazed, and swell up as they suck blood. The important thing is to remove them gently, without leaving the head in your skin because this can cause a nasty infection. Do not use petrol, Vaseline, lighted cigarettes, etc, to remove the tick; use a pair of tweezers to rock it out carefully. If travelling with children, check them over for ticks.

Jigger flea In areas of wet soil or sand the jigger flea can burrow its way into people's feet causing a painful itchy swelling which finally bursts in a rather disgusting fashion. Avoid these by wearing shoes and if they do become established have someone experienced winkle them out with a sterile needle.

Putsi flies Also known as tumbo or mango flies, these flies lay their eggs under the skin of sheep and cattle, but they can also lay their eggs in damp fabric including washing. The result is that the egg is transferred to the skin and a maggot grows and pops up as a boil. The best way to remove these is to cover the boil with oil, Vaseline or nail varnish to stop the maggot breathing, then to squeeze it out gently the next day. Avoid them in the first place by never laying clothes out to dry on damp grass; rather hang them in direct sunlight until crisp. They can also be eradicated from clothing by ironing.

Tsetse fly The tsete fly is present in most game areas in Tanzania, and can transmit sleeping sickness (African trypanosomiasis). However this disease is extremely rare in humans (although domestic animals can get it), but tsetse flies do administer a wicked bite and can be itchy for some time afterwards. The only way to avoid them is to wind up windows on a game drive. See also page 77.

Scorpions Bites from scorpions are very painful but rarely dangerous to adults. Seek medical advice if a young child is bitten. Do not immerse the bite in cold water as this increases the pain. If camping, shake out boots and shoes, and check backpacks before putting them on.

Snakes Most snake species are non-venomous and venomous snakes often inflict a 'dry bite' where no venom is injected. But if you are unlucky (or careless) enough to be bitten by a venomous snake, try to identify the culprit without putting yourself in further danger. Do not apply a tourniquet, suck or cut open the bite wound; victims should be taken to a hospital or a doctor without delay.

into the service and the **African Medical Research Foundation** (**AMREF**) behind it.

In Moshi
Kilimanjaro Christian Medical Centre (KCMC), 6 km north of town beyond Shantytown, T027-275 4377, www.kcmc.ac.tz.
Mawenzi Regional Hospital, just north of Kilima St, T027-275 2321.

In Arusha
Arusha International Conference Centre (AICC) Hospital, Nelson Mandela (Old Moshi) Rd, T027-2 05 0181-5, www.aicc.co.tz.
Mount Meru Regional Hospital, opposite AICC, East Africa Community Blvd, T027-250 3351-3.

Useful websites
www.btha.org British Travel Health Association.
www.cdc.gov US government site that gives excellent advice on travel health and details of disease outbreaks.
www.fco.gov.uk British Foreign and Commonwealth Office travel site has useful information on each country, people, climate and a list of UK embassies/consulates.
www.fitfortravel.nhs.uk A-Z of vaccine/health advice for each country.
www.travelhealth.co.uk Independent travel health site with advice on vaccination, travel insurance and health risks.
www.who.int World Health Organization, updates of disease outbreaks.

Insurance

Before departure, it is vital to take out comprehensive travel insurance. There are a wide variety of policies to choose from, so shop around. At the very least, the policy should cover medical expenses, including repatriation to your home country in the event of a medical emergency. If you are going to be active in Tanzania, ensure the policy covers whatever activity you will be doing (for example, trekking

Tip...
It is essential to have travel insurance as hospital bills need to be paid at the time of admittance, so keep all paperwork to make a claim.

or ballooning). There is no substitute for suitable precautions against petty crime, but if you do have something stolen while in Tanzania, report the incident to the nearest police station and ensure you get a police report and case number. You will need these to make any claim from your insurance company.

Internet

Despite the decreasing need for them, there are still a few internet cafés around Arusha and Moshi, but these days most online access is via Wi-Fi at hotels and coffee shops. However don't expect it at remote safari lodges and tented camps and in small out-of-the-way towns. Costs vary from free of charge, at coffee shops and at more expensive accommodation, to expensive, when you have to buy a voucher with a password, when it may cost up to US$5 for an hour's access. If you are using a 3G mobile phone or device, remember that data charges will be expensive if it's on roaming with your home service provider so be sure to disable data roaming on your phone and use local Wi-Fi instead. There's also the option of using a local Tanzanian SIM card (also see page 176) and a USB/dongle connection on your laptop, and use local pay-as-you-go data bundles. All this can be organized at any of the mobile phone shops (there are plenty in Arusha and Moshi) and there are several mobile networks – the 4 major operators are **Vodacom**, **Airtel**, **Tigo** and **Zantel**.

Language

Tanzania is a welcoming country and the first word that you will hear and come to know is the Kiswahili greeting '*Jambo*' – 'hello', often followed by '*Hakuna matata*' – 'no problem'! Lengthy greetings are important in Tanzania, and respect is accorded to elderly people, usually by the greeting '*Shikamoo, mzee*' to a man and '*Shikamoo, mama*' to a woman.

There are a number of local languages, but most people in Tanzania, as in all East Africa, speak Kiswahili and some English. Kiswahili is the official language of Tanzania and is taught in primary schools. English is generally used in business and is taught in secondary schools. Only in the remote rural regions will you find people that only speak in their local tongues. A little Kiswahili goes a long way, and most Tanzanians will be thrilled to hear visitors attempt to use it. Since the language was originally written down by the British colonists, words are pronounced just as they are spelt.

Media

Newspapers and magazines
Tanzania has several English-language newspapers. The best are the *Daily News* (www.dailynews.co.tz) and the *Guardian* (www.ippmedia.com), which both cover eastern and southern African news and syndicated international news and are available online. There are also a number of newspapers published in Kiswahili. An excellent regional paper, *The East African* (www.theeastafrican.co.ke), published in Nairobi, comes out weekly and has good Tanzanian coverage and provides the most objective reporting on East African issues. On a local level, the weekly *Arusha Times* (www.arushatimes.co.tz) has good local news and sports. Copies of international newspapers from Europe and the USA usually filter to the street vendors in Arusha a few days after publication.

Radio
Radio Tanzania broadcasts in Kiswahili, and news bulletins tend to contain a lot of local coverage. There are several popular FM stations that can be picked up in the cities, such as **Radio Free Africa**, **Clouds FM** and **Radio One FM**, which mostly broadcast imported pop, rap and hip-hop music. **BBC World Service** is broadcast to Tanzania; check the website for frequencies (www.bbc.co.uk/worldservice).

Television
Television Tanzania began to transmit in 1994, and it's widely believed that Tanzania was the last country in the world to get TV. Prior to that, Julius Nyerere believed (in accordance with his socialist principles) that TV would increase the divide between rich and poor. There are now numerous national and local stations which have a mixture of English and Kiswahili home-grown programmes and foreign imports. Most hotels have DSTV (Digital Satellite Television), South African satellite TV, with scores of channels including news and movies. The most popular with Tanzanians are the sports channels for coverage of European football.

Money

US$1=TSh2190, £1=TSh3130, €1=TSh2380 (Feb 2016)

Currency
The Tanzanian currency is the Tanzanian Shilling (shilingi), not to be confused with the Kenyan and Uganda Shilling, which are different currencies. The written abbreviation is either TSh or using /= after the amount, ie 500/=). Notes currently in circulation are TSh500, 1000, 2000, 5000 and 10,000. Coins are TSh50, 100 and 200. A TSh500 coin was issued in 2014, which will eventually replace the TSh500 note. As it is not a hard currency, it cannot be brought into or taken out of the country, however there are no restrictions on the amount of foreign currency that can be brought into Tanzania.

Changing money
There are plenty of banks with ATMs and bureaux de change (known as forex bureaux)

in the cities and international airports. All banks have a foreign exchange service, and bank hours are Mon-Fri 0830-1500, Sat 0830-1330. Forex bureaux are open longer hours and some open on Sun. The easiest currencies to exchange are US dollars, UK pounds and Euros. If you are bringing US dollars in cash, try and bring newer notes – because of the prevalence of forgery, many banks and bureaux de change do not accept US dollar bills more than 5 years old. Sometimes lower denomination bills attract a lower exchange rate than higher denominations. Many non-resident prices (see page 31) are published in US$, but they can be paid in TSh – just ensure that you are getting a reasonable exchange rate. Visitors should not change money on the black market as it is illegal. However, there is an exception to this rule – at land borders where there are no banks, there are informal moneychangers and it is deemed acceptable to make use of these to change a small amount of local or US$ cash to last until you reach the next bank. Be very careful during these transactions as scams and short-changing is common, and always have the required amount to change ready – you do not want to be dipping into your money belt in such a public place as a border crossing.

ATMs and credit and debit cards

Visa is the most widely accepted card, followed by MasterCard; AMEX and Diners far less so. ATMs are found in all but the smallest towns, but remember your bank at home will charge a small fee for withdrawing from an ATM abroad with a debit or credit card. Cards are accepted by the large hotels,

Tip...
ATMs generally only dispatch notes in increments of TSh10,000, which are often too large for people to have change – break bigger notes when you can and save small change for taxis, snacks and drinks, souvenirs and the like.

airlines, main car hire firms, tour operators and travel agents. An additional levy of 5% may be charged, so check first if paying a sizeable bill. Most Tanzania National Parks (TANAPA) entrance fees are quoted and paid in US$ cash, but TANAPA have an electronic ticketing system in place (see Park fees, page 82 for more information). If paying at 'point of sale' machines at park entry gates (which accept Visa and MasterCard), it will be your home bank that calculates the US$ exchange rate.

Currency cards

Pre-paid currency cards allow you to preload money from your bank account, fixed at the day's exchange rate, and are accepted anywhere that you can use a debit or credit card. They are issued by specialist money changing companies, such as Travelex, Caxton FX and the post office. You can top up and check your balance by phone, online and sometimes by text.

Opening hours

Banks Mon-Fri, 0830-1530, Sat 0830-1330. Forex bureaux are open longer hours, 7 days a week. **Post offices** Mon-Fri 0800-1630, Sat 0900-1200. **Shops** Generally Mon-Sat 0800-1700 or 1800. Larger branches of the supermarkets stay open until late in the evening and are open on Sun morning. Small shops and kiosks and markets in the bigger towns are open daily.

Post

Tanzania Post Office (www.posta.co.tz) has branches across the country, even in the smallest of towns. The postal system is fairly reliable, and letters to Europe take about 5-7 days and to the USA about 10 days. If sending parcels, they must be no longer than 105 cm and have to be wrapped in brown paper and string. There is no point doing this before getting to the post office as you will be asked to undo it so that the parcel can be checked for export duty. Items have been known to go missing, so post anything of personal value through the fast post service known as **EMS**, a registered postal service available at all post offices, or with a courier company such as **DHL** (www.dhl.co.tz), which has offices in the major towns.

Public holidays

1 Jan   **New Year's Day**
12 Jan   **Zanzibar Revolution Day** (Zanzibar)
Mar/Apr   **Good Friday; Easter Monday**
26 Apr   **Union Day**
1 May   **Labour Day**
8 Aug   **Farmers' Day**
14 Oct   **Nyerere Day**
9 Dec   **Independence & Republic Day**
25 Dec   **Christmas Day**
26 Dec   **Boxing Day**

Safety

The majority of the people you will meet are honest and ready to help you, so there is no need to get paranoid about your safety. However, theft from tourists in Tanzania does occur and it will be assumed that foreigners in the country have relative wealth. The most common crimes are pickpocketing, purse-snatching and thefts from vehicles, and many robberies happen in crowded places such as markets and bus stations. The general common sense rules apply to prevent petty theft: don't exhibit anything valuable and keep wallets and purses out of sight; always keep car doors locked and windows wound up; lock room doors at night as noisy fans and a/c can provide cover for sneak thieves; do not accept any food or drink from strangers as it may be drugged and used to facilitate a robbery; avoid deserted areas and always take taxis at night.

It's not only crime that may affect your personal safety; you must also take safety precautions when visiting the game reserves and national parks. If camping, it is not advisable to leave your tent or *banda* during the night. Wild animals wander around the camps freely in the hours of darkness, and a protruding leg may seem like a tasty take-away to a hungry hyena. This is especially true at organized campsites, where the local animals have got so used to humans that they have lost much of their inherent fear of man. Exercise care during daylight hours too – remember wild animals can be dangerous.

Telephone

> **Tip...**
> If you find a taxi driver or tour guide you like, get their mobile number as this is the best way to reach them.

Tanzania's IDD is 000 and country code 255. The landline telephone system is run by **Tanzania Telecommunications Company Ltd** (**TTCL**; www.ttcl.co.tz), but the need for public coin or card phones has become virtually non-existent, given that almost everybody carries a mobile phone. Many call boxes have been, or are in the process of being, decommissioned but you can still make a call from the **TTCL** office in Arusha (Boma Rd) and Moshi (Market St). While businesses still have landlines, they nearly always use an additional mobile phone too. You can use your own mobile phone in Tanzania if it's on international roaming, or you can buy a local pay-as-you-go SIM and top-up cards. There are several mobile networks – the 4 major operators are **Vodacom**, **Airtel**, **Tigo** and **Zantel** – and you can go to their phone shops, and also buy from roadside vendors anywhere, even in the smallest of settlements.

Time

GMT +3 (the same as Kenya and Uganda). There is a 1-hr time difference going westwards to Malawi, Rwanda and the DRC, which are GMT + 2.

Tipping

It is customary to tip around 10% for good service, which is not obligatory or expected but is greatly appreciated by hotel and restaurant staff, most of whom receive very low pay. You can make individual tips, or most large hotels and safari lodges have tip boxes in reception for you to make a contribution at the end of your stay, which is shared among all staff. Taxi drivers don't need tipping since the price of a fare is usually negotiated first. How much to tip the guide/driver (and on a camping trip the cook too) on safari is tricky. Remember that wages are low and there can be long lay-offs during the low season. Despite this, there is also the problem of excessive tipping, which can cause problems for future clients being asked to give more than they should. It is best to enquire from the company at the time of booking what the going rate is. As a very rough guide you should allow US$8-20 per guide/driver per day – more for a small group of two to four; less for a large group, or one that includes children. Always try to come to an agreement with other members of the group and put the tip into a common kitty. It is also expected (and important) that you tip guides and porters if climbing Kilimanjaro (see box, page 148).

Tour operators

If you book an organized tour with a travel agent in your own country, the advantage is that they may also be able to book flights and other transfers and accommodation arrangements too. However, within Tanzania there is a bewildering array of tour operators offering safaris in the region with many having offices in Arusha (see page 58). There is no reason why you cannot deal with them directly and they may often be cheaper and better informed than travel agents in your home country. Do ensure that the company is properly licensed and is a member of the **Tanzania Association of Tour Operators** (**TATO**, www.tatotz.org), which represents over 200 of Tanzania's tour operators and is a good place to start when looking for a safari. See also the box on page 58, 'How to organize a safari'.

UK and Ireland
Abercrombie & Kent
www.abercrombiekent.co.uk.
Acacia Africa www.acacia-africa.com.
Africa Travel Centre www.africatravel.co.uk.
Africa Travel Resource
www.africatravelresource.com.
Expert Africa www.expertafrica.com.
Explore www.explore.co.uk.

Global Village www.globalvillage-travel.com.
Odyssey World www.odyssey-world.co.uk.
Okavango Tours and Safaris www.okavango.com.
Rainbow Tours www.rainbowtours.co.uk.
Real Africa www.realafrica.co.uk.
Safari Consultants Ltd www.safari-consultants.co.uk.
Somak www.somak.co.uk.
Steppes Africa www.steppestravel.co.uk.
Tanzania Odyssey www.tanzaniaodyssey.com.
The Tanzania Specialists www.thetanzaniaspecialists.net.
Tribes Travel www.tribes.co.uk.
Wildlife Worldwide www.wildlifeworldwide.com.

Australia
African Wildlife Safaris www.africanwildlifesafaris.com.au.
Classic Safari Company www.classicsafaricompany.com.au.
Peregrine Travel www.peregrine.net.au.
The Africa Safari Co www.africasafarico.com.au.

North America
Adventure Centre www.adventure-centre.com.
Africa Adventure Company www.africa-adventure.com.
African Horizons www.africanhorizons.com.
Bushtracks www.bushtracks.com.
Ker & Downey www.kerdowney.com

Africa

African Budget Safaris www.african
budgetsafaris.com.
Go2Africa www.go2africa.com.
Pulse Africa www.pulseafrica.com.
Simba Safaris www.simbasafaris.com.
Wild Frontiers www.wildfrontiers.com.

Visas and immigration

Your passport must have at least 2 blank
pages and be valid for at least 6 months
after your planned arrival date in Tanzania.
You must also produce a yellow fever
vaccination on arrival at the airports and
land borders. Almost all visitors require a
visa, with the exception of some African
countries, including South African passport-
holders should who are allowed a visa-free
stay of up to 30 days. A transit visa valid for
14 days costs US$30 per person; a single-
entry visa valid for 3 months costs US$50
(the exception are US citizens for whom a
single entry is US$100); a multi-entry visa
valid for 12 months costs US$100. Single-
entry and transit visas can be obtained on
arrival at the border crossings or airports,
but multiple-entry visas can only be
obtained in advance through Tanzania's
embassies. Visas are paid for in US$ cash,
but the airports and borders frequented

by tourists, such as Namanga (between
Nairobi and Arusha) will also accept Euros
or UK pounds.

Visas can be extended (but before they
expire) to a maximum of 6 months at the
Immigration Department: Goliondoi Rd,
Arusha, T027-250 3569, Mon-Fri 0730-
1500; and Boma Rd, Moshi, T027-275 1557,
Mon-Fri, 080-1530. You will be asked to
show proof of funds (a credit card should
be sufficient) and your return or onward
airline ticket or tour voucher. Occasionally,
independent travellers not on a tour may
be asked for these at point of entry; those
travelling through Tanzania on the way to
somewhere else on a 14-day transit visa will
most certainly be asked for these. For more
information visit www.immigration.go.tz.

Weights and measures

Metric.

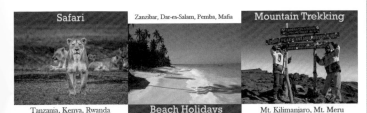

Index

Entries in bold refer to maps

FOOTPRINT

Features

Advertisers' index

About the author

Originally from London, **Lizzie Williams** has worked and lived in Africa for more than two decades and has visited 20 African countries. For several years she led trips across Africa as a tour leader on overland trucks from Istanbul to Cape Town. Now a full-time writer, she is the author of Footprint's Namibia, South Africa, Uganda, Kenya, Tanzania and Zimbabwe handbooks, as well as several other regional Footprint guides. She is also an author on African countries for other guidebook publishers and writes regularly for magazines and websites on African travel. When not on the road, Lizzie lives in Cape Town.

Acknowledgements

Many thanks to author Will Gray for his contribution to the colour section at the front of this book. The text in 'Safari adventures' was taken from his guidebook, *Wildlife Travel*, published by Footprint.

Credits

Footprint credits
Editor: Stephanie Rebello
Production and layout: Emma Bryers
Maps: Kevin Feeney
Colour section: Patrick Dawson

Publisher: Felicity Laughton
Patrick Dawson
Marketing: Kirsty Holmes
Sales: Diane McEntee
Advertising and content partnerships:
Debbie Wylde

Photography credits
Front cover: Sebastien Burel/
Shutterstock.com
Back cover top: Axiom Photographic/
SuperStock.com
Back cover bottom: Lizzie Williams
Inside front cover: Aleksandar Todorovic/
Shutterstock.com; Minden Pictures/
SuperStock.com; Steve Lagreca/
Shutterstock.com; Benny Marty/
Shutterstock.com

Printed in Spain by GraphyCems

Publishing information
Footprint Kilimanjaro & Northern Tanzania
2nd edition
© Footprint Handbooks Ltd
March 2016

ISBN: 978 1 910120 82 8
CIP DATA: A catalogue record for this book
is available from the British Library

® Footprint Handbooks and the
Footprint mark are a registered
trademark of Footprint Handbooks Ltd

Published by Footprint
6 Riverside Court
Lower Bristol Road
Bath BA2 3DZ, UK
T +44 (0)1225 469141
F +44 (0)1225 469461
footprinttravelguides.com

Distributed in the USA by
National Book Network, Inc.

Every effort has been made to ensure that
the facts in this guidebook are accurate.
However, travellers should still obtain advice
from consulates, airlines, etc about travel
and visa requirements before travelling.
The authors and publishers cannot
accept responsibility for any loss, injury
or inconvenience however caused.